ENERGY

A CRITICAL DECISION FOR THE UNITED STATES ECONOMY

by

Samuel M. Dix

Energy Education Publishers principals

Peter M. Wege
Peter M. Wege, II
Christopher H. Wege
Williams & Works, Inc.

Printing History
First printing January 1977
Revised edition June 1977

Published by Energy Education Publishers
P. O. Box 6488, 1432 Wealthy Street, S. E.
Grand Rapids, Michigan 49506
Telephone (616) 454-8261

Library of Congress Card Catalogue No. 77-784-03
ISBN 0-918998-01-8

S Y N O P S I S

The source of America's energy today is oil and gas
and our own is running out. Atomic power contributes only
3% of the total energy and an increase to 7% before 1985
is only a possibility. There will not be enough of it soon
enough to avert an energy crisis. Coal contributes less
than one-quarter of our energy today and it cannot be used
to replace oil and gas until a massive and expensive conversion industry is built. Oil and gas produced from coal
will quadruple the present retail price and it can be made
available in the required quantities at the end of the
century only if the plants are started now. Solar energy
will only be a minor contributor to our energy needs.

The United States does not have a constructive energy
policy. There are many reasons for this and they are important in understanding the resultant paralysis in the decision
process. Misinformation concerning the size of the U. S. oil
and gas resource and the amount that can be produced from
year to year is the principle cause. A long range projection
is imperative.

The immediate energy crisis will be caused by the supply
failure in natural gas. Price deregulation will be suggested
as a cure. It is not. The second and more serious crisis will
develop from the supply failure of imported oil. This will
occur during 1979.

We have become dependent on authoritative persons to give
us the answers. For energy, few honest answers have been
provided. The facts are available, but they take time to
interpret. Then the conclusions become obvious.

ACKNOWLEDGEMENTS

The financial assistance of Frederick G. Meijer and John W. Blodgett, Jr. made possible the completion of my research.

The encouragement and support of the founders of Energy Economics Education enterprise provided the necessary dialogue with the academic and business communities and extended my contact with the nationally recognized authorities who have contributed substantially to my resources. The principal contributors of time and direct assistance are:

Earl Cook, Geologist, Dean of the College of Geosciences, Texas A&M
   University
Herman Daly, Economist, Louisiana State University
John W. Duane, Petroleum Engineer, Consumers Power Company
Tom Edens, Economist, Michigan State University
Richard M. Fairbanks, III, Assistant to the Chairman, National Energy
   Project, American Enterprise Institute for Public Research, Washington
Donald D. Fink, President, University Consortium Center
Herman T. Franssen, Economist, International Law and Political Science
   analyst, Library of Congress, Washington
Harold Gall, Botanist, University of Chicago
Nicholas Georgescu-Roegen, Economist, Vanderbilt University
John Henderson, Associate Professor of Geology, Grand Valley State Colleges
M. King Hubbert, Geologist, U. S. Geological Survey, Reston, Virginia
Herman E. Koenig, Professor, Electrical Engineering & Systems Science;
   Director, Center for Environmental Quality, Michigan State University
Duncan E. Littlefair, Minister, Fountain Street Church
Dennis Meadows, Professor of Management, Dartmouth College
Richard F. Meyer, U. S. Geological Survey, Reston, Virginia
Betty Miller, Geologist, U. S. Geological Survey, Denver, Colorado
Jack Redding, Continental Illinois Bank, Chicago, Illinois
Wilhelm K. Shroeter, Director of Development Planning, Lear Siegler, Inc.
Harold Steketee, Jr., Biologist
Jay Wabeke, Minister
Richard Ward, Geologist, Wayne State University
Peter M. Wege, Corporate Secretary, Steelcase, Inc.
Joan Wolfe, Chairman, Michigan Natural Resource Commission

I am indebted to my assigned staff, Wayne Mares, Betty Rienks, and Ruth Scott; my editors, Mary Lee Taliaferro and Carolyn Medendorp; my cover artist, Michael A. Vander Wall; and to Tom Lee for his publishing assistance.

C O N T E N T S

PREFACE
                                                                              Page

P A R T   O N E

T H E   D E C I S I O N S

I   PERSPECTIVE   2

Petroleum and the physical economics prerequisite.
The bastions of the defense.   The democratic
dilemma.   The environmentalists and the confu-
sion of fact as to the remaining resource.   9

II   THE LITERATURE

III   OIL   11

The givens.   The source of confusion.   The remaining oil resource. Summation of historic petroleum
production parameters and projections. The significance of the petroleum imports requirement.

IV   GAS   21

The U. S. natural gas forecast.   The gas economy squeeze.

V   ATOMIC ENERGY, SOLAR ENERGY AND COAL   29

Nuclear power today.   Solar energy.   Coal and the
Kaiparowits experience.

VI   THE ENERGY BALANCE FOR THE NEXT TEN YEARS   39

World petroleum available to the United States.

Contents

VII   THE CRITICAL DECISIONS   46

The energy decision dilemma.   The gas price decision.
The petroleum substitution non-decision probability.
Federal financing of new energy resources.   States'
rights.   Individual rights.   Energy organization.

VIII   THE POLITICAL-ECONOMIC FUTURE   58

PART TWO

THE OIL AND GAS FIGURES

IX   THE PETROLEUM FIGURES   63

The consensus as to the remaining petroleum resource.
The U.S.G.S. geological estimates of remaining oil.
Dr. M. King Hubbert's forecast method.   Short term
forecast and identification of liquid hydrocarbons.
The proved reserves and their contribution to forecast
methodology.   Proved reserve withdrawal rate.
Total remaining resource withdrawal rate.   The petroleum production forecast.   The significance of gas
liquids.   Economic influences - supply and demand
versus price.   Domestic demand.   Federal Energy
Administration - Project Independence.   U. S. Department of the Interior and M. King Hubbert petroleum production expectancy.   Historic perspective on world
petroleum supply.

X   NATURAL GAS AND ITS SUBSTITUTES   105

Gas production and discovery history.   Comparative gas
forecast.   The first alternative to natural gas,
petroleum substitution.   Liquefied natural gas, LNG.
SNG, synthetic or substitute natural gas.   The gas
economy squeeze.   Potential future gas.

Contents

Page

XI   CONCLUSION   124

        Postscript.

P A R T   T H R E E

T H E   S H A P E   O F   T H E   F U T U R E

XII   THE GENERALS   129

XIII   THE INDUSTRY SPECIFICS   131

        Electric power.   Gas.   Transportation and oil.
        Atomic power.   Solar, wind, shale, and geophysical.
        Agriculture.

XIV   THE FUTURE FOR THE INDIVIDUAL   140

        Consumer attitudes and expectancies.   Home heating.
        Transportation.   Food.   Recreation.   Population.

XV   A BEGINNING FOR CHANGE   149

        Truth.   Education.

XVI   A POTENTIAL ENERGY POLICY   154

        The resistance.   Inventory of attitudes in the social
        structure.   The national constituency necessity.
        The elements of an energy policy.   The desirable but
        improbable energy authority.   Possible legislation.

Contents

XVII   THE ECONOMIC FICTIONS AND REALITY   169

           The reality of the earth.   The special nature of
           energy and waste.   The fiction of money and capital.
           The reality of inflation and its measure.   The
           inflation fictions.   The void in the nation's
           balance sheet and the fiction of the Gross National
           Product.   Labor, capital, and the inflation syndrome.

XVIII   THE SOCIAL CONTRACT AND THE LEADERSHIP DECISION   180

           The decision.   Time and the two economic disciplines.
           The conflict between the free economy and the free
           society.   The probability for survival and the signi-
           ficance of the national constituency imperative.

A P P E N D I X

TABULATIONS   190

           Oil: Past production, rate, forecast, comparative
                 forecasts.
           Gas: Past production, rate and forecast by regions,
                 comparative forecasts.
           World oil production and U. S. supply

BIBLIOGRAPHY
& LITERATURE
   REVIEW   General periodicals.   Scientific periodicals.   The   234
           academic press and resource books.   The Government
           Printing Office contribution.   Future literature.
           Author indexed listing of contributing books.

TABLES OF EXHIBITS, FIGURES, AND TABULATIONS   254

PREFACE

The energy supply problem faces the United States and the free world with the most critical decision since our Declaration of Independence. For two hundred years, our political and economic beliefs have been rooted in faith in man's initiative and ingenuity to build a civilization from the natural materials of this continent. Our free economy and free society made possible a miracle of production and construction. Some credit was given to the centuries of human progress in developing our scientific knowledge, but very little credit was reserved for the raw materials of the earth, the several hundred million years required to produce and store the fossil fuels that powered this civilization.

Today we are running out of oil and gas, the fuel that represents almost three-quarters of the energy upon which the United States economy depends. This is a physical fact, a physical problem. It is only secondarily an economic and a political problem, but we are in the habit of reversing this priority. Our economic system assumes that demand controls the balance of supply and price. If there is money, the materials will be forthcoming and energy is one of the economists' materials.

I am an engineer and an independent consultant to management with clients in thirty-one states. My assignments have included the petroleum industry. My concern with our energy supply problem began in 1971. Since the inauguration of Gerald Ford as Vice President, I have enjoyed the good offices of the White House in obtaining access to persons and records in my research to determine the origins of and the potential solutions to the developing energy problem. My reports were addressed to the President or his immediate Assistant for Economic Affairs.

This manuscript is the last report to President Ford, prepared for transmittal to President Carter, and acknowledged for the President by Mr. L. William Seidman December 28, 1976. In its present form, my analysis began with the development of the year to year U. S. oil and gas production expectancy, based on the ultimate resource estimates which I believe to be accurate. These became available in 1975. The analysis procedure for converting the resource base to expected annual production is ultimately simple but critical to my conclusions.

In the presentation of my conclusions, I have recognized the necessity for separating the overall view of energy in the economic analysis from the detailed proofs of the probable future energy supply. Part One of this study is concerned with this overview and economic conclusion. Part Two presents the energy supply data which was my beginning.

Part Three considers the immediate future in political-economic terms. A brief outline of general conclusions in Chapter XII is followed by specific immediate solutions to each of the critical energy segments of the economy. The final chapters are concerned with an approach to an energy policy and an analysis of the economic conflicts.

In the Appendix, I have reproduced the critical tabulations that represent my source material and my conclusions. The Bibliography includes a discussion of the available energy literature.

Energy Economics Education enterprise is a non-profit corporation organized to support and continue research in this field and encourage the dissemination of my findings.

March 1977   *Samuel M. Dix*

POSTSCRIPT

When President Carter took office, he inherited four independently prepared energy reports in addition to the on-going energy programs of departments charged with this responsibility. The independent reports had been prepared by the CIA, the State Department, the Treasury Department, and the privately financed report which constitutes — with minor updatings — the body of this book. President Carter's National Energy Plan and the reaction to that plan are critical elements in projecting the future United States economy.

PRESIDENT CARTER'S NATIONAL ENERGY PLAN

President Carter's energy plan was presented to the Joint Session of Congress on April 20, 1977 and published by the Executive Office with a transmittal letter dated April 29. The content of the President's message and his plan can be divided into two parts. The first is a statement of the physical facts of the United States and world energy supply as they relate to historic and projected consumption with the implication of energy attrition for the U. S. economy. The second is the proposed course of action and legislation to realize stated political and economic goals.

The importance of President Carter's recognition of the energy problem cannot be overstated. Energy limits were clearly identified during the Eisenhower Administration, but he and the four following presidents avoided facing the nation with its problem. Broad public understanding of the gravity of the situation, a commitment to action, and a willingness to endure some sacrifice are prerequisites to any significant governmental action.

The specifics of the recommended legislative action and the details of the economic projection make up the second part of the President's message and his plan. The proposed legislation is strongly influenced by economists and political advisors. The plan is a compromise between the problem which the President recognizes and the realities of political acceptance.

The compromise is necessary to begin positive thinking on a very critical problem. We have no peacetime planning experience, no tradition, no natural acceptance for the introduction of planning concepts into our market economy. For the great majority of economists and business administrators in the government and in the private sector, planning is anathema.

THE IMMEDIATE REACTION TO THE PRESIDENT'S PLAN

The negative reaction of the Congress and the economic press exceeded my expectations. The President's statements were clear and the facts which he presented can be documented without question. The proposed legislation requires little actual sacrifice, and there appeared to be considerable public acceptance. But acceptance did not develop with the leaders of the economic community.

President Carter's energy message threatens economic expansion, the cornerstone of the country's political and social structure. How do you get the economy going, control inflation, and reduce unemployment with a conservation program? The leaders of business and their economic advisors have not been able to find the answers. The media editors and the leaders of the leaders have attacked the plan. The nature of their attack is very significant. Heretofore, responsible representatives of business have recognized the heavy risk of confronting undeniable physical evidence, but the attack on the President's plan has been aimed at these undeniable facts. Exponential growth is not forever possible in a finite world. This is the undeniable fact. But our economic system is dependent on growth. This is the problem.

The Wall Street Journal editorial of April 27, 1977 identified 1,001 years of natural gas available to the U. S. economy, castigating the President for ignoring this claimed resource which was identified in quantities of trillions of cubic feet requiring only slightly higher prices to produce. The sources were Devonian shale, Western tight sands, coal seam gas, and geopressured methane dissolved in water at 15,000' below the Gulf region. These claims cannot be supported.

It takes energy to produce energy. Energy is represented in the heat required to release hydrocarbons from shale, to pump gaseous and liquid materials from the depth of the earth, to drill the wells, to produce the steel pipe which the wells and the pipeline-gathering system require, to pressurize the gas to move it through the pipeline system to the point of use, and to return or contain the by-products of energy production. Hydrocarbons can be produced from each of the identified resources, but energy cannot be reproduced when the energy balance is negative. More energy would go into the process than could be returned.

The net energy balance is totally independent of the economic price system. The energy employed to produce energy and the energy which is produced must be costed on the same basis. The employment of cheap oil to produce expensive gas would be profitable only as long as the underpriced oil and the unpriced energy component in the materials employed continued to be available for the hydrocarbon production. These elementary physical facts have been avoided in both the political and the economic attack on the President's plan.

The great expectations of the *Wall Street Journal* editors become minor and improbable additions to known gas reserves under objective analysis but the business community has flocked to the defense of the *Journal* and subsequent editorials have become more sanguine.

The Stanford Research Institute has consistently extolled the efficacy of economic incentives to produce resources, compromising the objectivity of their conclusions by avoiding physical evidence of limits. In a paper delivered to the annual meeting of the Scientists' Institute for Public Information, their manager for international projects, William J. Schumacher, carefully avoided recognition of the President's energy policy which had been announced nine days earlier. He deplored the "current energy shortage hysteria" in the United States.

Schumacher considers the oil reserve picture to be still "quite secure," glossing over his own reference charts identifying the decline in the world reserve to production ratios beginning in 1958 and the decline in absolute world reserves beginning in 1974. For oil, he is concerned with an "economically efficient price, less than current price levels." He concludes that "the supply picture for fossil fuels in the twentieth century remains strong and there are sufficient quantities of these fuels to get us well into the next century, giving us time for sound energy planning." Thus, planning becomes a subject for discussion by the next generation. He anticipates vigorous debate in this next century.

Barry Commoner, Chairman of the Board of Scientists' Institute for Public Information, directly attacked the President's plan at this same meeting, but his motivations are different. He proposes solar energy as a solution to the nation's energy problem. To realize his objectives, the age of oil and gas must be extended to accommodate the transition. Dr. Commoner deplores coal for its environmental depravations, and nuclear power is the ultimate evil.

Dr. Commoner attacks the President's energy plan in the name of science and environmental protection, but he is casual in his scientific references. He ridicules the interpretation that domestic oil production cannot be increased, citing the Federal Energy Administration's Project Independence report. (This report is analyzed in detail, primary reference Figure 15 on Page 95.)

Dr. Commoner's most serious violation of scientific ethics is his apparently deliberate misinterpretation of responsible references. In his paper, he quotes the reliable inventory of the U. S. oil and gas resources released in 1975 by the U. S. Geological Survey as Circular 725. He interprets this document as finding up to "289 billion barrels of economic oil.....which can be produced, profitably, at the cost made possible by current economic factors." He then finds additional domestic oil resources of up to 440 billion barrels at higher costs.

Circular 725 is not easy reading. Reserves are constantly depleted as they are used. Geologists refer to the original oil in-place to avoid this problem. Correcting the U.S.G.S. figures to January 1, 1976, their conclusions identify a minimum remaining producible reserve of 131 billion barrels with a 5% probability of finding their maximum 219 billion barrels. These are the bases of President Carter's conclusions. It is possible to reach Dr. Commoner's 289 billion barrels only by including in the future production potential all the oil we have used since the beginning of exploration and production in this country.

It is unreasonable to conclude that degreed economists and scientists cannot read or add. The answer must lie in motivation and the deep-seated nature of the conflict between the expansion ideology of western civilization and the physical facts of our finite world. This is the problem that must be resolved right now. This is the subject of my thinking and discussion.

June 1977   *Samuel M. Dix*

PART ONE

THE DECISIONS

The barbarian is not at the gate of western civilization.
He is in the marketplace and his form is not human.   He
has penetrated the thinking processes.   He inhibits the
decisions that are critical to the survival of our civilization.

Part One is concerned with the political-economics of the
decreasing energy availability and the social implications
of this physical fact.

I

P E R S P E C T I V E

Energy is a many dimensioned thing. It is visible only through what it does and what it was before it became energy. It is measured by engineers in units of power and work and heat and an esoteric word - entropy - which identifies its availability to do work. With the exceptions of nuclear and geophysical sources of heat, all energy on the earth derives from the sun. Man is solar energy dependent.

Today, the United States and the western world face an energy problem which can be identified as a developed dependence on oil and gas. The problem grew out of the industrial revolution and the successes of a scientific age. Petroleum was only one of many energy resources in this evolutionary process. Before oil and gas there was coal and before coal there was wood and before that animal power and man's own muscle. After oil, we have assumed an age of nuclear power, first atomic fission and then infinite energy from nuclear fusion.

Man's social history developed in parallel with his sources of energy. The free society and the free economy released economic man from virtually all restraints in building his civilization and populating the world in proportion to the energy that he was able to find. The energy source for the most spectacular period of growth was oil and secondarily gas. After discovery, they flowed from the earth in great quantities. It has been the purest form of energy available to man. It is almost all net energy.

We have known almost from the beginning that oil is not infinitely available but this fact has had no significance. Another energy source would replace oil. This was the accepted knowledge before there was any scientific basis for believing that atomic energy could be harnessed and now we are producing a substantial amount of this energy. Why then a fear of a developing energy crisis at this point in history? The answer lies in the numbers, the quantities in the remaining oil and gas resource, the time delay and limitations of the present atomic energy development, the human life span, and the human population. A second major contributor is our developed humanity. Early death is no longer an acceptable solution to the human problem.

In the United States, three-quarters of our day to day energy supply is represented by oil and gas, and we have used more than half of all the oil and gas that can be produced on this continent, including its undersea's shelf. As we proceed with the removal of the last half of this resource,

the day to day and year to year production decreases. From this time for-
ward, the North American continent, including Alaska, can be expected to
produce less oil and gas each year. Before the end of the century, the
free world will have passed the production peak. The world oil and gas
resource will have been half depleted and the world annual production will
begin to decline year by year.

The United States and the free world have become dependent on oil and
gas to support their economy, their population, their way of life. The replacement energy resource will not be available in time. We have developed
a civilization that is dependent on energy each hour of each day, and we
have assumed the origin of that energy to have been the ingenuity of man.
We have credited our social, political, and economic institutions with our
progress and we have measured this progress in population and wealth —
numbers of people and monetarily denominated materials and services.

Energy does not enter the economic and political equation. Only the
sources of energy — the quantities of oil and gas and coal which have been
consumed — are counted, and the counting only reflects the cost of the
removal of these energy resources from the earth and the cost of its
transport and conversion. Energy has remained the unseen, unthought-of
thing, unrecognized for its importance to man's continued existence. Energy
is provided by geologists who locate the diggings, engineers who remove and
transport and convert the material, and the businesses and political institutions that have organized the world based on its availability. The source
of energy is not costed. It has been given.

The energy problem is the running out of the given. Oil and gas were
produced on the earth several hundred million years ago under identifiable
conditions in which animal and vegetable materials were buried, compressed,
and preserved underground and under the floor of the sea. They are a non-
renewable resource, the product of time, a very long time. Today we can
identify the probable total quantity of this resource. We can determine
how little remains, and we can determine our limitations in replacing the
energy required for the continued expension of our own economy and the
world economy. The energy crisis today impresses only the individuals who
understand the numbers and understand the limitations of our scientific
development. The general crisis will occur when the facts are generally
recognized. This crisis may not occur until energy is no longer available
in the critical quantity and this will precipitate a social revolution.

The mini-crisis of the Arab boycott disappeared when the flow of oil from Africa and the Arabian Peninsula was reestablished. It was momentary and it did not affect the country's political and economic thinking. The failure to remain concerned indicates how determined Americans are to deny an energy problem.

We have developed an economic discipline and an economically dependent social and political system that is based on faith in our system. We have been carried away with the success of the system and we have ignored its limitations. The free society grew up with the free economy. The free society is assumed to be dependent on the free economy. The seats of power in both the political and economic societies are controlled by the believers. But the obvious dependence of the economy on energy cannot be discussed in economic terms. We lack a proper language. In the two hundred year development of the economic discipline, its physical origins have been lost. Material and pecuniary economics have been separated and the physical economics have been almost totally neglected, relegated to the responsibility of the physical sciences, cut off from intercourse with the decision-making powers of the state.

The energy problem has produced a paralysis in the social thinking process. The paralysis is subconscious, virtually unrecognized. The energy problem facing the United States is more critical than inflation or unemployment or the avoidance of war, but the energy problem was not discussed by any candidate for election in 1976. The avoidance of the energy discussion and the avoidance of decision has affected almost every element in our social structure: education, economic, and political. The paralysis takes on the form and appearance of a natural conspiracy. It is a conspiracy of the elements of society acting spontaneously to protect the past without regard for the future.

PETROLEUM AND THE PHYSICAL ECONOMICS PREREQUISITE

Petroleum is not the only non-renewable resource that threatens the expanding economy, but petroleum is the most obvious. Petroleum has a virtual stranglehold on the transportation systems of western civilization. Petroleum, along with its byproduct natural gas, has a large influence on the supply of power and heat critical to an industrial economy. Lacking oil and gas, the western world will not be reduced to the agricultural economy of the middle ages, but life in the advanced societies will be very different. The free society probably will not survive an unplanned transition.

Coal still is available, and coal can be converted to a gaseous or liquid state, but coal cannot replace oil and gas in the quantities required, within the necessary time without precipitating critical shortages of other non-renewable resources. Power supplied by renewable energy from the solar sources — wind, river flow, wood, vegetation, the direct utilization of the sun's rays — and energy from the atom are governed by their own restraints of conversion cost, resource limits, and technical feasibility. The broader discussion of these alternatives is mainly a cover for avoiding the recognition of this century's inescapable dependency on the fossil fuels.

No amount of money will produce energy from a resource that requires more energy in the production process than can be delivered. An energy resource is not a resource unless net energy can be produced. The energy balance can be determined and presented in pecuniary economic terms but only after the physical economic analysis has been completed. The energy balance is the critical fact in the projection and is the final arbiter of social power. Physical economics is preemptive in the conclusion.

Money will not be replaced as a storer of value and a medium of exchange, but the measure of all things in monetary terms may very well have to be recognized for its secondary importance before a real solution is found for the replacement of petroleum and natural gas and the recognition of the actual limitations of coal in energizing western man's economy. Stresses on the political structure are less dangerous than the avoidance of the physical economic problem. The unconscious and spontaneous conspiracy to avoid the realities of the physical economic limitations can be expected to be followed by the collapse of both our economic and our political structure as it exists today.

THE BASTIONS OF THE DEFENSE

The defense of the status quo requires a denial of the energy crisis. There is a conscious and subconscious gathering of the most responsible political and economic leaders committed to the non-recognition of a real energy problem. Their defenses are varied and numerous but some of these have become common.

Faith is the greatest of the defenses: Faith in the ingenuity of our scientists and the power of our industrialists, Faith in our free economy, Faith in our religious inheritance and God's admonition to go forth and multiply and take possession of all that is on the earth and in the seas, Faith in our children to solve their inherited problems for their own generation, and finally, Faith in ourselves. It is a betrayal of our every institution to deny the efficacy of Faith.

Hope is the second of the defenses, and in the absence of identifiable solutions to the energy problem, hope becomes a necessity. Hope is second only to faith in its universal appeal.

Momentum is the power behind the avoidance of the energy problem. Big government and big business are required to maintain course and speed; but actually, bigness has little to do with the working of momentum. Even the individual household, the lone man and his dog must eat and sleep each day and so long as there is a place to lie down at night and something to sustain the body for one more day, each will continue on his way. It is not a thinking process. Rational persuasion at the individual level can produce only minimum anxiety and the acceptance of sacrifice. But the sacrifice will not be made without visible necessity and leadership. The question then becomes what kind of a leader?

THE DEMOCRATIC DILEMMA

How can constructive direction be encouraged in the "government by the people," which is so sensitive to special interest persuasion, when virtually all of the special interests are conditioned to oppose recognition of the problem, and the most universally accepted special interest is unlimited fuel for the great American toy? Nineteen seventy-three was the awakening, thanks to the Arabs. Twenty-one years ago, in 1956, the peaking of the United States petroleum production was forecast with remarkable precision as the beginning of the 1970's. Actually, it occurred in November of 1970 and two years after that event the proof began to be recognized as production declined month after month. The decade of the 1950's provided much of the thoughtful research establishing material limits and the conflict with unrestricted economic expansion.

It is perhaps two years since the leading physicists of the country began to disclose the fact that there was no breakthrough in atomic fusion, that none could be expected for a decade, and that the breeder could not be counted on to carry the primary electric power load in this century. There has been no realistic discussion of the physical requirements for liquid petroleum to power the transportation system of the United States, the limitations of the U. S. and world supply, or the quantitative limitations on alternative liquid energy by the liquefaction of coal or production from other hydrocarbon resources. We only have discussions of potentially feasible processes without reference to when, how much, and at what physical cost.

THE ENVIRONMENTALISTS AND THE CONFUSION OF FACT AS TO THE REMAINING RESOURCE

The environmentalists have not yet effected positive political and economic responses. They have created anxiety. They were the first to recognize material limits and the necessity for social and political change. They have joined forces with the ultraconservatives in blocking legislation and stopping progress in the planning and building of energy production systems and energy transport systems by the petroleum and electric utility corporations. But they have offered no realistic planning alternatives and they have again joined the conservatives in overstating the United States gas and oil reserve potential. A leader of the environmental movement, Barry Commoner, is engaged in totally unscientific and indefensible claims as to the size and availability of the United States petroleum resource.

The exaggeration of the U. S. resource is based on materials published by the U. S. Geological Survey in 1972. This information is obviously still available in the libraries of the country, but it was never adequately supported and since 1975, it has been totally discredited. However, the theme of exaggeration has persisted.

The Federal Energy Administration publications in 1974 forecast production of gas and oil for 1980 which were totally irresponsible at the time of their publication and are now obviously ridiculous. In 1976, their optimistic projections were substantially reduced but they exceed realistic probability. Similarly, the Interior Department's Bureau of Mines in their

1976 forecast titled, "Petroleum and Gas Production Through the Year 2000", project production above the level that is physically possible based on current resource identification.

The American Petroleum Institute requires more careful identification in this perspective. It is the trade association of the major oil producers. It has been totally responsible for gathering petroleum production statistics from the producers and reporting to the government. It has been criticized, and its reports have been questioned, but the numerous investigations have only confirmed the accuracy of the reporting. The assumption that the government can perform this service is a critical illusion. Our oil has been produced by private companies from private resources on private property. Until and unless our basic ideology of private property and production is changed, the government cannot be expected to control petroleum production.

The forecasting of future petroleum production is another critical area, little understood. The A.P.I. only determines the quantity of proved reserves which the oil companies have identified. This term defines what amounts to the shelf inventory of the industry. Historically, it has no geological significance. However, the current failure to increase reserves does have significance.

When the United States petroleum reserves were actually declining in the 1950's and 1960's, world production, particularly in the Arabian peninsula and Africa, began to dominate petroleum economics and provide the basis for the petroleum geologists' claims of unlimited future supply, extending the hundred year history of relative excess despite the exploding demand for the product. Petroleum geologists are eternal optimists who are only interested in finding oil. They will be the last to accept a political or economic philosophy limiting exploration as there will always be some oil to find. But if the odds are reduced and the facts are known, the financing will dry up before the producing wells do. Even gold loses its allure in the face of the improbability of finding any. Thus, it is not surprising that the early and now demonstrably accurate forecasts of the limits of the petroleum supply have been denied by the professional geologists. The denial is their creed almost to a man.

II

THE LITERATURE

A free society determines the literature that it will pay for and in so doing, determines the literature that will be made available. The current Cassandras of the energy crisis have not been popular. The very best in writing, in authority, and in historic perspective has been rejected at the bookstand. As a consequence, the general books' editors have shunned this market.

The primary source of information on the developing energy problem from 1970 through 1973 is the scientific periodical press. These magazines anticipated the crisis and provided perspective for their special interest readers. After 1973, the general periodicals performed the same service. From this time on, there was much news and the daily papers covered the news, but the treatment of energy information was disparate. The economic faith and hope of publishers was often the primary ingredient in energy fact reporting. The news of the most unsettling events relating to the energy supply was released without fanfare, at odd holiday times, under camouflage of gratuitous misinterpretation, or carefully planned discouragement of readership and further publication. Critical events were not publicized. In 1975, when the U. S. Geological Survey found that its much publicized 1972 estimates of the oil and gas resource had been overstated by twenty-two times, only a few liberal newspapers carried the news item. When the Federal Power Commission increased the price of new interstate gas by almost three times in 1976, the news item was treated in the same way. No politician in this election year even mentioned it.

The academic press is controlled by the academic community. Books are published by the professors who are respected in the community and whose students can be expected to purchase the books. The dearth of academic treatment of the energy problem results from the absence of an academic discipline that recognizes energy as a whole subject. Discussions of energy and the implications of the limits of the energy resource are rejected by the economic discipline. It is not discussed in general economic texts except to mention limits as a theory not generally recognized by the profession.

The treatment of energy as a subject related to the survival of our modern society has been undertaken by academic persons in the physical science disciplines or by individuals writing outside of the academic community. I have placed great importance on the books from this source which have only just begun to appear. The limitations of the economic discipline must be faced. Economics as it has been taught is not a whole subject. The dichotomy of pecuniary and physical economics will have to be recognized. The economists must return to the earth.

The Government Printing Office is a major source of information on energy supply and demand, supported by the research efforts of the trade associations in this energy field which are often the primary source of much of the government data. The most significant characteristic of the government energy press is the unreliable nature of the publications. The departments of the government specifically charged with the responsibility for energy reporting and forecasting have produced contradictory reports. They can be interpreted only after extensive research, identifying the origins and the bias of the administrative offices and the research organizations. The departments with the highest authoritative credentials have produced the least responsible information. Organizations created and charged with the most specific energy responsibility have produced the most consistent and the most obvious misinterpretations of historic fact projecting the most unbelievable forecasts and economic prognostications.

Further discussion of our primary reference sources will be found in the introduction to the Bibliography. This Bibliography includes classic economic texts, universal histories, as well as the periodicals and government publications that have been specific to our analysis.

I I I

O I L

With the fading of optimistic anticipation of quickly replacing the fossil fuels with solar and atomic energy, the avoidance of energy decisions has been based on the overstatement of the remaining U. S. petroleum resource and its future production potential. The cover for these overstatements is the confusion in the numbers and the definitions. The known is presented as questionable or unknowable. The language and the mathematics which were employed to determine the facts of petroleum availability have been reemployed to produce uncertainty. The offices with the primary responsibility for measuring future resources have been divided.

But almost all of the actual confusion is now history. The facts are available and only elementary mathematics are required to interpret the numbers within the tolerance necessary for economic and political decision. Only a few hours are required to gain perspective on these numbers and definitions, providing one additional ingredient is supplied — a minimum confidence in the source material.

THE GIVENS

Before entering the jungle of petroleum numbers and definitions, a few basic facts that cannot be altered by persuasion or confusion should be set down:

(1) The supplies of petroleum and other fossil fuels are finite. We know their origin and where they are likely to be found. The geological time unit for their formation is one hundred million years and several are required. Petroleum is a non-replaceable resource.

(2) The mathematics of withdrawal from a fixed resource in uniform exponential growth is compound interest operating in reverse. Each time the rate of withdrawal doubles, the amount of the total withdrawal from the beginning also doubles. It took one hundred years to withdraw the first one hundred billion barrels from the U. S. resource on a growth curve of approximately 4% increase per year. The next hundred billion barrels will be withdrawn in eighteen years at this rate. The following doubling will require two hundred billion barrels, *in only eighteen more years.*

(3)   The U. S. was the world supplier of petroleum for the first one hundred years. This dominant position in supplying the world market continued through World War II.

(4)   U. S. transportation is almost totally dependent on liquid petroleum and accounts for 54% of all petroleum products used.

(5)   The lower 48 states are the most explored area in the world with more than three million wells drilled and the most sophisticated exploratory methods employed.

(6)   The north slope of Alaska is more remote economically than the Arabian Peninsula and it represents a separate exploratory universe in projecting future domestic production.

(7)   Historically, there has been a direct correlation between per capita income and per capita consumption of energy.

(8)   Petroleum production from established wells in the United States has been decreasing at the rate of one million barrels per day each year. This declining rate has been offset by only one-half million barrels per day of new oil for the last three years.

THE SOURCES OF CONFUSION

The conflict between the substantial evidence of a predictable U. S. petroleum supply and the broadly based rejection of this information can be explained. First, the terms for the identification of petroleum reserves are inexact and the remaining resource is constantly changing, reduced with each year's production. An average of only one-third of the identified petroleum can be produced, but the producible percentage is different for each geological formation and is affected by the organization of the field and the production methods. Secondary and tertiary production procedures are economically sensitive and open the door to exaggerated claims as to how much oil might be produced if the price were right.

Second, perspective on the significance of major trends that are not subject to much change is lost in short term projections that ignore both the historic past and the predictable future. Third, mathematical procedures and modeling methodology introduce a barrier to comprehension. Fourth, truncated graphic presentation and misplaced emphasis on the significance of selected relationships can introduce distortion which comes close to deliberate misrepresentation.

The close correlation between petroleum and power in the marketplace and in the political process encourages the use of misrepresentation and distortion. These are the ingredients of a general confusion of fact and a general acceptance of an unsupportable ideology which I have called the conspiracy. It has become necessary to begin with definitions and the basic facts of the remaining oil resource and prove each step of the year to year production forecast.

THE REMAINING OIL RESOURCE

We have employed three independent studies as a reference base for our conclusions as to the remaining recoverable oil in the United States:

The National Academy of Sciences study titled *Mineral Resources and the Environment* was completed in 1975, based on 1972 statistical data. Correcting their findings for January 1976, they concluded that 140 billion barrels of liquid hydrocarbons represented the remaining U. S. resource.

The United States Geological Survey study titled, *Geological Estimates of Undiscovered Recoverable Oil & Gas Resource in the United States, Circular 725,* was released in 1975. Correcting their findings to the same January 1976 date, they found a 95% probability of producing 131 billion barrels of liquid hydrocarbon from the U. S. resource. They also projected a 5% probability of future production at the level of 219 billion barrels.

Dr. M. King Hubbert, an independent oil geologist working for the Shell Oil Company accurately forecast the peaking of U. S. petroleum production in 1956. Dr. Hubbert was a member of the U.S.G.S. and vigorously opposed the Survey's 1972 and 1974 oil and gas reserve estimates. Adjusting his latest forecast to our January 1976 common date, Dr. Hubbert projects an expectancy of 126 billion barrels of liquid hydrocarbon.

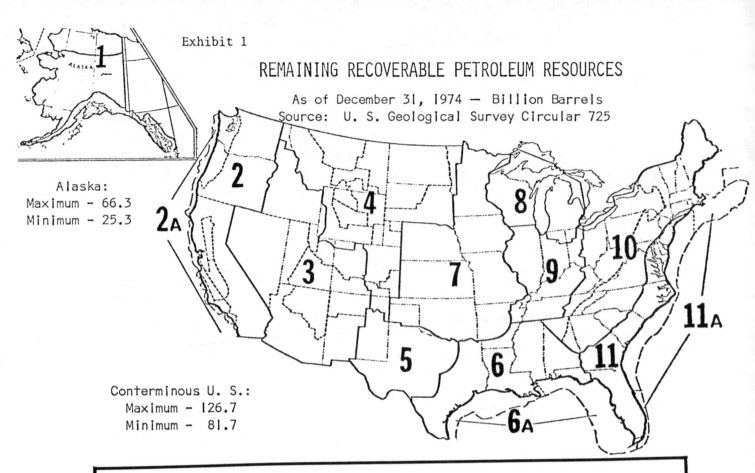

Exhibit 1

REMAINING RECOVERABLE PETROLEUM RESOURCES

As of December 31, 1974 — Billion Barrels
Source: U. S. Geological Survey Circular 725

Alaska:
Maximum – 66.3
Minimum – 25.3

Conterminous U. S.:
Maximum – 126.7
Minimum – 81.7

TABLE 4.—*Production, reserves, and undiscovered recoverable oil resources for the United States, December 31, 1974 (billion barrels)*

Regions	Cumulative Production	Demonstrated Reserves		Total Cumulative Production + Demonstrated Reserves	Inferred Reserves[1]	Undiscovered Recoverable Resources	
		Measured	Indicated			Statistical Mean	Estimated Range[2] (95%-5%)
ONSHORE							
1. Alaska	0.154	9.944	0.013	10.111	6.1[3]	12	6 – 19
2. Pacific Coastal States	15.254	2.699	1.091	19.044	0.3	7	4 – 11
3. Western Rocky Mountains	1.115	0.417	0.089	1.621	0.7	4	2 – 8
4. Northern Rocky Mountains	6.021	1.461	0.256	7.738	1.2	7	5 – 11
5. West Texas and Eastern New Mexico	21.385	7.060	1.991	30.436	1.6	8	4 – 14
6. Western Gulf Basin	31.345	7.082	0.587	39.014	8.6[4]	8	5 – 12
7. Mid-Continent	17.203	1.805	0.211	19.219	1.3	6	3 – 12
8. Michigan Basin	0.645	0.082	0.008	0.735	0.2	1	0.3 – 2
9. Eastern Interior	4.346	0.283	0.009	4.638	0.3	1	0.6 – 2
10. Appalachians	2.539	0.155	0.067	2.761	Negl.[5]	1	0.4 – 2
11. Eastern Gulf and Atlantic Coastal Plain	0.039	0.042	0.006	0.087	0.1	1	0.2 – 2
Total Lower 48 Onshore	99.892	21.086	4.315	125.293	14.3	44	29 – 64
Total Onshore United States	100.046	31.030	4.328	135.404	20.4	56	37 – 81
OFFSHORE (0-200 metres)							
1A. Alaska	0.456	0.150	Negl.[5]	0.606	0.1[3]	15	3 – 31
2A. Pacific Coastal States	1.499	0.858	0.258	2.615	0.2	3	2 – 5
6A. Gulf of Mexico	4.135	2.212	0.050	6.397	2.4	5	3 – 8
11A. Atlantic Coastal States	0.000	0.000	0.000	0.000	0.0	3	2 – 4[6]
Total Lower 48 Offshore	5.634	3.070	0.303	9.012	2.6	11	5 – 18
Total Offshore United States	6.090	3.220	0.308	9.618	2.7	26	10 – 49
Total Lower 48	105.526	24.156	4.623	134.305	16.9	55	36 – 81
Total Alaska	0.610	10.094	0.013	10.717	6.2	27	12 – 49
TOTAL UNITED STATES	106.136	34.250	4.636	145.022	23.1	82	50 – 127

Other independent geological studies produce estimates falling between the low and high U.S.G.S. finding. This is the only auditable inventory of the U. S. oil resources and the only complete study that has been undertaken by this organization which is charged with the responsibility of measuring and reporting the resources of the United States to its government. For these reasons, we have based our projections of the year to year production expectancy on U.S.G.S. Circular 725.

Exhibit 1 reproduces the summary of the remaining recoverable petroleum resource by the U. S. Geological Survey in their Circular 725 finding. The map identifies the regions which are the basis of the inventory and all production reporting. The table begins with the historic fact of cumulative production before 1975 and identifies each of the reserves and future resources, all stated in billions of barrels.

In referring to this table, it should be noted that statistical probability controls the mathematical summations. The measured, indicated, and inferred reserves are relatively precise and are generally confirmed by the American Petroleum Institute's estimates. The critical question concerns the estimated range of the undiscovered recoverable resource. The estimates of this resource are governed by the probability mathematics, first applied to the individual regions and then applied to the combinations which are summarized. The 95% probability estimate for the total country is not the sum of the identified regions.

In our forecast procedure, we have separately and independently projected the year to year production expectancy first for the high probability minimum estimate of the total resource and second for the low probability maximum estimate. These year to year production estimates were determined from an analysis of the historic withdrawal computed from the past, actual production divided by the total remaining resource each year.

Exhibit 2

Ref. Tabulations B,D,
G,H,I,J,K&L

FORECAST OF U. S. LIQUID HYDROCARBON PRODUCTION & DEMAND

Sources: American Petroleum Institute Published Data (1976)
             U. S. Geological Survey, Circular 725 (1975)

Resource Base	Maximum	Minimum
Conterminous U.S.	126.679	81.679
Alaska	66.307	25.307
Natural Gas Liquids	34.350	23.350
(As of 1/1/75)	227.336	130.336

Projections Based On: Consumption At Zero Per Capita Increase
                        1.5% Annual Population Increase
                        Alaska Pipeline Capacity
                        Maximum Probable Annual Production at 2% of
                            Remaining Recoverable Oil In Place
                        Minimum Probable Annual Production at 3-1/3% of
                            Remaining Recoverable Oil In Place

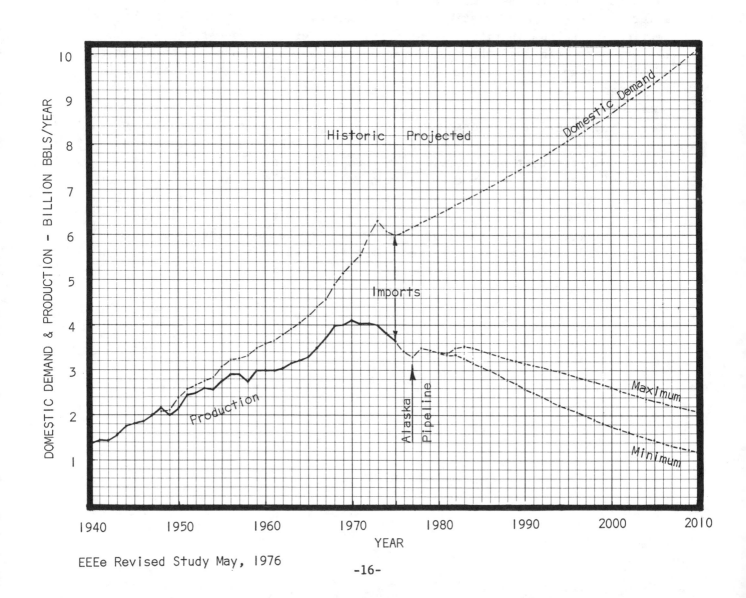

EEEe Revised Study May, 1976

The mathematical procedure which we have employed is a simple, logical extension of the remaining petroleum resource which has been established within narrow limits by the three independent research organizations. The ultimate resource is converted to annual production expectancy by computing the historic annual rate of withdrawal and applying this rate to the resource which will remain year by year. Interestingly, the withdrawal rate for both the maximum and minimum resource estimate peaked and began a slow decline within two years of the highest level this ratio has reached. We stabilized this rate at approximately its current level which is close to the average for the last twenty years. The relatively limited range of movement of this rate improves the reliability of the forecast methodology.

Exhibit 2 graphically presents the forecast conclusion from 1976 to the year 2010 and compares this forecast with past production and domestic consumption since 1940.

The projection of domestic demand is based on a 1.5% annual increase (compounded), recognizing that for the next decade the adult population will be increasing by this amount regardless of the birth rate (Cohort projection of existing sub adult population). The population expansion rate drops slightly in the second decade, and after that the current birth rate will become effective, but there is no great expectancy of a substantial reduction. Thus, the projection closely approximates a zero per capita increase in petroleum consumption over the next thirty-five years. Certainly, in the early years this will not be realized as consumption has been increasing at an average rate close to 4% per year and for the year 1976 the preliminary indications are an 8% increase, overcoming the 1974 decline which was the first significant year to year decline which was the first significant year to year decline since 1932.

The obvious conclusion from Exhibit 2 is the growing dependence on imported petroleum and the inevitability of an increase in this dependence.

Exhibit 3

Ref. Tabulations A,B,C,
D,G,H,I,J,K&L

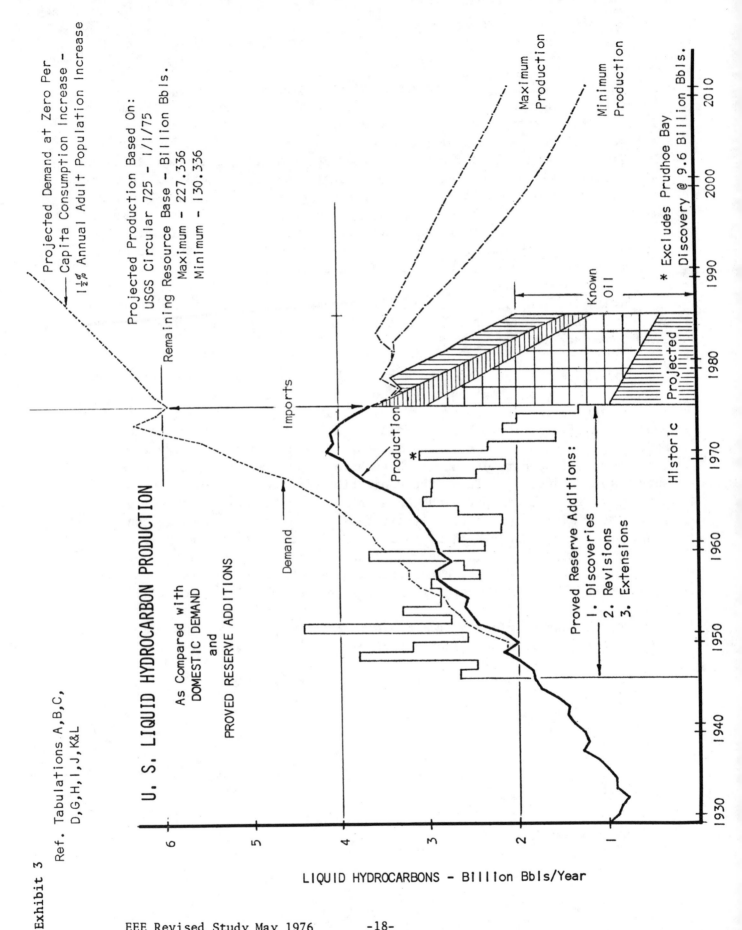

U. S. LIQUID HYDROCARBON PRODUCTION

As Compared with
DOMESTIC DEMAND
and
PROVED RESERVE ADDITIONS

SUMMATION OF HISTORIC PETROLEUM PRODUCTION PARAMETERS AND PROJECTIONS

Exhibit 3 is a summary of the most significant chronological facts relating to petroleum production and petroleum reserves. Each of these series
are presented and explained in Chapter IX, but an overall comprehension is
required to maintain perspective on the total U. S. energy problem at this
point in our discussion. Annual additions to proved reserves have been
decliding and declining substantially since 1951.

The Alaskan discoveries must be kept separate. Alaska is totally different from the lower 48 states both geologically and economically. The
Prudhoe Bay discovery is noted as to quantity but it is not shown on the
reserve addition graph. However, the upper, vertically crosshatched segment of the ten year known oil projection is Prudhoe Bay.

This ten year forecast of known oil has particular significance. It
is based on studies in the field by petroleum geologists familiar with the
production of the largest fields in the United States, including Prudhoe
Bay, Alaska. These fields represent 52% of the remaining proved crude oil
reserves of the country. In my projection, I have assumed that this 52%
sample is representative of the remaining fields and I have extended their
anticipated production through 1985 on the same ratio of decline. Known
oil is thus very specifically identified in this forecast.

THE SIGNIFICANCE OF THE PETROLEUM IMPORTS REQUIREMENT

No attempt was made to *forecast* petroleum consumption, recognizing
that the U. S. consumption will be determined by petroleum availability,
and this will depend on political actions by the Federal government or
by world events outside our control. The demand projection simply provides a reference point for 1½% annual increase corresponding to the
present increase in the adult population and equating to a zero per capita
consumption increase. This compares with an estimated 8% year to year
increase at the end of the second quarter of 1976.

The tremendous gap between the level of the U. S. demand and the
potential U. S. production accentuates the economic and political problem of petroleum supply. No combination of miracles can produce the
quantities required in the years ahead to satisfy this demand. There
is no alternative to the growing dependence on foreign imports except
drastic conservation through rationing controls or the price structure.
The present price structure will not support alternative sources of petroleum, encourage conservation, or discourage continued consumption expansion.

By the year 2000, import requirements will exceed six billion barrels a year if there is no significant increase in the U. S. per capita consumption of petroleum and at this zero growth in consumption, the limitation on the growth in the general economy has always equated with recession bordering on depression. Additional petroleum or replacement energy, with a reasonable probability of being produced during this period, do not add more than enough to provide part of the hoped for 4% economic expansion.

If we are dependent on imports at this six billion barrel per year level, they will represent close to 70% of our petroleum supply. This dependence on foreign sources would preclude a realistically dominant position as a world power. More important, this quantity may not be available in the world market between now and the year 2000. World production is expected to begin to decline only a few years before or after the turn of the century and six billion barrels would represent a little more than our share of a declining world energy resource. An absolute limit in the U. S. oil supply will precipitate a financial crisis.

I V

G A S

Both now and in the future, petroleum is and will be the critical
energy resource because of its versatility and because of its stranglehold on the transportation systems of the free world. But petroleum
will not be the first energy resource to adversely impact "business as
usual" in the United States and precipitate decisions on energy. That
honor is being reserved for natural gas and its replacements, LNG* and
SNG*.

The immediate energy decision — and it can be a critical one for
future generations — concerns the choice of alternatives for the maintenance of the natural gas supply to the U. S. economy. Natural gas production has been declining since 1973. Additions to proved reserves
peaked in 1967. The decline in production within the last two years was
12.8%. The phasing out of Canadian imports has been announced. "Three
quarters of the major pipelines cannot now meet their firm contract
quantities" according to John Nassikas, former chairman of the Federal
Power Commission at the Energy Technology III Conference in Washington,
March 29-31, 1976. At this same conference, evidence was introduced
refuting past estimates of the future production capacity of the U. S.
gas industry and the optimistic anticipations for offshore leasing which
have not been realized and must now be discounted.

The gas supply industry is a major component of the U. S. economy.
In 1975, gas production very nearly equaled petroleum production comparing the energy value of the two resources. Substantial segments of the
economy have become dependent on gas for heat and power, and conversion
to a reliable alternative source of energy is not economically possible
for some segments. The investment in gas transmission lines and delivery
facilities have little value in the absence of a fuel which can utilize
this system.

The gas related decisions involve public policy that is sensitive
both politically and economically. The importation of natural gas other
than from North American neighbors requires expensive liquefaction plants
in the foreign country, a fleet of refrigerated tankers, and an isolated

---

* Footnote on next page.

U. S. port for receipt and storage. The safety problems with the delivery system are extreme and dependence on a foreign source of supply will remain. The alternative, production of synthetic gas from coal, requires much more capital and it is not currently competitive with the imported liquefied natural gas. The cheapest free market substitute is oil and its products. Oil can either replace gas by the conversion of the user equipment and the installation of a tank, or petroleum can be used to produce a natural gas substitute, but both uses ignore the nation's vulnerability to an interruption in supply or international blackmail.

The process of substituting liquid petroleum for natural gas is well advanced. It is critical. If this substitution continues, our total energy problem will be much more difficult to resolve in only a few years' time.

The gas decisions will introduce a sequence of events which will set in motion decisions affecting the free economy and the free society. The economy is mixed today, partly controlled by government agencies and the complex of political prerogatives, partly controlled by corporation decisions and the uninhibited initiative of individuals. But the economy is unplanned in principle and the planning balance which has existed through trade associations and corporate control of market segments has been under attack by liveral ideologists while national planning is the greatest fear of the conservative interests. There have been few hard facts in the seventy-five year ideological battle. Now this is changing, and it appears that the natural gas supply and demand statistics will be the critical element in the conclusion.

---

* Liquefied natural gas (LNG) can be imported in a delivery system which maintains a temperature of 260° below zero F. Substitute or synthetic natural gas (SNG) can be produced from coal, and there is a synthetic gas producible from liquid petroleum.

THE U. S. NATURAL GAS FORECAST

There are substantial differences between natural gas and liquid petroleum requiring differences in the specifics of analysis and forecast procedure. In the beginning, gas was undesired, a by-product of petroleum exploration and production. Gas provided the pressure, raising petroleum to the surface, which pressure needed to be controlled to obtain maximum petroleum recovery. Gas can be pumped into oil fields to regenerate petroleum production in secondary recovery. Gas can be stored in pumped-out gas or oil fields. Gas may migrate horizontally and vertically far from its original location and its association with liquid petroleum. Commercial gas production may begin and end suddenly. Gas fields can be depleted faster than oil fields without reducing the amount of gas that the field will finally produce.

Because of the difficulty of transporting gas long distances or of storing gas - economically prohibitive in tanks or tankers - gas was originally burned in the field and still is in some areas remote from a user market. In contrast to the 125 year history of petroleum production in the United States, gas production records are reliable only for a little more than the last twenty-five years. For practical purposes, the gas industry is a post World War II phenomenon when petroleum pipelines were employed to test the economics of interstate transmission and a broadly based marketing system. The gas industry virtually exploded between 1950 and 1970. Every community wanted gas and the gas pipeline companies supplied these needs as rapidly as possible. Gas was cleaner and easier to burn than either coal or oil and it was cheaper. It was difficult to resist the temptation to depend on gas and the U. S. economy did not resist that temptation.

Coal burning facilities were abandoned, many of them demolished to make room for the non-polluting gas-fired boilers and generators. The conversion could be paid for in a few years and the process was, in more recent years, substantially assisted by governmental restrictions on the pollution from coal-fired boilers. Residential and commercial structures proliferated with an almost total dependence on gas fuel, no available area for the storage of coal or a stack to carry off the waste products of coal combustion. Even the reversion to oil is difficult. Central oil or coal based steam plants were often abandoned and their distribution lines were allowed to deteriorate beyond repair. And most of this occurred within a time span of only two decades.

Exhibit 4   Tabulations N-1 & P-1

FORECAST OF U. S. NATURAL GAS
PRODUCTION & DEMAND

Sources: American Gas Association Published Data - 1976
U. S. Geological Survey Circular 725 - 1975

Remaining Recoverable Resource	Maximum	Minimum
Lower 48 States	1018.065	625.965
Alaska	111.667	70.667
(As of 1/1/75)	1129.732 TCF	696.632 TCF

Production projection based on maximum and minimum probable
annual regional production at variable rates of withdrawal
as related to the fields in question and the alternative
transmission systems proposed.

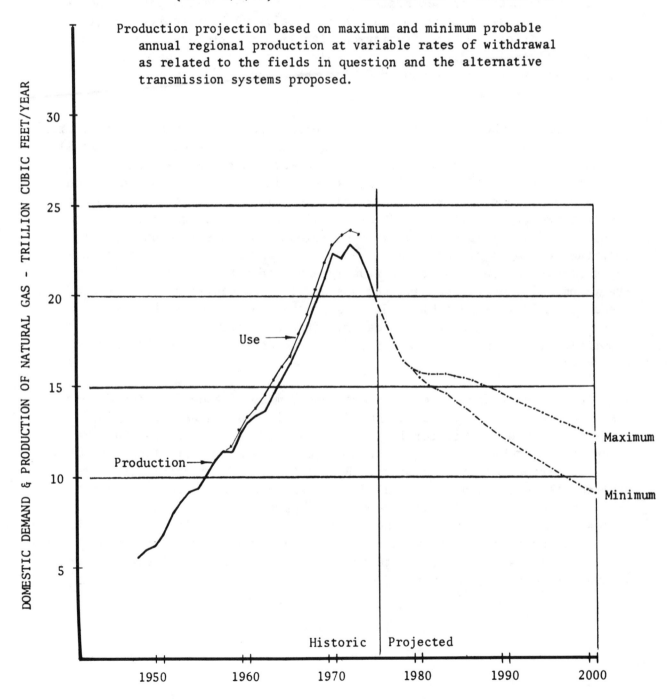

As a consequence, the increase in the supply of natural gas to the U. S. economy was much more rapid than petroleum. Similarly, the decline experienced to date has been much more rapid, and the projection of the probable future natural gas production in the United States continues this relatively rapid decline. Gas is more volatile than petroleum both physically and economically.

The gas production history and the gas reserves are also much less consistent because of its physical and economic characteristic. Past production and future expectancy differs substantially from region to region, with the consequence that future projections are much less reliable on an annual basis than they were with petroleum. Fortunately, the U.S.G.S. inventory of the future gas resource was compiled on a regional basis and the production history is available on this same basis. Thus, I have been able to relate my forecast on a regional rather than on a national basis for natural gas. This regional treatment requires ten separate forecasts, as only the regions in the eastern third of the country could be combined without sacrificing too much accuracy in the conclusion.

Each gas region forecast follows the same procedure employed for oil. The year to year production is based on the stabilized rate of withdrawal applied to the remaining resource. The rate of withdrawal developed from the record of past production divided by the resource which actually remained that year, accepting the accuracy of the U.S.G.S. 725 ultimate resource forecast. The forecast thus produces the logical year to year gas production expectancy and the forecast becomes more accurate each year. Since the inventory spread actually represents the probable maximum and minimum eventual resource, the forecast has a high confidence level.

It should be noted that both my gas and oil forecasts have recognized the specific limitation of the actual oil pipeline and the projected gas pipeline. On an annual basis, no more oil can be delivered and the analysis indicates that additional pipelines cannot be justified. Further discussion of the natural gas forecast will be found in Part Two.

THE GAS ECONOMY SQUEEZE

Exhibit 5 introduces the profile of gas use in the U. S. and the forecast of maximum availability through 1995 identifying the substitutions which may be available. The impingement of reduced gas supply on the economic segments dependent on gas are indicated by comparing the upper and lower graphs of this figure. As with all of the projections, my forecast of U. S. produced gas is indicated as the primary reference.

The gas use profile recognizes the prior claim of the gas industry on any production, followed by residential and commercial, but it should not be assumed that the priority segments will be immune from the gas squeeze. The industrial sector has demonstrated its ability to move rapidly to find substitute fuels in the same manner that it moved rapidly to take advantage of the economics of gas availability. Neither the utility segment nor the industrial segment can immediately abandon gas and in an actual gas shortage in any specific community, an electrical blackout or a total shutdown of the industry would be more devastating than discomfort in the commercial and residential segments for lack of heating and air conditioning. As we are rapidly approaching the critical areas in gas availability, the problem with these decisions should become apparent very soon. At the top of Exhibit 5, the numerical basis for the gas consumption profile is indicated in trillions of cubic feet per year from 1950 through 1985. The imports represent the net balance of Canadian receipts after subtracting our exports to Canada. These can be computed by comparing total consumption with the previous tabulations of historic production and our projections of the maximum and minimum future expectancy.

The lower section of Exhibit 5 identifies the estimates of substitute sources of natural gas equivalent, beginning with the tapering off of Canadian imports. Even the minimum estimates include fairly optimistic anticipations for a development of the liquefied natural gas industry, synthetic gas from coal, and the existing synthetic gas from liquid petroleum, naptha produced from natural gas liquids (the by-product of petroleum production.) There is a reasonable spread between these maximum and minimum natural gas substitutes which add to our projected maximum and minimum domestic production.

The conclusion should be obvious. Even with optimistic expectancy for the development of natural gas substitutes, the gap between supply and demand is rapidly increasing. The gap spells physical shortage, economic losses, and inadequate heating for the immediate future, 1977.

Exhibit 5

U. S. GAS DEMAND BY PRIORITY AND TOTAL PROJECTED SUPPLY SOURCE

Sector Consumption:	1950	1955	1960	1965	1970	1971	1972	1973	1974	1980	1985
Electric Utility	.63	1.15	1.73	2.32	3.88	3.99	3.98	3.61	3.43	1.81	1.07
Industrial	2.04	2.78	3.76	5.12	7.20	7.44	7.42	7.98	7.56	7.50	7.50
Commercial	.39	.63	1.02	1.44	2.06	2.17	2.29	2.29	2.26	2.25	2.25
Residential	1.20	2.12	3.10	3.90	4.84	4.97	5.13	4.88	4.78	4.75	4.75
Gas Industry Use:	-	-	-	-	-	-	-	-	-	-	-
Transmission Loss	.18	.25	.27	.32	.23	.34	.33	.20	.29	.32	.30
Venting & Flaring	.80	.77	.56	.32	.49	.28	.25	.25	.17	.20	.10
Field Use	1.19	1.51	1.78	1.91	2.31	2.30	2.36	2.41	2.36	2.50	2.75
Refinery Use	.46	.63	.78	.86	1.03	1.06	1.07	1.07	1.04	.90	.85
Pipeline Fuel	.13	.25	.35	.50	.72	.74	.77	.73	.67	.60	.55
TOTAL CONSUMPTION:	7.02	10.09	13.35	16.69	22.76	23.29	23.60	23.42	22.56	20.83	20.12

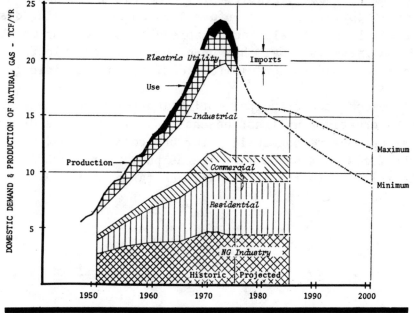

Projected Gas Supply	1975	1980		1985		1990		1995	
	Actual	Max.	Min.	Max.	Min.	Max.	Min.	Max.	Min.
Domestic NG Production	19.72	15.75	15.48	15.47	13.81	14.43	11.99	13.30	10.42
Canadian NG Imports	1.00	.50	.30	.20	0	0	0	0	0
LNG Imports	0	.60	.20	1.00	.50	1.50	1.00	2.00	1.00
Coal Gasification	0	.30	.20	1.10	.70	2.20	1.20	3.00	2.00
Naptha (NGL's)	.40	.40	.30	.40	.20	.30	0	.20	0
Storage Losses	-.09	-.15	-.10	-.15	-.10	-.15	-.10	-.15	-.10
U. S. Exports	-.07	-.04	-.02	-.01	0	0	0	0	0
Total Supply (TCF/Yr)	20.96	17.36	16.36	18.01	15.11	18.28	14.09	18.35	13.32

The critical time for decision on alternatives to the natural gas supply is already in the past. So far, the decision has been avoided and there is very little public awareness of the decision default. Canadian gas has continued to be available and petroleum has been substituted for gas in the industrial and utility segments. The 1974-75 recession and abnormally warm winters contributed to maintaining the balance. More important to the explanation of the deferred decision, the alternatives have been politically unacceptable. The democratic process has no machinery for accepting advanced information on an impending disaster. Munich was the only politically acceptable alternative for Chamberlain's England and "business as usual" has been the only scenario for the U. S. economy's acceptance of the precipitous decline in available gas energy.

Gas will become the principal motivation for recognizing energy limits, but alternatives will not be chosen as long as the decision makers can escape the responsibility for the consequences. In the final analysis, the decision must be made in the public arena and thus, the hurt must be felt before the action will be taken.

V

A T O M I C   E N E R G Y ,   S O L A R   E N E R G Y   A N D   C O A L

Nuclear fusion and extraterrestrial solar power are the hope of the future, but this hope requires analysis. It is based on the assumption that money will buy success in scientific discovery. The problem with this optimistic expectancy derives from the limitations of the scientific community. No amount of money will produce a scientific miracle.

The unfortunate fact is the limited area of the real scientific successes. The miracles have been confined to electronics and there has been very little actual progress in the energy field. Money can buy progress in developing the application of a scientific breakthrough, but the kind of scientific discovery required to achieve a controlled nuclear fusion reaction has resisted both time and very substantial quantities of money.

The laws of thermodynamics have not been altered by new discoveries in the last 150 years. Even the most advanced and most efficient system for producing electric power through magnetohydrodynamics was discovered by Michael Farraday in the mid-1880's. We are simply waiting on the pedestrian process of finding metals which will contain the 5,000°F. gases to put this scientific principle into practice and produce electricity in a single process avoiding the conventional boiler and electric generator. Although this was not accomplished in the first hundred years, it can be anticipated in the second.

A controlled atomic fusion reaction presents a very different problem. The required temperatures are measured in millions of degrees, fifty to one hundred million centigrade. Scientists are still trying to make it happen in a laboratory situation. Competent engineers are unable to conceive of a controllable process. Atomic fusion is observable in the universe and in a bomb which employs atomic fission for initiation, but that is where we are. No responsible scientist can promise a delivery date for the controlled process. After that, all agree that twenty years are required to develop an industry able to deliver fusion power.

The light water atomic reactor which is responsible for most of the U. S. electronic power generation today was recently observed as a natural phenomenon. An African excavation uncovered the evidence of water seeping through fissionable natural uranium elements, producing energy and the expected uranium isotope over a ten thousand year time span. All of today's electric generating plants represent relatively minor improvements on James Watts' 1769 condensing steam engine and Michael Farraday's 1831 electric generator.

NUCLEAR POWER TODAY

It is with this perspective that we must view the more than $40 billion expended on atomic research for the peaceful generation of power since the bombs were developed. The scientists have not been unemployed these last thirty years and the specific problems of our energy needs had been anticipated for at least two-thirds of this time span. Light water atomic reactors are in operation producing electricity. We can build more of these reactors but we don't have enough fuel. An energy economy based on this process cannot be supplied from known American resources much after the turn of the century.

The breeder reactor is in substantial trouble in this country, but in recent years, European scientists and Russian scientists have developed working models producing electricity. Thus, we can anticipate an atomic breeder but we must accept with it the by-product, plutonium, available for the proliferation of atomic bombs and incompatible with the free society that we know today. The question then becomes our ability to withstand the temptation to join the world of breeder energy when the plutonium bomb producing by-product of that world is available outside our borders and could hardly be kept out.

The acceptance of the atomic breeder reactor is not a simple decision that will result in the immediate availability of energy. If American scientists approved the processes which appear to be available in the world, and the American society withdrew its objections, it would take twenty years to replace any significant portion of our electric power generating capacity with the atomic breeder reactor, and some materials are in critical supply and might not be available for the completion of this process.

SOLAR ENERGY

Solar energy is a renewable source of power. It is the power source
that created the fossil fuels over a few hundred million years with the
assistance of the continental drift and the internal energy of the earth
that buried the animal and vegetable materials. Solar energy is responsible for wind energy, hydraulic energy, and the energy from wood and vegetable materials. Solar energy is largely non-polluting, and above the
earth's atmosphere and the earth's own shadow, it is equally distributed.

The uses of solar energy as a source of heat or power vary with the
gathering process. On the surface of the earth, solar energy is limited
by atmospheric interference, the diurnal rotation of the earth, the latitude of the observer, and the season of the year. Solar energy in space
is not limited by these factors, but the transmission from a satellite
station of enough power to significantly help the U. S. energy supply is
economically beyond reach. The theory of a space station generating
electric power and transmitting it to the earth in quantities sufficient
to power the U. S. economy is just as remote in the combination of scientific and economic feasibility as atomic fusion.

The scientific processes required to build a solar plant in space
are available today but refinement of several of the elements will be
necessary before the cost will become reasonable. Large scale solar
energy collection from above the earth's atmosphere requires a space
platform 22,000 miles from the earth's surface and microwave transmission
of ten million kilowatts of direct current power to a receiving station on
earth. The reflectors in space would be two miles wide and the receiver
on the earth would occupy a number of square miles plus a no-man's land
for safety. The system multiplies by ten thousand the largest space power
system in existence today.

The costing of solar power from space does not appear reliable. It
will depend on a space shuttle and technology which is conceivable but
not available.

The real barrier to extraterrestrial solar power is the environmental danger. Power transmitted from the satellite would represent a death
ray capable of unbelievable damage if its focus strayed from the target
receiver. The microwaves would be partially dispersed by rain, adding
both to the danger of the dispersion of radiation and the tenuous reliability of the power source.

Solar energy must be recognized as the power that can be gathered from two kinds of terrestrially based gathering systems. Flat bed collectors absorb solar energy in proportion to their area and they are limited by the temperature generated by the sun's rays after penetrating the earth's atmosphere at a specific location over a specific period of time. The most economical flat plate collectors have a fixed orientation, but the same principle applies to a manually or automatically oriented collector. By these means, more of the sun's rays can be captured on the horizontal surface. However, the directing of a flat bed collector does not increase the ultimate temperature of the system, and this ultimate temperature controls thermal efficiency.

The second type of collector requires curved mirrors which concentrate the rays of the sun on a small target, producing very high temperatures. Solar energy gathered by a number of mirrors adding together to equal an acre of reflecting surface can focus on a few square feet and produce temperatures that are limited only by the effective temperature of the sun itself. These generating systems are complicated, expensive to install, and they are not free of operating cost as the system must be maintained. Obviously, with unlimited temperatures, high efficiency power production is possible, but only for short periods of time.

The solar energy concept has captured the imagination of the American public. The complexity of the process produces intriguing discussion with new terms and opportunities for hyperbola. But the hard facts of solar energy come down to its limitations. Photosynthesis, nature's method of converting solar radiation to usable sources of energy employing the chlorophyll of plants, is only one percent efficient. The practical availability of solar energy very closely approximates that which can be felt and seen. On the days that the sun does not shine, the wind blows, and water freezes, the largest solar collector that is economically conceivable for an individual family unit will scarcely warm water for tea. If you do not feel warm standing in front of a window that faces the sun, a solar heat generator will not do very much for you.

There is little question about the potential efficiency of solar heating systems for individual homes in the southwestern United States. We need only to improve on the Indian's adobe huts and modern materials to produce solar heated houses. There is a time lapse in the transfer of heat through all materials. Stone and masonry constructions can be built of a thickness which requires a twelve hour time lag. The southwest Indians used this principle. The heat of the day reached inside their adobe huts during the cool of the night. Solar rays pass through glass but the heat generated when the rays impinge on solid objects is trapped. If there's enough sun, these two principles can be effectively employed to maintain reasonable comfort levels.

In the northern quarter of this country, solar heat is not an obvious solution and, in fact, may be no solution at all. The Indians at these latitudes burned wood to maintain the minimum requirements of animal existence during the winter season and I can personally attest to the significant air pollution of their camps in all seasons.

Exhibit 6 introduces the basic parameters of the solar heating problem of the northeast quarter of the United States. The United States Weather Service records the power of the sun on an hourly basis at their major weather stations. The unit of measure is the Langley, one gram calorie per square centimeter which equates to 3.687 Btu per sq. ft. The measure is taken in a horizontal attitude which has been corrected for an optimum fixed orientation of 55° to the horizontal, due south azimuth. There is no significance to the assumed 50% collector efficiency except to establish a reference base.

Only the collection of low temperature, solar energy for home heating and hot water heating is economically feasible. Silicon cell electric power collectors would cost $20 a watt of peak capacity and only a few hours would be available in the northern latitudes to produce the average electrical load of 18.6 kwh per day. By the same token, the cost of focusing flat plate collectors or high temperature parabolic collectors is prohibitively expensive and too complicated for the home operator. Thus, only the fixed orientation flat bed collector can be considered and I have found no evidence of a collection system which is competitive with fossil fuel costs today or in the immediate future.

The physical problems of developing and operating an efficient collector are multiple. First, only the available solar power can be collected. This limitation is indicated on Exhibit 6 which identifies the heat which could be collected at the assumed 50% efficiency and the cost of the average unit available on the market today. The 500 sq. ft. collector represents a cost of a little less than $12,000 and should produce enough solar heat for the average day of the five month heating season for a 1,250 sq. ft. home, but this is only the beginning. The first problem is with the averages. It will produce only 60% of this theoretical average during the month of December if all December days are average. On minimum December days, less than 1% of the

Exhibit 6

PERSPECTIVE ON SOLAR POWER POTENTIAL

For Existing Homes in Northern United States
Latitude 42° to 43°

Based on records of U. S. Weathern Bureau at Lansing, Michigan
corrected for optimum fixed flat plate collector
(55° to horizontal, south orientation)
and 50% collector efficiency

Unit Measure		Total Energy Per 24 Hour Day	
		Sun Power Langley*	Heat Power Btu Flat Plate
Collector		Bolometer	Fluid
Efficiency of system for horizontal collection			13%
Efficiency at optimum fixed orientation			33%

AVERAGE DAY OF FIVE MONTH HEATING SEASON:

	Sun Power Langley	Heat Power Btu Flat Plate Fluid
Horizontal (Reading) Collection	183	337/sf
Optimum Fixed Orientation Collection	457.5	843/sf

96 S.F. COLLECTOR (3 - 4'x8' PANELS) at Opt.
  Fixed Orientation   80,928 Btu

PRESENT DAILY USE:

Average heat used in 1,500 sf home	828,000 Btu/day
Same home with total insulation (min.elect.std.)	387,200 Btu/day

SOLAR HEATING SYSTEM SIZE & COST:

Solar Collector Size in	Sq. Ft.	100	300	500	700
Collection & Storage System Cost	Dollar	4,000	8,400	11,500	14,700
Nominal Living Area for Solar Panel	Sq. Ft.	250	750	1,250	1,750
Solar Heat Av/Day 5 mo. Heating Season	Btu	84,300	252,900	421,500	590,100

MONTHLY & DAILY VARIATION IN SOLAR HEAT:

	Horiz. Meter Langley	Btu	Per	Day	
December average day	111	51,143	153,429	255,715	358,001
March average day	303	139,607	418,821	698,035	977,240
Minimum day December	.6	276	552	1,380	1,932
Maximum day December	250	115,188	345,564	575,940	806,316

AREA VARIATION:

Grand Rapids, 42° 58 min. north is 94% of Lansing, 42° 44 min. north
Detroit   42° 20 min. north is 102% of Lansing
Detroit sunshine percent of possible: December 32%, March 49%

* One Langley=3.687 Btu/sq.ft.

five month heating season average can be expected, and Michigan can register one minimum day after another with no break.

The next problem is with the efficiency of the collection system. Efficiency is defined in terms of the amount of heat that can be collected relative to the amount of heat that is available as measured by the Weather Bureau's bolometer. For low temperature heat collection, we need to be concerned only with the first law of thermodynamics, the non-reversibility of the process. During the winter months, the radiant heat loss exceeds the radiant heat input for all parts of the United States. The collector must be designed to receive radiant heat when the sun is shining and avoid the loss of radiant heat as soon as the solar flow is reduced for any reason to the point where the losses exceed the gains. At all stages in the process, the energy flows both ways: the solar collector receives radiant heat and the collector loses heat to the surrounding atmosphere by radiation, conduction, and convection. The limited flow of solar heat for reason of atmospheric interference is measured by the bolometer, but this instrument does not measure the radiant heat that is unavailable for reason of the short time span of the radiant flow. Several hours are required at the beginning of the solar heating day to bring the solar collector up to temperature and compensate for the inherent losses in the collection process. The system must be warmed up, and when the sun shines all day, this warming up occurs as the sun rises and obtains a path sufficiently free of atmospheric interference to register positive radiant heat. The system cannot be efficient at marginal levels of radiation and the system cannot be efficient with intermittent radiation.

Finally, the value of the heat collected by the system is limited by the temperature that it is able to produce. The solar collector may be very efficient in raising the temperature of the ambient air from zero degrees Fahrenheit to 50°F., but the water or the rocks that are warmed by the system to only 50° will produce a limited amount of comfort.

Solar energy can provide hot water during the summer months and contribute to reducing the cost of hot water during the winter season. Solar energy provides the foundation for other systems of heating including off-peak load electrical employment of the heat pump and the storage of heat in insulated water tanks. The low temperature heat produced from the solar process could be stored in liquid form. The temperature could be raised with electrical input, stored again, and circulated through hot water heat exchangers in the living area. This becomes an expensive system. It requires optimum off-peak electrical rates. The efficiency of the solar collector itself will approach zero in terms of delivered comfort when there is intermittent cloud cover and the temperature is low.

COAL AND THE KAIPAROWITS EXPERIENCE

In 1977, coal moved into the center of the energy solution controversy. For years the producible U. S. coal reserve was conservatively estimated at something over six hundred billion tons. Only the Russian reserves were greater. Coal was the U. S. energy insurance policy. With production substantially below one billion tons per year, the supply was considered to represent five hundred years of potential energy, but that was before oil and gas began to run out and atomic power lost its luster.

When coal began to become important enough to require checking the reserve figures, the reserve began to shrink. The veins were not as thick as they had been thought to be, much of the coal was found to be uneconomical to produce. With energy costs exceeding the energy value, there was no net energy. The confident six hundred billion tons became two hundred and fifty billion tons with no assurance from any source of the reliability of the estimates.

The really chilling revelations related the coal reserve to current energy requirements. Western coal has a much lower heat value than eastern coal, and lignite has less than half the average coal value. By 1990, the effect of western coal production will reduce the average heat value from the present 12,000 Btu's per pound to 10,000. At this level, fifty million tons of coal will be required to produce one quadrillion Btu's, and in 1975, we used 75½ of these quads, or the equivalent of 3.75 billion tons.

But this is only the beginning of the calculations. Coal is the only resource available to replace oil and gas, and this replacement depends on its conversion in an expensive process which loses 40% of the coal's original heat value. The 53.7 quads of oil and gas which were used in 1975 would require ninety quads of coal at this 60% conversion efficiency, representing 4½ billion tons. When you add more than a billion tons anticipated for electric power production between now and the end of the century, a coal economy would require five or six billion tons a year and the presently estimated coal reserves would represent only forty or fifty years.

Coal is dangerous to produce, costly to produce, and costly to burn without substantial pollution. The technology is available to reduce the coal burning effluent to tolerable levels but very little progress has been made in the last fifteen years in resolving the problem of defining and administering pollution standards at costs which the total society can agree upon.

The thirteen year history of the planned coal generating plant on the Kaiparowits Plateau in Utah is particularly instructive in its relationship to the nation's declining natural gas producing capacity. The plant was planned by a group of utilities including Southern California Edison and San Diego Gas & Electric Company to supply power to this west coast market. The plant was planned for a capacity of six million kilowatts, burning 60,000 tons of coal a day. This capacity is $3\frac{1}{2}$ times the 1971 rating of the combined Hoover, Parker, and Davis Dams on the Colorado River.

This compares with the installed capacity of the electric power industry in 1972 of 418 million kilowatts or 1.4%. This capacity also compares with 31 million kilowatts of added capacity between 1971 and 1972, twenty-seven million kilowatts added in each of the two previous years, and it is less than half the minimum annual capacity added since 1960.

The Kaiparowits plant would have served the area now supplied largely by gas burning utilities and would have made possible the retiring of these gas burning generators or their conversion. Further, the Kaiparowits plant supplied an area of the country which is extremely sensitive to the problems of air pollution associated with a coal burning utility. The plant would have avoided dependence on both gas and liquid petroleum to generate electricity. In terms of petroleum imports, which will be the ultimate consequence of not building the plant, the original plant represented .4 million barrels per day.

The most inefficient use of natural gas is burning it to produce electricity. With available gas transport lines, twice as much usable heat can be delivered through gas lines as through electric power lines. The unnecessary thermodynamic conversion cost (40% reasonable maximum efficiency) can be avoided, and the natural gas obviously avoids the efficiency loss (60% expected efficiency) of the conversion of coal to gas. Thus, there is approximately a three to one advantage in the conversion to coal of a gas burning electric generation plant, which is supplying heat to its customers.

But after thirteen years of attempts to meet environmental qualifications, the plan for the Kaiparowits plant was abandoned. Its planned coal consumption is approximately six times the basic SNG* plant. The nation needs the energy in some form. More, smaller plants will lose economic advantage and will not reduce the environmental impact very much.

---

* Synthetic natural gas and oil plants are currently planned for a coal input of 10,000 tons/day, producing .048 quadrillion Btu per year at capacity which equates with a requirement of 21 plants to produce one quad. The cost of one plant unit is estimated at $1.5 billion. If we were to replace half of the 1975 oil and gas usage with synthetic oil and gas, 567 of these plants would be required and it would take 22 years if we completed one every two weeks.

To replace the Kaiparowits plant with solar energy having six thousand megawatts of peak capacity would require 23 square miles of photovoltaic cells at a present cost of $120 billion. If ERDA and the Mobil Tyco Solar Energy Corporation* are successful in meeting their cost reduction objectives with their new process, this cost would be brought down to $14 billion, but at the optimum location on the U. S. southwest border, the solar system would be productive only 24% of the time, requiring a 4.2 multiple on costs and area to provide the equivalent annual capacity of Kaiparowits. Three-quarters of the power generated during the sunny hours of the day would have to be stored for use when the sun power is not available; and hydraulic storage is the only practical solution to this problem, a reservoir into which water would be pumped an optimum elevation with a generator to produce the hydraulic power when required. As the capacity of Kaiparowits is 3½ times the Colorado River flow through Hoover Dam, Parker and Davis Dams, a very substantial proportion of the Grand Canyon would be needed to provide this reservoir and equivalent vertical lift.

The significance of Kaiparowits is not the environmental impact. The impact is social, political, and economic. The attack is aimed at the planning function in our economy, the same planning function that the economists deny. Industry must plan to provide services for the future and the Kaiparowits plan which began thirteen years ago for the supply of power to Southern California was not premature in its timing. The plant should have been built within the five to ten year time spectrum. As was anticipated when it was planned by the utility industry, it is now needed to reduce dependence on oil and gas, an uneconomic source of fuel today which will soon be unavailable.

Energy is required to build the world of the future as well as continuing the operation of the world we have already built. With reference to solar cells, Dr. Martin Wolfe of the University of Pennsylvania has noted that the cells require so much power to build, that it will take forty years to recover this energy from the cells' own production to balance their cost. The question must then be raised as to the life expectancy of the cells. Are they in fact capable of producing net energy? The sun's energy is free in nature but not in its economic employment.

---

* The photovoltaic generation of electricity by Bruce Chalmers *Scientific American,* October, 1976.

V I

THE ENERGY BALANCE FOR THE NEXT TEN YEARS

Only a short time span has political and economic significance in
our free society. Ten years is a maximum. Only one, two, four, six,
and eight years are important for the business executive and the politician. The time span which has significance is the length of time that
a man is responsible for the consequences of his own decisions. Only
the President is required to look eight years ahead and then only when
he begins his term. It is difficult to overstate the significance of
the actual planning limits of our free economy and political system.
Ultimately, this problem must be faced and the decision can be more
critical than the decisions I am identifying with the energy problem.
We will have to find a way of representing the future of man and his
society in the political and economic process.

The natural world operates on time cycles that extend beyond man's
economic and political horizons, and it is the relationship with this
natural world that is involved in the availability of energy. There are
very few doubts as to the direction of physical change and the consequence
of physical actions in the natural world, but there are questions as to
when these events will take place. In my analysis of energy availability
I began with the known physical facts of the remaining resources and projected the inevitable sequence of probable year to year production over
the total time span. Then I considered the immediate future.

This approach accounts for the primary difference between my conclusions
and the conclusions of the Federal Energy Administration, the Interior Department, the General Accounting Office, and the other organizations directed by
the Administrative and Congressional branches of the government. They have
begun with the present. They have *not* been concerned with the decreasing resource and its inevitable effect on year to year production potential. They
have concentrated on the month to month extrapolation of economic demand.
They have considered political influence but ignored physical fact. In
assuming an infinite resource, they have neglected the reality of even the
next five years.

My ten year projection brings the facts of the U. S. energy problem
into political and economic focus, and this projection is integrated with
my long term forecast. The critical nature of the problem becomes obvious.
Both immediately and as far as we can see into the future, there is not
enough energy to support the expanding U. S. economy.

Exhibit 7   Ref. Tabulation Q,R,S,
                                                          T,U,

U. S. ENERGY SUPPLY AND DEMAND

1975 through 1985

Quadrillion Btu/Yr.

1×10^{15}

	1975 Actual	1980 Maximum	1980 Minimum	1985 Maximum	1985 Minimum
SUPPLY					
Domestic Production:					
Petroleum	21.17	19.72	19.72	19.95	17.92
Natural Gas	20.20	16.13	15.85	15.83	14.14
Coal	15.36	17.20	15.30	20.85	17.20
Nuclear @47,100 Btu/watt capacity	1.83	3.50	2.50	7.20	4.80
Hydro @47,500 Btu/watt capacity	3.21	3.40	3.20	4.10	3.40
Domestic Synthetics:					
Syngas, Naptha, and Syncrude	.41	.72	.51	1.54	.92
Other Domestic Sources:					
Shale Oil	-0-	-0-*	-0-*	.58	-0-
Geothermal	-0-*	-0-*	-0-*	.07	.04
Solar: Electric	-0-*	-0-*	-0-*	.02	.01
Heating & Air Conditioning	-0-*	-0-*	-0-*	.13	.07
Solid Wastes	-0-*	-0-*	-0-*	-0-	-0-
Net Imports:					
Natural Gas	1.03	.51	.31	.21	-0-
Liquefied Natural Gas	-0-	.62	.21	1.03	.51
Subtotal Supply, except Petro.Imports	63.21	61.80	57.60	71.51	59.02

*Negligible Production

DEMAND

Actual in 10^{15} Btu	75.51		
Projected @2.2% increase per year		83.96	93.40

REQUIRED PETROLEUM IMPORTS

	1975	1980 Max	1980 Min	1985 Max	1985 Min
Actual in 10^{15} Btu	12.30				
Projected max + min 10^{15} Btu		22.16	26.38	21.89	34.38

Petroleum in Billions of Barrels per Year					
Net Imports Required	2.12	3.80	4.55	3.77	5.93

AVAILABLE PETROLEUM IMPORTS

Actual past imports (gross)	2.20		
Estimate future potential (max.)			
Free world)(See Exhibit 8)		3.32	4.61
Sino-Soviet contribution)		.02	.04
Total Estimated Imports available to U. S.		3.34	4.65

Exhibit 7 summarizes the total energy supply and demand for 1975, 1980, and 1985. The reference base in quadrillions of Btu's is beginning to become familiar, but the significant fact in this analysis is the relationship between alternative sources of supply and the overall energy demand. The limits of energy convertibility from one source to another become critical after considering the total energy availability.

In this supply projection, I employed our own estimates of domestic petroleum and natural gas availability. The nuclear plants over this short time span are under construction or in planning. The coal estimates for 1980 and 1985 are based on the Library of Congress research study currently in progress, which is based on the country's physical capacity to develop the mining facilities and the electrical plants during this time span. In 1980, the conversion from tons to heat value is based on 10,600 Btu per pound; in 1985, 10,100.

Exhibit 7 develops the requirement for imported petroleum, the only energy resource that will be available in the next ten years to meet the net energy requirements of the U. S. economy. At the bottom of Exhibit 7, the net requirements in common energy units is converted to equivalent barrels of petroleum stated in billions per year. The question then becomes the availability of this quantity of petroleum in the world market.

The conclusion is astounding. The total quantity of oil required by the United States in 1980 is not available in the world market. We will be short one million barrels per day under the maximum U. S. oil and gas production expectancy, and we will be short three million barrels a day if the more conservative minimum forecast of U. S. production proves accurate. A great push to get more oil and gas for one or two years will only compound the problem after that short time span. U. S. energy depends on the petroleum supply.

Petroleum is the only energy resource immediately available to the United States' economy by importation from the world supply. It is also the only energy resource that possesses the versatility to satisfy the actual specific requirements of our various energy systems. Oil can be substituted for gas as a boiler fuel with minor conversion costs and pipeline grade gas can be produced from the light ends of liquid petroleum. Oil will do most anything that coal will do with less cost. The converse is not true. Very substantial costs are involved in the conversion of coal to serve the petroleum or gas energy purpose.

The common measurement of all energy resources is the British thermal unit (Btu), the amount of heat required to raise one pound of water 1°F. The conversion for nuclear energy is based on the Atomic Energy Commission's average for 1974 of 10,660 Btu per kwh. The thermal equivalent for hydro-electric production is based on the average for the fossil fuels of 10,389 Btu per kwh. Thus, there are very small differences in the common measure between alternative sources of energy. The basic conversions are:

1 cu. ft. of gas	=	1,024 Btu
1 bbl. of oil	=	5,800,000 Btu
1 short ton of coal in 1975	=	24,000,000 Btu to 20,000,000 in 1990*
1 kwh electrical output	=	3,413 Btu

The conversion of heat energy to electrical energy entails a loss of very nearly two-thirds of the energy input (the consequence of the second law of thermodynamics). Electrical energy identified as capacity of the generating plants is measured in watts or multiples of watts without the hour designation. There are 8,760 hours in the year which would be the multiple to convert watt capacity to watt hours of potential output, but only a little more than half of the capacity can be employed in the average year as electricity cannot be stored and production must be cut back when it is not in demand.

Tabulations R, T and U (Appendix) identify the energy forecast in terms of barrels of oil, cubic feet of gas, tons of coal, and electric generating capacity of the nuclear and hydro plants. The nuclear and hydroelectric energy contribution in 1980 and 1985 is based on these estimates. The electric power production spectrum (Tabulation T) identify the sources of electric power for the last twenty-five years, converting power from each source of energy for both input and output value. In 1975, the heat value of the electrical output of the country represented 6.5 quadrillion Btu or 8.6% of the nation's power. The heat input was 20.4 quadrillion Btu or 27% of the total energy available to the country. This is the base from which projections must be made for a future dependence on nuclear power or electricity generated from any other fuel or power resource. The electrical generating capacity of the country and the electrical distribution system accounts for only a little more than one-quarter of our energy use.

WORLD PETROLEUM AVAILABLE TO THE UNITED STATES

The potential imports of petroleum in 1980 and 1985 cannot be precisely determined by any individual or organization, but the availability has definite physical limits. The oil which will be available for shipment nine years from now almost certainly has been identified and almost certainly is included in production planning. The ongoing development is indicated in the past production history. The practical limits of future world production expectancy can be found in the production records of the immediate past, and it is possible to estimate the probable maximum exports to the United States. The estimate must consider all available information for each country, and only the total estimate will approach accuracy. The overly optimistic or pessimistic individual estimates will balance out. Finally, the estimate must be based on the assumption that there will be no disruption in international relationships. Thus, only an optimistic forecast is possible.

With these qualifications, I have undertaken an analysis of the available petroleum in the world market. Exhibit 8, identifies the reported production and estimated production from each of the principal petroleum supply countries for the years 1972, 1974, and 1976. For the first two of these years, exports to the United States are recorded. The measured reserves of each country are indicated. Finally, the 1975, 1980, and 1985 estimates include the preliminary record of these exports for 1975 as actual.

This estimate represents simple, logical deduction from the available facts. Optimistically, there will be only a small reduction in oil from Venezuela and a continuation of oil from the Caribbean refineries. It should be noted that the source of oil from these refineries is not identified but that the total world oil production is accounted for. Thus, the Caribbean refined oil is an addition to exports from identified countries not otherwise reported.

I have assumed a rapid increase in receipts from Mexico with 1980 representing 20% of their current production. Similarly, I have anticipated very substantial increases from Indonesia, more than double their present contribution by 1980, 64% of their current total production and the same kind of increase from Nigeria. Angola is now giving us nearly 100% of their production and I have projected an increase, but the measured reserve is too small to expect much more. I have doubled receipts from the Congo and Zaire each five years. A three times increase in receipts from Norway is projected. On the basis of the available information, these assumptions appear to represent the limit in optimism, the ultimate in diplomatic arm-twisting of the countries who are not involved in ideological conflict with the United States. We are faced with the loss of nearly one million barrels per day from previous sources in the Western Hemisphere. This is the crux of the immediate problem with our friends.

---

* Western coal is cleaner burning (less SO_2) but it has a lower heat value. As western coal begins to dominate the U. S. supply, the average Btu/ton will decrease.

Projections from the Arab countries are equally optimistic. An
increase is projected for every country except Algeria where a very
small decrease is indicated to recognize a much more substantial decrease in their production the last three years. In 1980, I have indicated 8% of Iranian production and ten times increase in receipts from
Iraq, a three times increase from Kuwait, and a five times increase from
Oman. A Saudi Arabian supply estimate is approximately equal to the
Alaskan pipeline expectancy in 1980 and almost a million barrels a day
more than this in 1985. I doubled shipments from the United Arab Emi-
rates in 1980 and again in 1985 and more than doubled expected receipts
from Qatar in 1980. Libyan receipts are projected for 1980 at 66% of
their 1976 production estimate, a five times increase in four years.
Egypt's contribution is increased five times in these four years.

The Soviet bloc is expected to approximately double its contribution to the United States in 1980 and double again in 1985. More than
this amount of oil may be available from the Soviet bloc but it also
seems probable that the sum total of these optimistic anticipations
will not be realized in some part of the free world or the Arab Middle
East. Specific projections for Saudi Arabia substantially exceed the
limits which this country's representatives have advised in their warn-
ings to the United States.

In total, I have projected an increase of available imports 52%
more than the imports this country received in 1975. This estimate
totals 3.343 billion barrels a year, over nine million barrels a day
in 1980, the critical year in the projection. Returning to Exhibit 6,
the import requirements under our maximum U. S. production expectancy
of oil, gas, and all other sources of power is 3.80 billion barrels.
This produces a short-fall of .46 billion barrels per year, more than
one million barrels a day on the basis of the maximum expectancy in
U. S. produced oil and gas. With a minimum U. S. oil and gas production, the short-fall will be three million barrels a day in 1980.

Very obviously, the projections indicate a problem of major proportions. During the Arab boycott, U. S. oil short-fall was less than
one million barrels a day and the country could afford to run down its
inventories in anticipation of a termination of the boycott from month
to month. My 1980 forecast includes the maximum flow from Alaska. Thus,
the projected short-fall is not a temporary thing and can only be met by
planning now to reduce our energy requirements before the crisis develops.

Exhibit 8

Ref. Tabulation Q

INTERNATIONAL PETROLEUM PRODUCTION ANALYSIS - U. S. IMPORT POTENTIAL

Billion Barrels Per Year **

Country	1972 Prod'n	1972 Exports To U.S.	1974 Prod'n	1974 Exports To U.S.	1976 Prod'n (Est.)	1976 Exports To U.S.	1/1/76 Measured Reserve	Actual & Estimated Exports to U.S. 1975	1980	1985
Non Arabic										
Canada	.561	.406	.617	.390	.467		7.10	.308	.050	0
Venezuela	1.178	.351	1.086	.357	.803		17.70	.255	.250	.250
Remaining S. America	.424	.015	.463	.114	.444		8.17	.117	.110	.100
Caribbean Refineries	0	.464	0	.425	0		0	.360	.400	.400
Mexico	.185	.008	.238	.003	.300		9.50	.026	.060	.600
Indonesia	.396	.060	.502	.110	.548		14.00	.142	.350	.350
Remaining SE Asia	.295	.007	.314	.007	.339		7.23	.009	.020	.040
Nigeria	.665	.092	.823	.260	.730		20.20	.278	.450	.720
Angola	.051	.006	.061	.018	.030		1.30	.027	.030	.030
Congo & Zaire	.003	Neg.	.022	.001	.022		2.95	.001	.002	.004
Remaining S. Africa	.046	.001	.074	.010	.091		2.50	.011	.015	.020
United Kingdom	.003	.003	.003	.003	.063		16.00	.004	.005	.006
Norway	.012	Neg.	.013	Neg.	.110		7.00	.006	.020	.020
Remaining Europe	.420	.059	.406	.064	.120		2.50	.026	.023	.020
Subtotal Free World	4.239	1.472	4.622	1.762	4.067		116.15	1.570	1.785	2.560
Soviet Bloc w/China	3.252	.007	3.997	.011	4.453		103.00	.011	.020	.040
Subtotal Non Arabic	7.491	1.479	8.619	1.773	8.520		219.15	1.581	1.805	2.600
Arabic & Middle East										
Bahrain	.026	.005	.025	.005	.022		.31	.006	.020	.020
Iran	1.839	.052	2.198	.171	2.008		64.50	.102	.170	.150
Iraq	.529	.001	.721	-	.700		34.30	.001	.010	.020
Kuwait	1.098	.016	.831	.002	.600		68.00	.006	.020	.040
Oman	.103	Neg.	.106	Neg.	.135		5.90	.001	.005	.010
Qatar	.177	.001	.189	.006	.178		5.85	.007	.020	.040
Saudi Arabia	2.098	.069	2.997	.168	2.982		148.60	.261	.630	1.000
United Arab Emirates	.441	.027	.616	.027	1.147		40.80	.043	.100	.200
Yemen	0	Neg.	0	Neg.	0		0	Neg.	Neg.	Neg.
Algeria	.385	.034	.368	.069	.350		7.37	.103	.100	.100
Tunisia	.032	.003	.032	.005	.030		1.07	.001	.003	.005
Libya	.820	.045	.555	.002	.680		26.10	.085	.450	.450
Egypt	.085	.003	.054	.003	.113		3.90	.002	.010	.010
Subtotal Arabic	7.633	.256	8.692	.458	8.945		406.70	.618	1.538	2.045
Total Production & Exports to U. S.	15.124	1.735	17.311	2.231	17.465	2.400	-	2.199	3.343	4.645
U.S. Production*	3.456		3.203		2.885		33.00			
World Totals	18.580	-	20.514	-	20.350	-	658.85			

* Excluding NGL's

** See Tabulation S, Pg. 231

for Million Barrels Per Day

V I I

T H E   C R I T I C A L   D E C I S I O N S

The U. S. energy problem is identified in the specifics of the remaining fossil fuel reserve and the history of man's relationships on the earth. The problem will become a crisis when the decision to recognize energy limits can no longer be avoided.

The resistance to economic and political decision is a more important measure of the critical nature of that decision than the extrapolation of the fossil fuel supply and the demand trends. No solution of the energy problem is possible without sacrifice in every segment of society. All stand to lose and there are no identifiable winners. The fossil fuel energy resource has been the slave of the rich and the poor without discrimination. The wealth which has trickled down and lubricated the social structure has been energy wealth.

Adam Smith is truly the prophet of the 19th and 20th centuries. He released the human energy for the exploitation of the new world and the development of the economy that shaped a civilization which has come to dominate the world in this modern era. But Adam Smith had little knowledge of the fossil fuels which are principally responsible for the power and hence the physical progress of this world. Gas had been distilled from coal and kerosene from oil but it is doubtful that Smith was aware of the potential contribution of these resources when he wrote *The Wealth of Nations*. His economic philosophy was based on an agricultural economy of renewal resources, man's labor, and capital represented by money and bank credits. Whale oil was the principal lighting fuel produced by man's daring adventures at sea in ships powered by wind and muscle.

There may be a direct parallel between the scriptural acceptance of Smith's instructions and the difficulties that have developed from the emphasis on yesterday's solutions to tomorrow's problem. The blasphemy of the last two centuries stems from the substitution of the parables of Smith for the more profound wisdom of both the ancient and modern society that includes the constantly renewed and corrected laws of science.

The energy problem is an uninvited guest in the society of elected kings and judges. Energy represents the constituency of the material world not usually represented in these high councils, and the material

world is not accustomed to the accommodations and deferences that are
customarily granted in this court. The material laws cannot be compromised. Material resources cannot be persuaded to yield one more
unit for the glory of the country or the reputation of the political
representative. As long as the decision makers could find another
oil well and another petroleum engineer to produce oil at their
request, there was no need for considering the intransigence of
materials and their scientific laws. There is no precedence for
such consideration.

The energy problem actually represents the conflict between these
two worlds, the material world governed by intransigent laws and the
political world of compromise and flexible ideologies. However, this
perspective is of limited utility in finding a solution to the problem.

The magnitude of western civilization's dependence on gas and oil
combined with the false presentation of energy information by otherwise
responsible governmental organizations is terrifying. The bending of
the truth is not itself a very serious social error. Our humor and our
social amenities seem to depend on a relaxed acceptance of hyperbole.
It is the lubricant in social relations and a test of intellectual competence with just the required ingredient of danger. But hyperbole
that gains acceptance and threatens the future of a society is quite
another thing.

In 1972, when the U. S. Geological Survey published its estimates
of the future producible petroleum and natural gas resource at four times
the level supportable by contemporary evidence, scientific respectability
was abandoned. The highest resource authority in the U. S. government
had abdicated.

The year 1972 was also the time when the evidence of the accuracy
of the forecast of oil and gas production limits was available for any
observing scientist. Petroleum production had peaked at the end of 1970
as it had been forecast. The only basis for the U. S. Geological Survey
multiple of the remaining resource base was the compromise of this evidence.

The petroleum flow is meaningful only in terms of the consequences
of its unavailability, and no American wishes to consider this turn of
events. How can I get to work the morning the gas pumps go dry? Despite
the actual practice in the exercise of this reality in a few cities during

the Arab boycott, the thought has little meaning today. Why should I be concerned with my own transportation problem when the factory or business could not operate even if I were able to get there? I really do not wish to contemplate the relocation of my home, my business, my source of work materials or my work product even though by this means our society could save a third of the petroleum consumed in the American economy.

This is the psychological reason for resistance to change. It is not an economic problem because economics as they exist today are so totally dependent on growth that the recognized science becomes useless. The main-line economists abhor the alternatives to their econometric models for monetary stability and the invisible hand of market pricing and control of material flow. Pain which the body cannot tolerate is blocked and life goes on or life ceases without further response. It is no different with the body politic.

Every generation and every segment of the American population has a stake in the growth economy. The retired have spent their lives earning the reward they believe they deserve. Would you suggest to them a 50% reduction in their effective income? The energy adjustment could be that much in economic terms. The active labor force and its union representative would be hard to sell on a reduction in their material income by the same amount. The manufacturer would prefer that the government support the demand for his products without proof of their need. And the wives of America with their dishwashers and frost-free refrigerators and ample cooled and warmed homes and shopping malls. Are they ready to abandon these amenities?

The advantages of cereal protein in feeding the world has been explained and the energy intensiveness of our agricultural system will require some adjustment even if no consideration is given to the starving Africans and Asians. But who in America wishes to be the first to implement a cereal diet?

It does not matter when the adjustment will have to be made, whether within the next five years or the next twenty-five or longer. Probability controls successful business decision, but probability is abandoned in the context of energy conservation. Atomic fusion power at the end of the century provides only an excuse for ignoring the evidence of an energy shortage that is now inevitable before that time. But responsible men in the political and economic world are hypnotized by the thought of a scientific rescue that will avoid the realities of the social and economic adjustment, an adjustment which is all too obvious.

The foreign source of petroleum is the obvious short term remedy. The United States supplied the world with petroleum for a hundred years and now it is the world's turn to supply America. The fact that foreign dependence already exceeds national security limits must be discounted. We still have atomic power for war and a war to secure the material resources required for our use would be an old-fashioned war, the kind that always has been won by the stronger. But strangely, our generals are not enthusiastic. No one has thought to ask the geologists, who would point out the fact that the world resource is not so much greater than our own. More than a very short war would consume more scarce energy than it would produce.

The petroleum problem is not just an American problem. It is a world shortage with only a few small countries benefiting for a relatively short time in the perspective of man's years on this earth. It is an unfortunate coincidence that the Communist world is less dependent on these energy resources and more abundantly supplied with the resources that remain.

THE ENERGY DECISION DILEMMA

There is no single energy decision, only a complex of decisions all relating to energy and many not identified with the relationship. There is no politically safe ground if the relationship with energy is recognized. The identifiable chain or probable sequence of decisions leads to a political never-never land with no recognizable economic landmarks. It is the world of physical limits introduced by energy limits.

Limits cannot be accepted nor can they be denied. The Congress and the Administration are equally deprived of confidence and decision power when faced with a choice between laissez-faire and energy planning. Both prefer growth versus a steady state economy. Neither will relinquish traditional authority and the alteration in the balance between the rights of the individual and a monolithic concentration of power and authority which is the hallmark of planning. How can energy planning be kept under control? How can the free economy be maintained in the presence of, and in subordination to, a planning authority that will determine the availability of energy, without which very little actually can happen?

Thus, the dilemma is defined and the indecision in the face of mounting evidence is explained. But the surface of the political scene appears very different. The arguments concern solutions to the fragments. The problem solving machinery of multiple administrative authorities and the courts have been employed in a great multitude of conflicts between the

energy producing organizations and the organizations and individuals concerned with the protection of the environment, the protection of the right
to the use of private property, public safety, the preservation of parks
in the wilderness areas, and the preservation of specific wild life species.
There is no national debate to determine energy policy and coordinate this
policy with conflicting national goals. The limits of economic expansion
cannot be directly discussed. The real conflict is not recognized.

The idealists put their faith in atomic fusion and the open road to
unimpeded economic expansion. Their appeal is almost universal. No one
opposes the American history, the American way, or the American future;
and if there is a way to assure this future without compromising the battle for the present, who can be found in opposition? The improbability
of atomic fusion appearing on the scene in time to serve its purpose is
lost in the euphoria of the argument. Very few of the orators comprehend
the scientific problem or its potential solution.

The realists recognize the vulnerability of dependence on an ultimate solution through atomic fusion, but they are few in number and they
cannot agree on a course of action. The scientists agree that the atomic
breeder would solve the energy problem and maintain the potential economic expansion of the future, but they know that it has an immediate problem. The problems are technical, sociological, and political. The free
society would be substantially compromised in protecting itself from the
unlimited availability of individually manufactured atomic bombs, and the
material available for this manufacture is a by-product of the breeder
technology.

The environmentalists are totally opposed to any extension of the
nuclear power industry. They must be given credit for drawing the country's attention to the problem of limits, but they are not contributing
to solutions which industry can accept. They have become the focus of
opposition to the growth in all energy resources, a position which may
prove to be necessary, but it is a position that creates barriers to the
solution-finding process.

Federal financing of the energy industry which must be developed in
the future has created new oppositions to the solution process. Virtually
none of the new sources of energy can be practically financed in the free
economy, and public control is almost inevitable with public financing.
The outright grant or thinly veiled public underwriting through loan
guarantees are unacceptable to the left, and the danger of creeping control is unacceptable to the right. The representatives of the extreme

political philosophies have united in blocking the development of the new energy industry.

Beneath the conscience of this political infighting, a nightmare lurks. The energy resources, coal, oil, gas, are unthinking Things, chips in the poker games of the frontier that built constituencies and created the political fabric of the country. But their owners were not their creators or even their masters. Now, it is the Thing that is in control and the Thing has been there all along. The government can take possession of the Thing and employ its value for the public good. No other tax would be required, but the thought is terrifying. Then who would be in control?

Centralized energy planning cannot be openly discussed even though its implementation involves only relatively simple political mechanics and limited transfers of power and authority. A few years ago the cost of the primary fuel measured only one or two percent of the Gross National Product, and its importance is still discounted by economists in proportion to this measure. Its influence is very much greater.

The decision process will not begin with either discussion or understanding of the overall energy problem. That opportunity has passed. The decision process will begin with specific, critical economic situations that must be remedied by the political process. These decisions will involve both the withdrawal of political interference in the free market and an extension of federal financing and control. Only after the majority of the critical decisions have been made will a comprehensive pattern develop.

THE GAS PRICE DECISION

It is very difficult to conceive of a delay beyond the first quarter of 1977 in political action to relieve the gas shortage which has been foreseen for several years and is now developing to a critical stage. The federally established price for gas of 52¢ per thousand cubic feet in interstate commerce represents only a little more than one-quarter of the market price identified in intrastate contracts and the price anticipated for Canadian imports. Interstate suppliers did not have enough gas to meet their expected commitments early in 1976.

---

* Interstate gas is presently pegged at 52¢/M ft.[3]   On 7/27/76 the FPC allowed gas produced from wells opened after 1/1/75 to be priced at $1.42. The court review of this price increase is still in process, but the new price can be employed subject to court-ordered rebate. The statute limits the FPC prerogatives to "cost based increases" which are almost impossible to prove in this industry.

Decontrol will cause a four times increase in the cost of new gas to
the consumer and the same four times multiple of the income of those segments of the economy who are producing old gas. The political pressure
on the gas price change will become all too obvious, but under decontrol,
Congress and the Administrators will gain some insulation, particularly if
the increase is gradual.

The alternative to the release of price control is the continuation
of control at a higher level. This alternative is less attractive politically than the first. It is improbable that minor changes in the price of
natural gas will have any significant effect in increasing supply except
for the short time span when shut-in gas can be expected to be released,
and gas now reserved for intra-state can move into the interstate market.
After this short time span effect has been exhausted, the decline in the
supply of natural gas must be expected to continue. In the free market,
there is no limit to the price that may be required to find equilibrium
between the demand for gas and its availability. Where alternative
sources of energy are not available, gas can be a necessity of life. The
political pressure to reestablish controls can be anticipated.

The only real advantage of the decontrol of gas pricing is the free
market efficiency in the transition period. Price will be effective in
stimulating conservation and reducing the net natural gas demand. This
is the process that is politically unattractive and is best suited to the
private economy.

The danger in this process is the illusion that the price structure
will make a contribution beyond the short time span. The actual increases
in the supply of pipeline grade gas require the development of synthetic
natural gas from coal (SNG) or the development of a liquefied natural gas
(LNG) industry based on importation. It will take years to develop these
industries. They should have been in the process of development for at
least the last five years with gas prices increasing to cover the capital
cost of building the industry. But that time is now gone and the individuals capable of developing the industry are probably not the individuals
who will benefit from the increased price in the short time span of a sudden price release. In the absence of the development of a synthetic or
liquefied natural gas industry, there is no identifiable ceiling on gas
prices in the free market.

Synthetic gas from coal will have to cost between $4 and $5 per thousand cubic feet and very possibly $6. A liquefied natural gas industry
may be able to provide gas for half this amount. Both will require some

five years for the development of the industry, and both industries will
be needed. These are the facts that must be considered in the gas price
debate. The debate that is now two years overdue. But the debate is not
an event that is waiting for an official opening. The debate has been in
process and all of the economic and political influences have been contributing to the present state of confusion. However, there is not even agreement on the simple fact that increased price will not produce the energy
that is needed.

THE PETROLEUM SUBSTITUTION NON-DECISION PROBABILITY

The most critical contributor to the acceleration of the energy problem is the substitution of imported petroleum for U. S. produced natural
gas. The rapid decline in the availability of natural gas is visible in
the record and it is well understood by the industries whose supplies have
been cut off. But the projection of this trend has not been recognized
politically. More important, its significance is little understood.

There is a limited supply of world petroleum which can be made available to the United States. When this limit is reached, the real crisis
will begin. Until that time, decisions can be deferred and the economy
can continue to function as it has functioned in the past. In the meantime, both the government and the free economy have been acting to encourage the acceleration of dependence on imported oil and petroleum products.

The substitution of petroleum and gas for coal to eliminate air pollution has been encouraged by the federal, state, and local governments
from the beginning of environmental conscience, before the laws and the
organizations became effective. Federal, state, and free market forces
acted together in creating economic advantages for the burning of gas and
oil, creating the national dependence on these sources of fuel and the
international disadvantage which our country faces today. Although there
is recognition of the need to reverse these influences, the economic factors in the equation have not yet been corrected and the political decisions have not been made.

There is only one natural response to the gas limitation in the
free market. Unless there are definite, political restrictions on the
replacement of natural gas with oil, this is the course that will be
followed. A variation on the conversion prohibition would be the
accurate dissemination of facts on the limits of oil availability in
the future and immediate clarification of the requirements for burning coal, including incentives to balance the very high capital cost
of realizing this desirable conversion.

At the bottom of this political stalemate is the fifteen year failure of the air pollution administrators and the utility industry to resolve the economic problems of coal burning emissions clean-up. That problem is little nearer its solution today than it was when the Air Pollution Control authority was established. As a consequence, the decision on petroleum substitution is still in abeyance, and there are no effective restrictions on a shift to oil. The total shift to oil will double the country's dependence on foreign imports.

FEDERAL FINANCING OF NEW ENERGY RESOURCES

Gas and oil are cheap in an economy that recognizes only the costs of finding and producing the natural material so long as it is available. Synthetic oil and gas from coal, synthetic oil from shale, and the processing of the fuels required in the atomic energy processes are not cheap. More important, these processes require enormously expensive manufacturing facilities in addition to research costs for processes which have not yet been proved. Month by month during the last few years, the evidence has been accumulating that the private economy cannot undertake the financing of these new energy sources and there is no longer enough time for these new energy sources to be made available before oil and gas become critically unavailable. Lead times run from three to five years to more than twenty years on completing the research and testing of new processes, the building of new plants, and the mass production of the energy resource in the quantities required.

Private industry has given up on the production of substitute petroleum from shale oil. Private industry has given up on the high energy gas reactor, a much more efficient concept than the light water reactor. Private industry has given up on the secondary processing of atomic fuels for the light water reactor. Atomic fuel costs have increased ten times and promise to continue to increase.

Synthetic oil and gas production from coal is not economical in competition with natural gas and oil. The free economy has no way of handling a five year time span of undeterminable price due to the dual costs of alternative gas replacement when both must be employed. The free economy cannot commit the tremendous sums to an unknown period of financing to build these plants. It is ridiculous to anticipate that any industry, any corporation, or any individual will sacrifice funds totally under his control for an unknown future of this dimension. Current energy profits will not be invested in this way. Time has run out on the private economy and its independent control and financing of the country's future supply of energy.

STATES' RIGHTS

The authority of the state to represent the interests of area inhabitants directly conflicts with the national interest in resolving the energy problem. The evidence of this conflict began to accumulate at an accelerating rate before 1970. At least five years of the current delay in developing alternative sources of energy can be credited to the privilege of local governmental organizations to deny the license or the zoning privilege or some other requirement for building or operating an energy facility. The Kaiparowits, Utah coal generating station plans ended after thirteen years of debate and delay. Most of these delays related to local interests even though the plant site is a virtually uninhabited desert. Now, the coal remains with no plans for its employment while the country's need for energy increases day by day.

More specific state interests have been involved in the denial of plans for an ocean port and offshore drilling on the eastern Atlantic coast. These plans involved a major complex of refineries in the Deleware, New Jersey, New Hampshire, and Maine areas. The frustration of planning for nuclear installations are too numerous to mention. Most recently, the State of California has questioned the desirability of transshipping Alaskan oil through the port facilities in that state.

State privileges in the area of air pollution control have combined with federal law to virtually terminate the expansion of coal-fired generators in the Midwest where the principal coal supply has a high sulphur content. Coal, which will become the most reliable national energy resource in the next fifty years, is located in states which would prefer tourism and agriculture to the excavation of their land and the influx of developers, miners, and pollutants of every kind.

The privileges and prerogatives of the local community now stand as a barrier to national progress in resolving the energy problem. The decisions are multiple and involve the developed law as well as current legislation.

INDIVIDUAL RIGHTS

The rights of the individual to restrain industrial planning and industrial operations have been magnified in recent years. The environmental programs have been based on both individual rights and community or state's rights. This development has been aided by specific legislation as well as court decisions. The development is not confined to the areas of energy and as a consequence, it is most difficult to conceive of decision patterns which will reverse the process.

The buildup in individual rights and privileges has coincided with the developing necessity to curtail individual rights and privileges to permit energy planning and development to meet the minimum requirements for the nation's economic survival. This survival is defined in terms of a very substantial reduction in the energy requirements for the expansion that has been assumed to be necessary in the traditional economics.

The nation's interests have been on a collision course with individual interests and the decisions are difficult to even identify. We will be involved in a whole complex of ideological conflicts. The entire democratic process and the cultural development of the last three hundred years is involved. Energy is a necessity for the support of the nation's economy and a breakdown in the economy will carry the political and social structure with it. The minimum energy requirements have not been identified nor has the retreat from individual privilege been charted.

ENERGY ORGANIZATION

The organization of the nation's response to the developing energy problem will be an evolving process. We must begin with the present divided authority and responsibility. Coordination of this responsibility will be a first step, but an energy policy that has any real significance must involve the nation. It is not simply a problem of structure.

The present state of organization is the legacy of the Arab boycott. Congress has failed in every attempt to even recognize the problem to say nothing of finding solutions. The Administration has shifted and divided authority over the energy problem, encouraged irresponsible administrators, and discouraged the development of competent individuals. Congress relieved the Administration of responsibility for developing an effective energy program after its first step.

There is no basis for anticipating a solution to the energy problem under the presently constituted authorities in the Congressional and Administrative organizations.

The developing energy crisis will create the necessity for decision and leadership may emerge in the process. The information is available and it can be assumed that there are many individuals presently involved in the energy organization who are competent to pull together the parts of the whole and develop an energy administration policy.

Organization for solution of the energy problem requires a release of authority by the Congress and by the Administration. The representation of every individual interest in developing energy policy has been demonstrated as a failure. Barriers must be provided to shield the decision-making process from the political process in this most sensitive of all areas. An independent energy authority must be created.

There is a close parallel between the history of the control of the money supply of the country and the control of the sources of energy. Pecuniary economic controls have preceded physical economic controls by fifty years in the nation's development. In this context, the history of the development of the nation's banking system and the independent Federal Reserve Board can be instructive. The authority of the Federal Reserve Board cannot be returned to the Congress or to the President. Pragmatic development of this separation of power can be repeated with the development of a very similar energy authority with the power to maintain the supply of energy to the nation, but the exercise of that authority would be substantially different and it would appear to be substantially greater.

The energy authority must have complete control over the importation of all energy resources. The energy authority must have the capacity to plan for the future development of internal energy resources and conversion capacity. The energy authority must be able to identify the practical limits of energy availability and make the energy limits known to the public and private sectors of the economy. Energy cannot be produced and expended today at the expense of future generations.

Energy planning introduces economic concepts which are totally unacceptable to the nation today. But there is no inevitable conflict between the continuation of a free economy and a free society in an energy controlled political-economic environment. Actually, the alternative to the control of the energy problem and the creation of an energy authority is the incorporation of the energy power in a total political dictatorship. Energy will become the ultimate source of power if it is not identified and isolated and controlled within the free political society.

V I I I

T H E   P O L I T I C A L - E C O N O M I C   F U T U R E

The energy decision process has been delayed and is held back at each stage for lack of a positive social-political-economic future for America and for western civilization. Our society has no picture of life without virtually unlimited energy supplies. The frontier still dominates American thinking. Our leaders are historic persons, all deceased.

The decision wheel suggests the necessity for ideological choice. In analyzing the alternatives, the future of our free society depends on atomic fusion. We have developed *no* alternative to an expanding economy for the support of our free society and this is *the critical fact* in the discussion of energy and the future of western man.

But atomic fusion is not the answer. It is a mirage. In the immediate future — the next thirty years — it is not available. In the next thirty to a hundred years it may not be available as time may run out on western civilization before the technological problems are resolved. In the long time perspective, complete success with atomic fusion is only a stop-gap in the collision course of the forces of nature with man's civilization. Unless man learns to accept the environment and turns his intellectual powers towards learning to live in the world as it is, his great accomplishments will count for very little. The immediate decision process must proceed with this in mind.

The burden of an expanding economy is intolerable in any long range future planning. The sources of energy which meet the unlimited expansion specification threaten the open society and all individual freedom. The by-product of the atomic breeder reactor is plutonium which makes available the atomic bomb to every terrorist group. A single, unstable individual with the combination of a technical education and a grudge against some part of the social fabric can destroy our largest city. Solar energy from a space platform presents the same danger to a larger segment of the population. In transmitting the tremendous quantities of power required for our economy, a death ray must be focused on the earth located receiver. Redirection of this death ray by accident or by manipulation would incinerate humanity systematically, almost without limit.

As the western world's oil and gas resources run out, and as science proceeds with its development of the breeder reactor, hope is focused on the ultimate fusion power and the realities of a free society run through the sands of time. Lacking a positive image of a social order, our political leaders are faced with a choice of lies. They can lie about the availability of oil and gas, or they can lie about the future of a free society in a plutonium world. Before this, they must lie about the solutions to our immediate social problems which will be resolved with an expanding economy, totally dependent on energy resources that we now know will not be available.

These are offensive thoughts and they will be resisted. No individual can be tagged with these kinds of responsibilities, but the problem is not with the individuals. The problem is with our social order and the demands we place on our political leaders. They are required to misinterpret the facts.

The American body politic is not ready for the energy decision. The future of man, energy, and society is no longer in doubt, but the doubt persists. By definition, the time of crisis is the time of decision, when the life or death evidence is available and the choice must be made. Although future events may move the identifiable time of decision into the past, or into the future, the time spectrum is rapidly narrowing. The decision must be made between a free society with limits or a continuation of economic expansion, but the expansion alternative is not infinite. When time is introduced into the economists' equations, the ultimate necessity to abandon expansionists' ideologies is delayed by a very small amount of time.

Thus, the ultimate lie in the politics of today can be qualified as ignorance of the time dimension in our economic ideology. Ignorance is more socially acceptable than deliberate distortion. Also, the locus can be shifted to the academic community providing society and its political institutions with a limited degree of respectability.

The free society of western civilization is not doomed yet. The academic community can awaken from its slumbers. Leadership may emerge. The materials, the scientific method, and the basic knowledge are available to present the western world with a future, free society that is compatible with the facts and conditions of energy availability. Many myths will have to be abandoned and powerful individuals and institutions will be threatened, but these are the problems of implementation, not the problems of the architect of the future. The immediate problem is finding some academic group, one university, one academic discipline that will undertake the leadership responsibility.

As individuals, as a nation, and as a civilization, today is the beginning of the rest of our existence. The time of decision is now and it will become more difficult and the options will be more limited as time passes. It will be more important to learn to smell the flowers if we choose an end to expansion, but there will be less time. More of man's labor will be required when the energy slave is less available. Labor will become more important but its rewards in monetary things will be greatly reduced and the society will need a larger proportion of workers. The current value system and the current economics have to change and herein lies the problem with the decision.

Recognition must be given to new political alignments. Uninhibited population expansion is not compatible with limited economic expansion. Terrestially collected solar energy is a daytime, sometime, someplace phenomena. Solar energy will not support the present expansionist economy. Conservatives and liberals must find new identifications in the real world of fact and possibility.

Energy planning must be recognized as a partner of the free economy. Neither need to be in jeopardy, but both must accept the limitations of the material world. The opportunities for man as an individual, thinking, working, person have never been greater. Out of the earth's crust, man has built a material civilization in the western world that is a credit to the millions of years of his existence. He only has to learn to live in it without destroying it. But the decisions are difficult.

PART TWO

THE OIL AND GAS FIGURES

No combination of energy alternatives can replace the
oil and gas serving the United States today. We now
depend on a world resource that is not within our control. The specifics of the quantity available to this
country will control the economic and political options.

Part Two is concerned with a statistical analysis of
the geological facts controlling the availability of
producible oil and gas in the United States.

I X

THE PETROLEUM FIGURES

We began with the numbers, the hard facts of the quantity of oil in the ground and the sources of information, the records and the people best able to know. We found contrived confusion and less than candid responses. We also found very solid information, responsible geologists, and a consensus of opinion by the middle of 1975 as to the remaining oil and gas resource.

In Part Two we will identify the step by step process of reaching our conclusion as to the availability of oil and gas to the U. S. economy, year by year. This is a long range forecast focused on the end of the century. Graphic presentations were cut off at the year 2010 only to maintain a readable scale. Our forecast method permits extension to the end of the petroleum age.

In Part Two, I have duplicated three primary exhibits, two for oil and one for gas in order to provide immediate reference opposite the discussion.

THE CONSENSUS AS TO THE REMAINING PETROLEUM RESOURCE

Figure 1 provides historic perspective on the petroleum resource estimates of the U. S. government organizations charged with the responsibility for this geological information. The U. S. Geological Survey has the permanent responsibility for maintaining these records. The National Academy of Sciences conducted its year-long survey as a special assignment. Dr. M. King Hubbert is the leading independent petroleum resource forecaster and he is a member of the U.S.G.S., but was not a member in 1956 when he developed his forecast procedures as an employee of the Shell Oil Company.

Very substantial interchanges of geological information between geologists representing the petroleum companies, the financial institutions, and the geological organizations have contributed to these conclusions. Many independent forecasts have been made, but none have exceeded the optimism of the U. S. Geological Survey's 1972 estimate. Neither earlier U.S.G.S. forecasts nor the independent forecasts have developed the data bank and the auditable methodology of the 1975 U.S.G.S. conclusion.

ESTIMATES OF ORIGINAL RECOVERABLE OIL IN PLACE   Figure I

Including Crude Oil, Lease Condensate, & Natural Gas Liquids

By: United States Geological Survey
National Academy of Science
Dr. M. King Hubbert

-64-

The modern history of petroleum resource forecasting begins with Dr. Hubbert's 1956 predictions which were confirmed in 1975. The current consensus based on the three identified forecasts can no longer be ignored. On a minimum basis, the remaining recoverable U. S. resource at the beginning of the year 1976 falls between 126 and 140 billion barrels. There is only a 5% probability of producing the 219 billion barrels identified by the U.S.G.S. analysis as maximum. Further, this maximum estimate is sufficient to cover virtually all independent estimates currently recognized as having validity; and the maximum estimates include, in addition to the statistical judgment base, a hedge for possible major findings on the Continental Shelf of the east coast of the United States and the Gulf of Alaska where insufficient data are available to reliably estimate future discoveries. Thus, the 219 billion barrel ceiling and the 131 billion barrel safe minimum provide reliable and generally accepted limits to the ultimate U. S. production potential of petroleum.

A few minutes may be required to interpret Figure 1. The legend in the upper right quadrant identifies each of the numbers that appear in the bar graph for the individual forecasts. The National Academy of Sciences estimate was employed in this legend. The only stable reference is the original oil in place and only the recoverable oil has significance. The estimates have been corrected to include all liquid hydrocarbons, crude oil, lease condensate, and natural gas liquids. Lease condensates are derived from small amounts of hydrocarbons that exist in the gaseous phase in natural underground reservoirs but are liquid at atmospheric pressure after being recovered from oil wells (casing head gas) in lease separators. Natural gas liquids are produced as a byproduct of gas wells where they are recovered prior to the transport and use of natural gas. These gaseous contributors to the total liquid hydrocarbons can be as much as 20% of the total.

The Figure 1 graphics identify visually the magnitude of the differences in petroleum estimates and their historic relationship. Only the minimum U.S.G.S. estimates can be employed in any conservative forecast of the nation's resources. The maximum estimates are most useful to individuals and institutions wishing to subvert the reality of the U. S. energy short-fall. The 1972 U.S.G.S. estimate serves this purpose. Additionally, the 1972 forecast included reference to a non-recoverable resource estimated at two trillion three hundred ninety billion barrels, totally unsupported. The 1974 U.S.G.S. estimate appears to be a poorly disguised retreat, and even the maximum estimate in 1975 carries the danger of the omission of its qualification. A 5% probability must be recognized as a statement of a remote possibility.

Figure 2

ESTIMATES OF ORIGINAL RECOVERABLE OIL IN PLACE
(Billions of Barrels)

Date - Report	Cumulative Production		Measured		Indicated		Inferred		Undiscovered		Total Original Recoverable Oil In-Place
	Oil	NGL's	Oil	NGL's	Oil	NGL's	Oil	NGL's	Oil	NGL's	
1956 M. King Hubbert:											
Conterminous US Only	52.4	-	30.0				117.6				200.0
Alaska (Circ. 725 Mean)	-	-	10.7	1.1	6.2	.6	-		27.0	2.8	48.4
Revised Hubbert	52.4		41.8				154.2				248.4
1972 USGS - Circular 650 (1970 Data)	106.0		47.0		5.3				459.0		617.3
3/26/74 USGS News Release (1972 Data)											
Maximum	115.3		48.3			35.0 Ave.			400.0		598.6
Minimum	115.3		48.3			35.0 Ave.			200.0		398.6
1974 M. King Hubbert (1973 Data)	118.0				67.0				55.0	12.0	252.0
1975 National Academy of Science (1972 Data)	115.0		37.5				113.0				265.5
1975 USGS - Circular 725 (1974 Data)											
Maximum	106.14	15.73	34.25	6.35	4.64	-	23.10	6.00	127.00	22.00	345.21
Minimum	106.14	15.73	34.25	6.35	4.64	-	23.10	6.00	50.00	11.00	257.21

PAST — Cumulative Production
PROVED — Measured
REMAINING RESOURCE / TOTAL UNDISCOVERED — Indicated, Inferred, Undiscovered

EEEe Revised Study - May 1976

Figure 2 identifies the audit path of our derivation of the quantities employed in Figure 1. Here we are concerned both with the resolution of the definitions' problem and the combination of numbers. The two principal sources for petroleum definition are the U. S. Geological Survey and the American Petroleum Institute. There is perhaps more general use of the American Petroleum Institute's terminology, but the U. S. Geological Survey spectrum of terms is more precise. The nine terms employed by the U. S. Geological Survey begin with the most definitely identifiable resource and proceed to their conclusion of the largest probable quantity to which is added past production and finally the non-recoverable resource to establish the original oil in place. The following tabulation identifies these terms as used by the two organizations:

U.S.G.S.	A.P.I.
Measured reserves	Proved reserves
+ Indicated reserves	
= Demonstrated reserves	Established reserves
+ Inferred reserves	
= Probable reserves	
+ Past cumulative production	
= Original producible oil in place	
+ Non-recoverable resource	
= Original oil in place	

It should be noted that non-recoverable resource is defined as those quantities estimated to be present but that cannot now be produced if found, or that might never be found because of small size or remote location.

Natural gas liquids (N.G.L.)are a particular source of problem in reconciling alternative petroleum estimates. They are the by-products of natural gas production which add significantly to crude oil. The total of crude oil, natural gas liquids, and lease condensate (a by-product of crude oil production) are referred to as total liquid petroleum. The old term, total oil in-place, usually implies total liquid petroleum.

THE U.S.G.S. GEOLOGICAL ESTIMATES OF REMAINING OIL

The how much and where of past and future oil production are identified in the 1975 U. S. Geological Survey estimate Circular 725. I do not
believe there is any better basis for determining these quantities and I
have listened carefully to the detractors of the survey as well as the
geologists who were involved in the work and have attested to the objectivity of the conclusions and provided the background for the interpretations
of the data. Circular 725 is available at the U.S.G.S., Reston, Virginia
without cost and will become our primary reference in the development of
annual production projections and comparisons with other forecasts.

Figure 3 reproduces the primary petroleum resource table of past production reserves, and recoverable resources which constitute the U.S.G.S.
Circular 725 conclusion. The regions are identified on the map. These
estimates exclude natural gas liquids and reference should be made to
Figure 2 for the detailed accounting of each contributor to the total
resource which we have employed in our forecast. As previously mentioned,
the sum of the regions does not equal the U. S. crude oil resource conclusion as the U.S.G.S. team employed statistical procedures in the combining
of their regional conclusions to develop the probabilities in their undiscovered recoverable category. The minimum resource represents a 95% probability of being produced whereas the maximum resource represents only a
5% probability.

There is no escape from the subjectivity of these estimates but
every mathematical and geological method has been employed in reaching
the conclusion and this conclusion is supported by our two other fore-
casters, who employed totally different methods to reach a very similar estimate of the remaining quantity of oil. This was the National
Academy of Sciences in their 1975 analysis and M. King Hubbert in his
1974 revision.

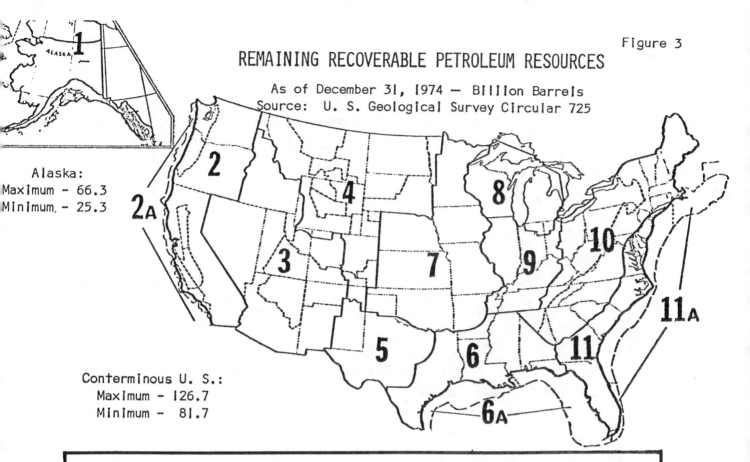

Figure 3

REMAINING RECOVERABLE PETROLEUM RESOURCES

As of December 31, 1974 — Billion Barrels
Source: U. S. Geological Survey Circular 725

Alaska:
Maximum – 66.3
Minimum – 25.3

Conterminous U. S.:
Maximum – 126.7
Minimum – 81.7

TABLE 4.—*Production, reserves, and undiscovered recoverable oil resources for the United States, December 31, 1974 (billion barrels)*

Regions	Cumulative Production	Demonstrated Reserves		Total Cumulative Production + Demonstrated Reserves	Inferred Reserves[1]	Undiscovered Recoverable Resources	
		Measured	Indicated			Statistical Mean	Estimated Range[2] (95%-5%)
ONSHORE							
1. Alaska----------------------	0.154	9.944	0.013	10.111	6.1[3]	12	6 – 19
2. Pacific Coastal States-----	15.254	2.699	1.091	19.044	0.3	7	4 – 11
3. Western Rocky Mountains---	1.115	0.417	0.089	1.621	0.7	4	2 – 8
4. Northern Rocky Mountains--	6.021	1.461	0.256	7.738	1.2	7	5 – 11
5. West Texas and Eastern New Mexico----------------	21.385	7.060	1.991	30.436	1.6	8	4 – 14
6. Western Gulf Basin--------	31.345	7.082	0.587	39.014	8.6[4]	8	5 – 12
7. Mid-Continent-------------	17.203	1.805	0.211	19.219	1.3	6	3 – 12
8. Michigan Basin------------	0.645	0.082	0.008	0.735	0.2	1	0.3 – 2
9. Eastern Interior----------	4.346	0.283	0.009	4.638	0.3	1	0.6 – 2
10. Appalachians--------------	2.539	0.155	0.067	2.761	Negl.[5]	1	0.4 – 2
11. Eastern Gulf and Atlantic Coastal Plain-----------	0.039	0.042	0.006	0.087	0.1	1	0.2 – 2
Total Lower 48 Onshore---	99.892	21.086	4.315	125.293	14.3	44	29 – 64
Total Onshore United States----------	100.046	31.030	4.328	135.404	20.4	56	37 – 81
OFFSHORE (0-200 metres)							
1A. Alaska----------------------	0.456	0.150	Negl.[5]	0.606	0.1[3]	15	3 – 31
2A. Pacific Coastal States----	1.499	0.858	0.258	2.615	0.2	3	2 – 5
6A. Gulf of Mexico-----------	4.135	2.212	0.050	6.397	2.4	5	3 – 8
11A. Atlantic Coastal States---	0.000	0.000	0.000	0.000	0.0	3	2 – 4[6]
Total Lower 48 Offshore--	5.634	3.070	0.303	9.012	2.6	11	5 – 18
Total Offshore United States---------	6.090	3.220	0.308	9.618	2.7	26	10 – 49
Total Lower 48-------	105.526	24.156	4.623	134.305	16.9	55	36 – 81
Total Alaska---------	0.610	10.094	0.013	10.717	6.2	27	12 – 49
TOTAL UNITED STATES-	106.136	34.250	4.636	145.022	23.1	82	50 – 127

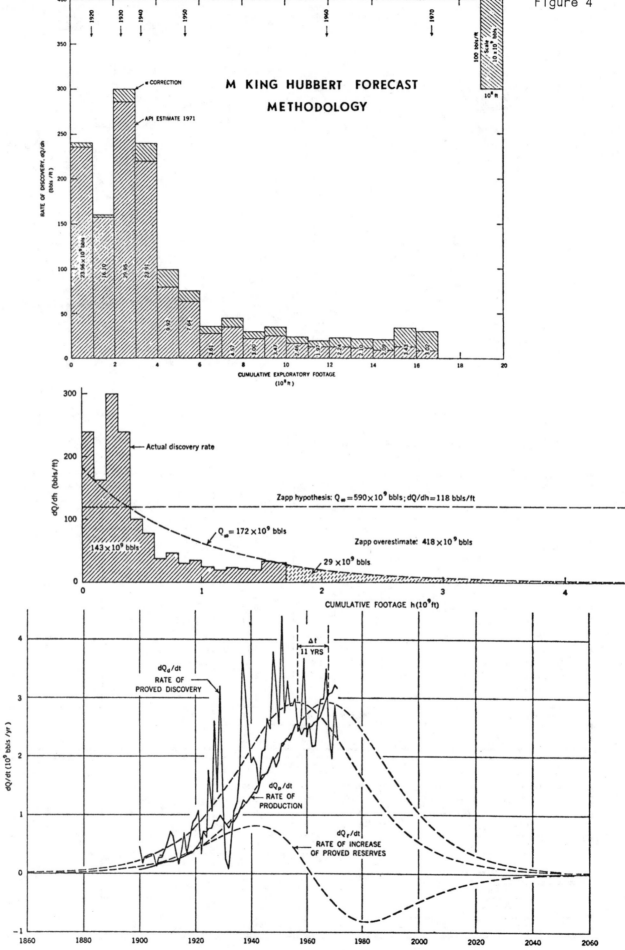

Figure 4

DR. M. KING HUBBERT'S FORECAST METHOD

No discussion of petroleum production forecasting would be complete without reference to Dr. M. King Hubbert's methodology and the history of his 1956 forecast which identified the peaking of U. S. production as well as the ultimate quantity of oil expected to be discovered. That peaking occurred in November of 1970 within the timespan of Dr. Hubbert's estimate in 1956. Alaskan production was not included in these early projections, but there's no current evidence that the addition of Alaskan production will be sufficient to affect the decline in U. S. petroleum production from 1970. Alaska represents a separate statistical universe in estimating the U. S. petroleum reserves and the year to year production from those reserves. Figures 4 and 5 reproduce five of Dr. Hubbert's charts which demonstrate his mathematical procedure and identify the principal historic inputs. The bar graph at the top of Figure 4 plots the rate of discovery stated in barrels per foot of drilling against cumulative exploratory footage. The cumulative figure relates to the time scale that is indicated across the top of this graph, and this horizontal axis represents one hundred million feet of drilling for each bar, a convenient division of the historic record.

The middle bar graph develops the rate of discovery and incidently compares the rate with the hypothesis employed by the U. S. Geological Survey in its 1972 Circular 650 release. Alfred D. Zapp was a senior geologist with the survey and he is credited with or held responsible for the hypotheses that supported the survey's exaggerated estimates of the remaining resource. Alfred Zapp died after the publication of Circular 650 eliminating the evidence and frustrating any investigation of the unsupported theory. In this projection, the rate of discovery stated in barrels of oil expected to be found for each foot of exploratory drilling was assumed to be a constant based on the historic average, ignoring the well established downward trend. He then projected this discovery rate for all future drilling to produce an estimate 418 billion barrels more than Dr. Hubbert's evidence will support. The director of the survey has made only oblique references to Dr. Hubbert's findings maintaining his support of the Zapp projection. This is the bureaucratic abuse of discretion, still not recognized by political appointees.

Dr. Barry Commoner, a principal speaker for the environmentalist movement, employed the Zapp hypothesis in his attack on the oil industry and the facts of the declining U. S. petroleum production. Dr. Commoner claims an adequate petroleum resource to carry the U. S. economy until the day when he thinks solar energy will be available. Dr. Commoner's attack on Dr. Hubbert is a part of his book

At the bottom of Figure 4, we have reproduced Dr. Hubbert's complete cycle of U. S. petroleum production from the lower 48 state universe that plots the rate of increase of proved reserves, the rate of proved discoveries, and the rate of production year by year.

At the top of Figure 5, is Dr. Hubbert's complete cycle of crude oil production for his primary universe and we have added his contribution from natural gas liquids expected for the remaining years of the cycle. These are a byproduct of the natural gas industry not represented in the crude oil production statistics.

At the bottom of Figure 5, the combination of crude oil and natural gas liquids is plotted and we have added his estimated quantities for both crude oil and natural gas liquids for Alaska. Dr. Hubbert's estimate of the Alaskan potential preceded the completion of the U. S. Geological Survey study that places the approximate maximum and minimum for Alaska at 28 to 74 billion barrels of liquid hydrocarbon. Thus, Dr. Hubbert's estimate of 48 billion barrels appears realistic for this state.

The complete record of Dr. Hubbert's analysis is available from the U. S. Government Printing Office in the Report of the Committee on Interior and Insular Affairs of the United States Senate "U. S. Energy Resource — A Review of 1972", Serial Number 92-40(92-75) 1974.

Dr. Hubbert's projections of world production employs the same methodology as his U. S. complete cycle. In this projection, world production of crude oil peaks in the 1990's and 90% of the crude oil resources will have been produced before the year 2025 unless restraints are introduced to conserve some part of this resource for future generations.

Figure 5

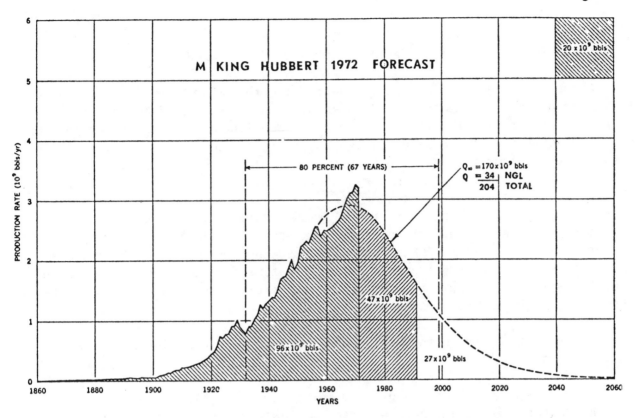

Complete cycle of crude-oil production in conterminous United States as of 1971.

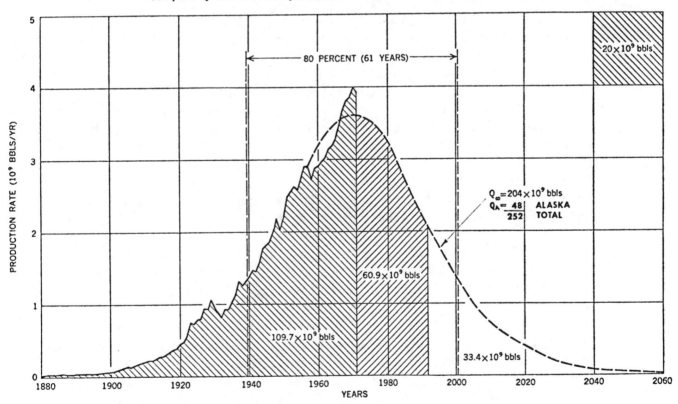

Estimate as of 1972 of complete cycle of petroleum liquids production in the conterminous United States.

SHORT TERM FORECAST AND IDENTIFICATION OF LIQUID HYDROCARBONS

Figure 6 serves the purpose of identifying the several sources of liquid hydrocarbon and relating the expected production from each of the identified segments for the next few years. As can be seen from Dr. Hubbert's projections which are confirmed in subsequent figures, petroleum production lags the finding of petroleum or the increase in proved petroleum reserves by approximately eleven years. This fact limits the potential increase or decrease in petroleum production over the short time span. Additions to proved reserves that result from the extension of existing fields can be brought into production in a much shorter time and the pressures on supplying the U. S. petroleum market during the last few years have resulted in a compression of this time sequence, but the consequence of reducing the time from discovery to production necessitates the pulling-down of proved reserves and reduces the availability of petroleum for future years.

Figure 6 is based on the most specific current information from the following sources:

(1) Past production divided among crude oil, lease condensates, and natural gas liquids is a matter of historic record in the published data of the American Petroleum Institute and the reports of the Interior Department's office of oil and gas which publishes summaries each month with a compilation delay of three or four months. 1973,'74,and '75 plotted.

(2) The bottom segment of Figure 6 for the years 1975 through 1985 represents the summation of the petroleum consultants' forecast for each of the 55 selected major U. S. oil fields identifying 44% of the U. S. proved reserve in the lower 48 states. This report was prepared by the Federal Energy Administration - dated October 1975 - in compliance with Public Law 93-275, Section 15(b). The north slope of Alaska - the Prudhoe Bay field - is included in this report but it is separately identified on Figure 6 with the Alaskan production from the Panhandle and southern slopes. Alaska's 1974 production is reported as history.

(3) The production of natural gas liquids is estimated for the years 1975 through 1985 based on historic production records together with forecasts of natural gas production from which these liquids result as a byproduct.

(4) Production from the remaining oil fields onshore and offshore of the lower 48 states completes the statistical universe, and it is projected on the basis of the 44% sample which we have assumed to be representative of this universe. If this assumption is correct, the

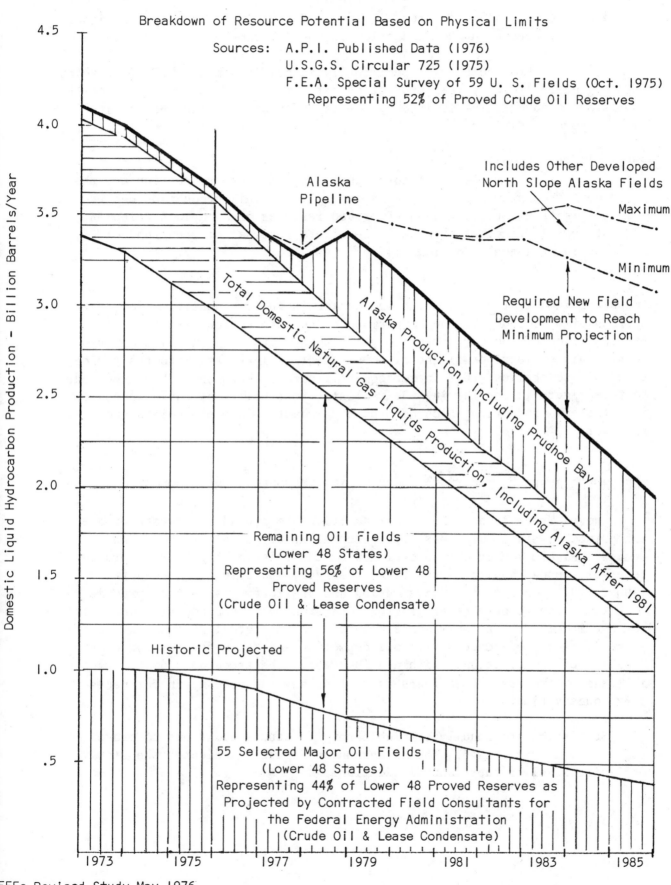

SUMMATION OF POTENTIAL U. S. PETROLEUM PRODUCTION
THROUGH 1985

Figure 6
Ref. Tabulations
A,D,G,H,I,J,K&L

Breakdown of Resource Potential Based on Physical Limits

Sources: A.P.I. Published Data (1976)
U.S.G.S. Circular 725 (1975)
F.E.A. Special Survey of 59 U. S. Fields (Oct. 1975)
Representing 52% of Proved Crude Oil Reserves

Includes Other Developed
North Slope Alaska Fields

Maximum

Minimum

Alaska
Pipeline

Required New Field
Development to Reach
Minimum Projection

Total Domestic Natural Gas Liquids Production, Including Alaska After 1981

Alaska Production, Including Prudhoe Bay

Remaining Oil Fields
(Lower 48 States)
Representing 56% of Lower 48
Proved Reserves
(Crude Oil & Lease Condensate)

Historic | Projected

55 Selected Major Oil Fields
(Lower 48 States)
Representing 44% of Lower 48 Proved Reserves as
Projected by Contracted Field Consultants for
the Federal Energy Administration
(Crude Oil & Lease Condensate)

Domestic Liquid Hydrocarbon Production - Billion Barrels/Year

1973   1975   1977   1979   1981   1983   1985

EEEe Revised Study May 1976

-75-

decrease in production from all lower 48 fields should be proportional to the decrease in the production in the 44% sample.

(5) Prudhoe Bay is specifically identified in the F.E.A. petroleum engineers' year by year production estimate. Most important, north slope production is limited by the capacity of the pipeline and its proposed additions.

(6) Finally, production from new fields is indicated by the gap between our estimate of future minimum and maximum production and the identified production from existing fields. This production can represent either a pulling down of proved reserves or a rapid development of new oil findings which will require a reversal of the trend of declining annual additions to reserves.

The significance of the Figure 6 projection is in its identification of the sources of petroleum and the comparison of our projection with a visual extrapolation of the current history for each of these identified contributors. This projection will be given perspective in relation to the period from 1975 to the year 2010 in subsequent figures. Reference should be made to this figure in considering the realistic possibility of rapid increases in petroleum production which have been forecast by the economists and their followers.

THE PROVED RESERVES AND THEIR CONTRIBUTION TO FORECAST METHODOLOGY

Proved reserves and the annual additions to proved reserves have been the principal statistical base for discussions of petroleum supply and demand. Figure 7 provides an overview of the relationship between proved reserves, annual additions to proved reserves, and domestic demand from 1900 to 1975. For most of this period and the forty years which precede this time span, proved reserves grew consistently with production and total petroleum demand. The only scare occurred in the late 1920's which precipitated a flurry of concern with oil depletion and the necessity for consideration of conservation. Within a few years, the tremendous discoveries in Texas put to rest these fears as well as any future concern for necessary conservation.

Statistics are readily available for the annual additions to proved reserves only since 1946. The bar graph on Figure 7 indicates the slowly declining level of these annual additions.

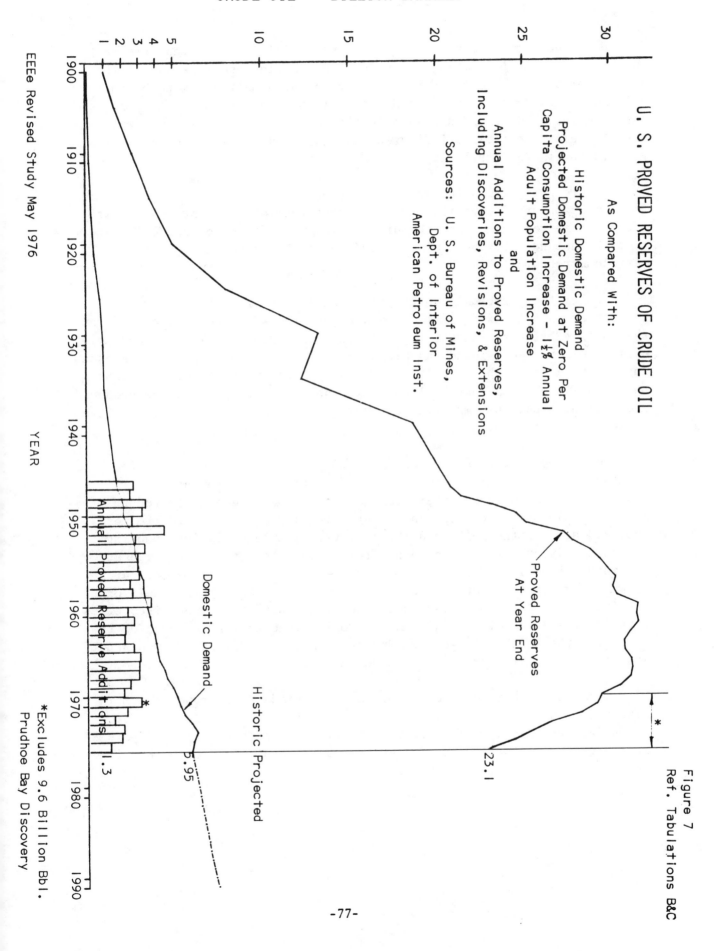

CRUDE OIL — BILLION BARRELS

U. S. PROVED RESERVES OF CRUDE OIL

As Compared With:

Historic Domestic Demand
Projected Domestic Demand at Zero Per
Capita Consumption Increase – 1½% Annual
Adult Population Increase
and
Annual Additions to Proved Reserves,
Including Discoveries, Revisions, & Extensions

Sources: U. S. Bureau of Mines,
Dept. of Interior
American Petroleum Inst.

Proved Reserves
At Year End

Annual Proved Reserve Additions

Domestic Demand

Historic Projected

23.1

5.95

1.3

EEEe Revised Study May 1976   YEAR

*Excludes 9.6 Billion Bbl.
Prudhoe Bay Discovery

Figure 7
Ref. Tabulations B&C

U. S. domestic demand eclipsed annual additions to proved reserves in the middle 1950's putting pressure on production and forecasting the decline of proved reserves. From this time on, domestic demand began to pull away from domestic production as indicated on Figure 8 and subsequent charts. The rapid decrease in the level of proved reserves relative to demand is clearly indicated on Figure 8 and the ratios are developed on Figure 9 following.

Figure 8 magnifies the annual additions to proved reserves which are the summation of discoveries and the corrections of the past year's estimate of reserves, comparing the discoveries with domestic production and domestic demand. Figure 8 also introduces perspective on the Alaskan petroleum resource.

One of the principal sources of confusion in projecting petroleum production is the mixing of the Alaskan resource with the production from the lower 48 states. Alaska is a separate area geologically and economically. Oil has been found and produced in the Panhandle and lower Alaskan coastal area since the late 1950's, but the great majority of the Alaskan potential lies on the north slope or in the interior which can be produced and delivered only by employing the most expensive pipeline system in the world.

More important than the economic and geological isolation of the Alaskan reserve is the separation of the statistical information. The lower 48 states including their coastal waters have been subjected to intense exploration for 115 years, beginning in 1860. This is the most explored area in the world and there is very little basis for doubting the conclusive nature of the identification of the ultimate reserve and the future annual production from these lower 48 states. The only area in which exploration data is not available is the Continental Shelf off the Atlantic coast. Surprises could occur in this area, even discoveries rivaling the Texas fields which have supplied the nation and much of the world for the last forty years. But even this quantity of oil would not last a decade in the present world demand situation.

The natural barriers to exploration and production of petroleum in Alaska are formidable. In any realistic treatment of future production potential, the Alaskan resource must be treated independently. Figure 8 indicates the distortion created by the addition of the Prudhoe Bay finding as a part of the U. S. universe.

Figure 8
Ref. Tabulations B,C&D

HISTORIC U. S. PETROLEUM DISCOVERIES

As compared with

DOMESTIC DEMAND ALL PRODUCTS

PRODUCTION OF LIQUID HYDROCARBONS

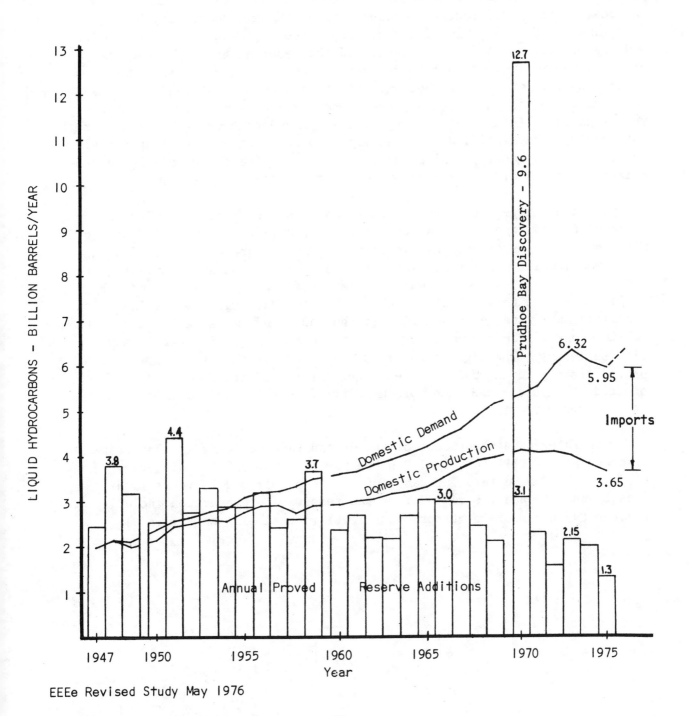

EEEe Revised Study May 1976

PROVED RESERVE WITHDRAWAL RATE

Proved reserves have been the basis for determining the withdrawal rate which is simply the annual production quantity divided by the quantity of the proved reserve. The withdrawal ratio is the reciprocal, indicating the number of years remaining in the proved reserve if annual production remains constant. For almost a hundred years, the withdrawal rate has centered on 8% or a ratio of proved reserves at 12½ times current annual production. As indicated in Figure 8, the withdrawal rate moved up to 9% in 1964, dropping the reserve to eleven times annual production; but by this time, U. S. production could no longer keep up with U. S. consumption and the production ratio which indicated the reserves holding steady at eleven times production in 1965 represented only 7½ years at the current level. By 1975 with the withdrawal rate holding steady at 13%, the demand rate was twice that amount and proved reserves represented less than four year's supply. In the late spring of 1976, advanced measures of the increase in petroleum consumption were registering consumption growth at an annual increase of 8%, happily confirming the end of the recession and the reestablishment of the old pattern of petroleum consumption increase.

There has never been great significance to the withdrawal rate or the ratio of proved reserves to annual production and it has virtually no significance today as an economic indicator. The withdrawal rate guided the petroleum industry in its development of new fields and in maintaining its capacity to supply the U. S. and world markets. So long as the industry could accomplish this objective, the withdrawal rate was their thing. As the withdrawal rate began to climb in the '60's and '70's, it reflected the pulling down of the proved reserve and the demise of U. S. petroleum production supremacy. The significant statistic today is the ratio of the U. S. proved reserve to the U. S. market requirement, and the basic figures plotted in Figure 7 are much more meaningful than the ratios indicated in this Figure 9 plotting.

One interesting byproduct of the demand rate plotting is the perspective on the 9.6 billion barrel Prudhoe Bay discovery. This discovery reversed the demand rate increase for only one year and 2½ years later the demand rate and the ratio of proved reserves to production including Prudhoe Bay was back to its previous level (dotted line on Figure 9).

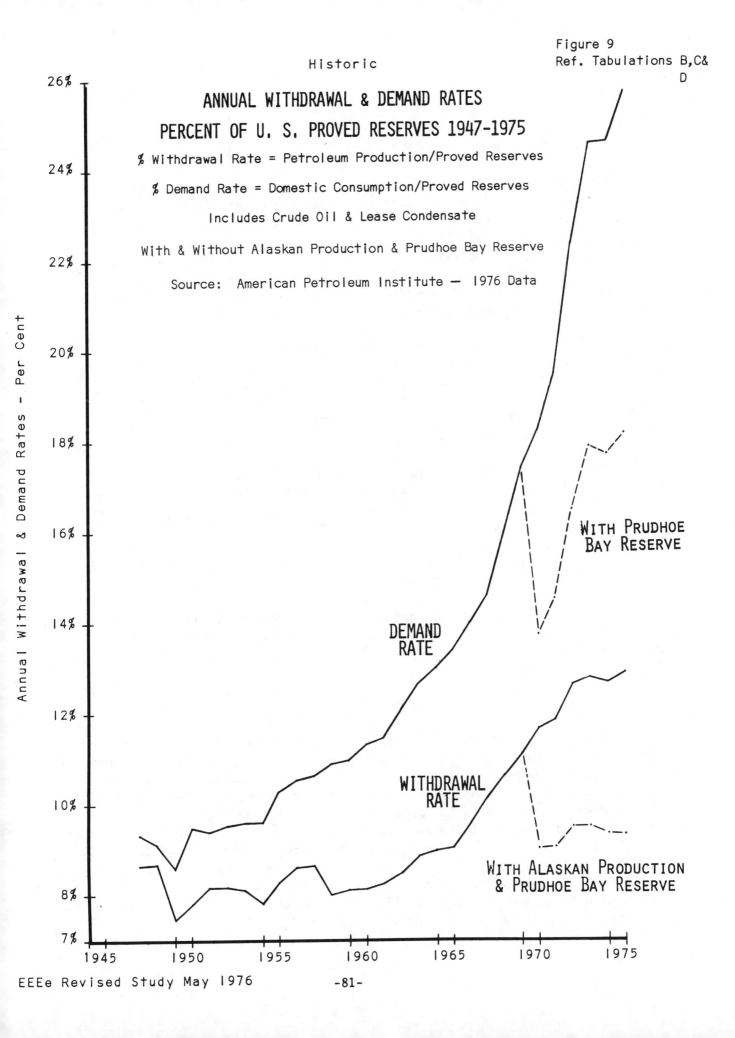

ANNUAL WITHDRAWAL & DEMAND RATES
PERCENT OF U. S. PROVED RESERVES 1947-1975
% Withdrawal Rate = Petroleum Production/Proved Reserves
% Demand Rate = Domestic Consumption/Proved Reserves
Includes Crude Oil & Lease Condensate
With & Without Alaskan Production & Prudhoe Bay Reserve
Source: American Petroleum Institute — 1976 Data

Annual Withdrawal & Demand Rates - Per Cent

WITH PRUDHOE
BAY RESERVE

DEMAND
RATE

WITHDRAWAL
RATE

WITH ALASKAN PRODUCTION
& PRUDHOE BAY RESERVE

26%
24%
22%
20%
18%
16%
14%
12%
10%
8%
7%

1945   1950   1955   1960   1965   1970   1975

TOTAL REMAINING RESOURCE WITHDRAWAL RATE

There is no tradition or precedence for relating current production
to the remaining petroleum resource as the American Petroleum Institute
has never recognized estimates of the total resource beyond their determination of proved reserves, and there had not been enough agreement as
to the quantity of the ultimate producible reserve until the completion
of the 1975 inventories by the U.S.G.S. and the National Academy of
Sciences. Dr. Hubbert's figures which have been available since 1956
could have been employed, but they had not been accepted.

We have computed the remaining U. S. petroleum resource — crude oil,
lease condensates, and natural gas liquids, onshore and offshore including
Alaska — based on the U.S.G.S. 1975 inventory (Circular 725). Assuming
this inventory to represent the beginning of the year 1975, production
each year before 1975 was added to the remaining inventory and the projected production after 1975 was subtracted from the inventory.

Alaska has contributed very little in the past and will contribute only
a small percentage of U. S. production until the Alaskan pipeline is completed. After that time, the bulk of Alaskan production will be restricted
to the capacity of the pipeline. In projecting future production, we have
employed the petroleum engineers' estimates of annual north slope production up to the limit of the pipeline capacity in its present design, including the presently planned expansion.

Figure 10 identifies the beginning of this computation process and the
historic withdrawal rate from 1940 through 1975 for the lower 48 states,
separating out past Alaskan production and the estimated ultimate Alaskan
resource. In this process we are maintaining our independent treatment of
the lower 48 universe and the Alaskan contribution. Figure 10 is supported
by tabulation E&F.

In the Alaskan projection, the pipeline limitation is controlling through
1998. After that, the present estimates of the undiscovered resource and our
expectancy of the rate of discovery and production results in insufficient
annual flow to the planned pipeline system. Thus, we could not find evidence
to support an increase in the capacity of this planned pipeline system. As
planned it will remain the effective limit to annual production. The summation
of all contributors to U. S. petroleum production is shown in Appendix tabulation G-L. The capacity of the pipeline is based on the Federal Energy Administration's, "1976 *National Energy Outlook*" (FEA-N-75/713) released in February
1976 with reference to Figure 11-13 which identifies pipeline capacity including the first loop at 2.5 million barrels per day.

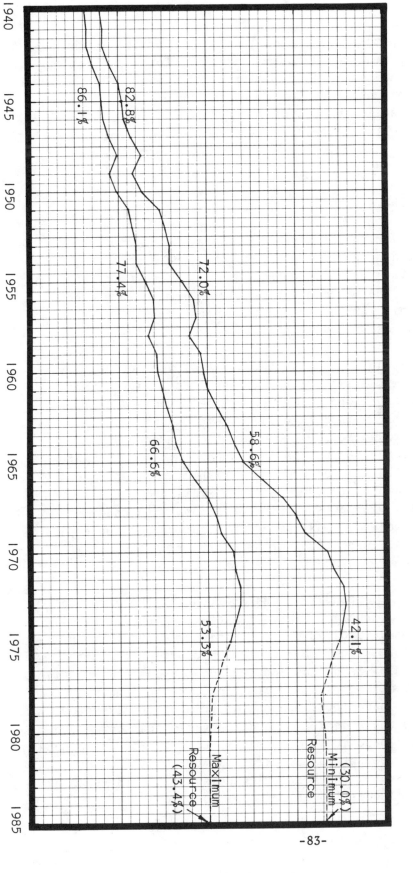

Figure 10
Ref. Tabulations E&F

CONTERMINOUS U. S. HISTORIC RATE OF WITHDRAWAL FOR CRUDE OIL
With Reference to % Original Recoverable Oil Remaining

Resource Base (U.S.G.S.,Circular 725)	Maximum	Minimum
Measured Reserves	24.156	24.156
Indicated Reserves	4.623	4.623
Inferred Reserves	16.900	16.900
Undiscovered Reserves	81.000	36.000
(As of 1/1/75)	126.679	81.679 Billion Bbls.

(Includes Both Onshore & Offshore Reserves)

EEEe Revised Study May 1976

-83-

Figure 10 graphically projects the annual withdrawal rate for the minimum resource and the maximum resource and indicates for each decade the percent remainder of that resource by numerical notation. The decline in the withdrawal rate is extrapolated for the next three years, tapering to 1980 when it is stabilized in our projection. By 1985, 30% of the minimum estimate of the U. S. ultimate producible resource will remain compared with 43.4% of the maximum estimate.

THE PETROLEUM PRODUCTION FORECAST

The stabilized and projected withdrawal rates have been applied to the maximum and minimum remaining resource, tabulated and graphed for annual production through the year 2010 on Figure 11. Then 26% of the maximum estimate and 13% of the minimum estimate will remain in the conterminous U. S. resource while 59% of the maximum Alaskan resource and 32% of the minimum Alaskan resource will still be available.

The year 2010 appears to be close to the limit of the reliability of this methodology as the withdrawal rate will begin to behave erratically as annual production approaches the last of the petroleum reserve. The principal advantage of the methodology is its employment of simple arithmetic computation in producing the geometric decline and in demonstrating the limits of variance beyond the maximum and minimum estimates. When the rate of withdrawal begins to become unreliable and theoretically will climb rapidly, the remaining resource will be small and the error in the actual annual withdrawal will be small in comparison with today's production. Further, the projected maximum and minimum production expectancy increases with time, allowing for increasing error in the estimate as the withdrawal rate loses relevance.

Tabulation G bound in the Appendix is as important as the graphical presentation for more than a casual consideration of the methodology of this projection. Here, we have indicated quantitatively each of the principal contributors to the total liquid hydrocarbon production that is expected, eliminating ambiguity in definition and identifying the relative importance of each of the contributors. As crude oil, lease condensates, and natural gas liquids each have their own characteristics or expected production rate relative to their depletion and the geological formation of the hydrocarbon reserve, these individual estimates are subject to substantial variance, and no agreement can be expected for any individual figure. We have simply presented the best evidence available in reaching our conclusion. The critical question is not the significance of a var-

Figure 11
Ref. Tabulations B,D,
G,H,I,J,K&L

FORECAST OF U. S. LIQUID HYDROCARBON PRODUCTION

Sources: American Petroleum Institute Published Data (1976)
           U. S. Geological Survey, Circular 725 (1975)

Resource Base	Maximum	Minimum
Conterminous U.S.	126.679	81.679
Alaska	66.307	25.307
Natural Gas Liquids	34.350	23.350
(As of 1/1/75)	227.336	130.336

Projections Based On: Consumption At Zero Per Capita Increase
                        1.5% Annual Population Increase
                        Alaska Pipeline Capacity
                        Maximum Probable Annual Production at 2% of
                           Remaining Recoverable Oil In Place
                        Minimum Probable Annual Production at 3-1/3% of
                           Remaining Recoverable Oil In Place

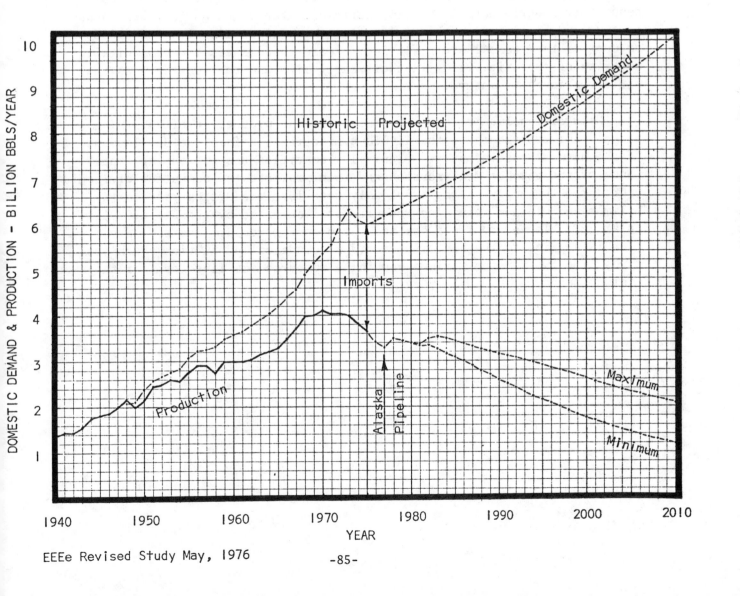

iance in one or more individual hydrocarbons in its contribution to the over-all conclusion. What is important is the total hydrocarbon production year-by-year and confidence in the inclusion of all contributors at somewhere near their expected dimension. The conclusion should be obvious in the Figure 11 graph and all subsequent graphs, the U. S. is ever increasing its dependence on imports! These imports represent a U. S. trade deficit which must be balanced and these imports may not be available in the quantities indicated.

THE SIGNIFICANCE OF GAS LIQUIDS

One of the sources of confusion in terminology is petroleum defined as all liquid hydrocarbons and petroleum defined as only crude oil. This differentiation was not important before 1940 and it may not be too signi-ficant after 2010, but in between it can introduce substantial differences. Figure 12 identifies and quantifies this difference for the seventy-year time span centering on 1975.

Lease condensates, the byproduct of crude oil production, were not separately identified in the early petroleum statistics as they were added to the crude oil flow in the field after their separation from the gaseous product or they were lost in flaring. Lease condensates increase with the maturity of specific fields in their early life and then decrease as the field continues to mature.

Natural gas liquids are a byproduct in the production of natural gas and did not contribute to the liquid hydrocarbons before the development of the natural gas industry. Figure 12 identifies the increasing impor-tance of the gaseous contribution and then projects the summation of liquid hydrocarbon by applying the previously described production rate to the maximum and minimum remaining resource as identified by the U.S.G.S. Cir-cular 725. These are lines one and three on Figure 12. The same projec-tion is applied to the historic record of crude oil production which pro-duces line two for the maximum remaining resource and line four for the minimum resource.

Figure 12
Ref. Tabulations B,D,
G,H,I,J,K&L

SUMMATION OF US LIQUID HYDROCARBONS & CRUDE OIL PRODUCTION

Sources: American Petroleum Institute Published Data (1976)
U. S. Geological Survey, Circular 725 (1975)

Resource Base	Maximum	Minimum
Conterminous U.S.	126.679	81.679
Alaska	66.307	25.307
Natural Gas Liquids	34.350	23.350
(As of 1/1/75)	227.336	130.336

Projections Based On: Consumption At Zero Per Capita Increase
1.5% Annual Population Increase
Alaska Pipeline Capacity
Maximum Probable Annual Production at 2% of
Remaining Recoverable Oil In Place
Minimum Probable Annual Production at 3-1/3% of
Remaining Recoverable Oil In Place

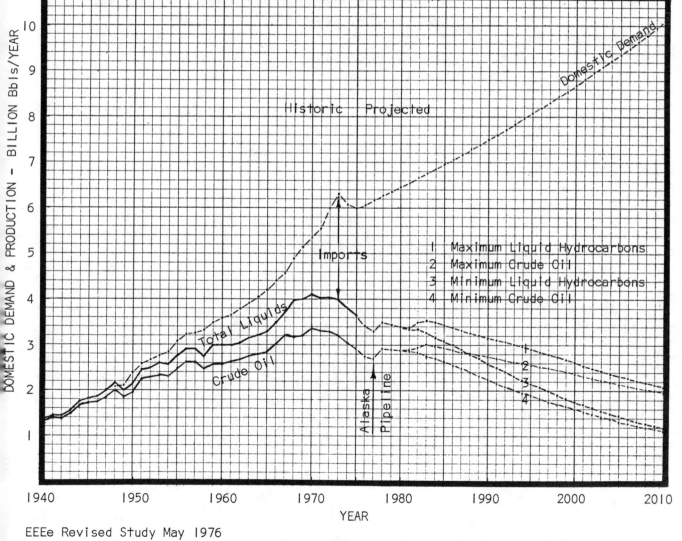

ECONOMIC INFLUENCES - SUPPLY AND DEMAND VERSUS PRICE

It would be foolish to question the interdependence of supply, demand, and price in a free economy, but it would also be somewhat foolish to expect the theory of the prescribed relationship to pertain in the absence of either a free economy or a material supply which can be influenced by price.

The physical facts of the petroleum market precondition this market to an isolation from the price mechanism, and the history of the petro'eum industry supports the conclusion that the petroleum price has been responsive to supply and demand only during short periods of the 125 years since it began to be produced and used in quantity.

Petroleum supply depends on exploration which precedes production by a longer time span than can be handled in the free market response without organized control. In a really free market, the price response to successful exploration would bankrupt the producer and the subsequent cycle of shortage would dry up the market for the product before the supply could be reestablished. Dr. Hubbert identifies an eleven year lag in his statistical projection of additions to reserves and production at the peak of U. S. petroleum development. Today, there are physical limitations on the expansion of U. S. production which depends on offshore and Arctic exploration, and less than eleven years, but more than half that amount, will be required. Theoretically, production increases should be felt approximately six years after price stimulation, but the importance of this observation is its relationship to the expectancy of a short time response of petroleum production to price stimulation. There is no historic or geological basis for this expectancy.

Figure 13 traces the history of the price-demand relationship for the sixty years from 1915 to 1975. This includes the period after the breakup of Rockefeller's Standard Oil Company and the influence of the Organization of Petroleum Exporting Countries on U. S. domestic price.

Before 1932, the price of petroleum gyrated from 50¢ to $3.50 a barrel and in the single year 1921, the range was from $1.00 to $3.50. Still, the organized forces in the market kept the price from dropping to 10¢ a barrel as had been the market situation prior to its organization by Mr. Rockefeller in the previous century. After 1932, the Texas Railway Commission and the major oil companies controlled the price of oil and that price moved very slowly in response to the rapid and steady increase in the U. S. market. From 1972 on, the control of price shifted from the market-conscious international producers to the production-conscious Organization of Petroleum Exporting Countries.

Figure 13
Ref. Tabulation 3

WELLHEAD PRICE OF DOMESTIC PETROLEUM
U. S. CONSUMPTION OF ALL PETROLEUM PRODUCTS
1915 — 1975

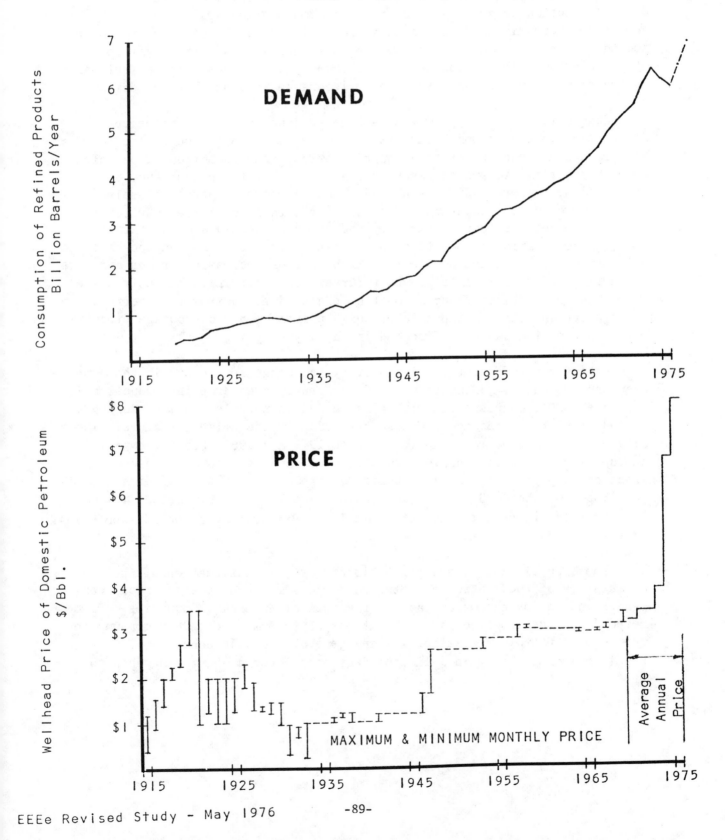

EEEe Revised Study — May 1976

There is no period in this history when supply or demand can be demonstrated to have been responsive to price. The 1974 illusion that the 2½ times increase in the average wellhead price of domestic petroleum would increase U. S. production or greatly decrease U. S. consumption disappeared with the end of the recession and the rapid increase in petroleum consumption in the second quarter of 1976. Petroleum consumption responds to the availability of petroleum and the prosperity of the country and is very little influenced by the price of petroleum within the price range that has been experienced.

Concentrating on supply, the lack of evidence of price influence is devastating to the economic theorists. Figure 14 projects the same price history against the two critical supply series, the production of petroleum, and the additions to proved reserves that represent the consequence of exploration. Before 1950, annual additions to proved reserves closely parallel production, maintaining the 12½ times ratio discussed earlier. There was excess production capacity and price reflected demand. After 1950, no correlation can be found between reserve additions and the historic price structure. We are now in the sixth year of increasing prices and both production and additions to proved reserves are declining. The only price influence or elasticity conclusion that can be derived from this correlation is negative and this is impossible. High prices do not discourage production if the production can be influenced in any way by price.

Attempts to offset the price history to recognize the lag in the supply response are equally unsuccessful. Coincidently, the drop in production in the late 1920's corresponded with a reduction in petroleum prices during a period of history when there was some freedom in the price structure. The mild increases in petroleum price between 1945 and 1965 which accompanied the decline in proved reserves could be explained as price response to contracting supply, but this was a period of expanding world production, the actual end of the U. S. market dominance of world petroleum prices, and the beginning of the domestic market isolation. Prices rose as world supply increased.

The significance of the price history is its confirmation of the economic history of the control of petroleum prices first by the major oil companies and now by the Organization of Petroleum Exporting Countries. Price responds to the supply or availability of petroleum. Demand or consumption responds to petroleum availability and general economic conditions, but supply is responsive only in a limited degree and over a short time span to price.

Figure 14
Ref. Tabulations C&D

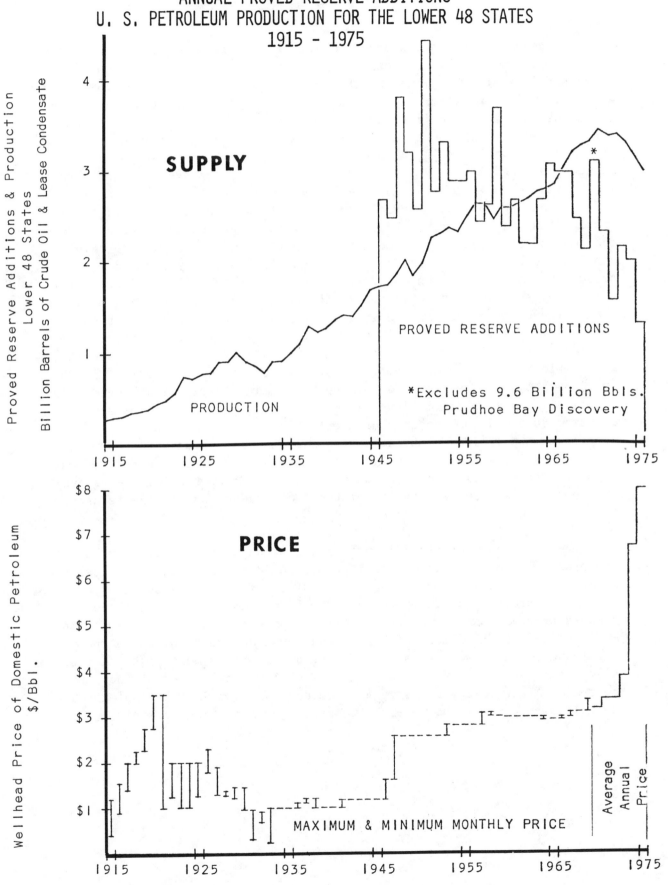

WELLHEAD PRICE OF DOMESTIC PETROLEUM
ANNUAL PROVED RESERVE ADDITIONS
U. S. PETROLEUM PRODUCTION FOR THE LOWER 48 STATES
1915 - 1975

SUPPLY

PROVED RESERVE ADDITIONS

*Excludes 9.6 Billion Bbls.
Prudhoe Bay Discovery

PRODUCTION

Proved Reserve Additions & Production
Lower 48 States
Billion Barrels of Crude Oil & Lease Condensate

PRICE

Wellhead Price of Domestic Petroleum
$/Bbl.

Average Annual Price

MAXIMUM & MINIMUM MONTHLY PRICE

The petroleum price history on Charts 13 and 14 was projected in historic dollar values. A correction could be made in the correlation of this price supply history by indexing the price structure. On the basis of the wholesale price index for all commodities, 1975 prices are four times the prices of 1930 and five times the prices of 1910. If these corrections were applied with appropriate index year by year, the price swings between 1915 and 1934 would be in the same range as the price demands of the OPEC between 1973 and 1976. But this would produce a price history with a sag in the middle roughly balancing the big umbrella of proved reserves which built up during this same period and began its descent in the late 1950's, accelerating rapidly after 1968. The decline in proved reserves handed the control of price to the producing countries and price will certainly continue to be responsive to the level of this proved reserve and the world consumption or demand trend, but the price influence will be filtered through control by the dominant influence on the market, now the supplier organization. There has been a controlling influence on the petroleum market for most of its history and that is not apt to change. It is a fundamental characteristic of the physical economics of this natural product and its many employments. The OPEC reserves are now the principal factors in the world market, and the isolation of the U. S. market will be achieved only relatively and with difficulty. No matter how sophisticated the statistical procedure and the economic argument, the controlling fact in the U. S. petroleum supply will be physical economics and not pecuniary economics, and price stimulants can be anticipated to have very little effect except over very short periods of time when price can effect the release of available reserves and permit tertiary methods of production and the transport of small quantities from remote fields.

The importance of price is not in the production of petroleum but in the production of petroleum substitutes, liquid hydrocarbons from coal and shale. Persistence in promoting the illusion of increased supplies of U. S. produced petroleum and independence from petroleum importation through increased price appears to be principally responsible for the stalemate in legislation and the demise of reason and constructive thinking in the political and social disciplines. U. S. petroleum prices must rise and rise significantly if the free economy is to survive, but the expectancy must be real. A new energy industry must be born and the last half of the U. S. petroleum supply must be reserved to make the transition possible.

DOMESTIC DEMAND

No actual attempt has been made to forecast the U. S. demand for petroleum products. Historically, the annual increase has centered on 4% each year almost from the beginning of the petroleum age with only two significant reversals, 1931 and 1932, and 1974 and 1975. At the end of the second quarter of 1976, the growth was estimated at 8% over the previous year which would quickly eclipse the two year decline. A 5% or 6% annual increase is certainly possible in the immediate future, but the return to a declining consumption is also possible and actually probable if the petroleum supply is restricted for any reason. There is substantial physical elasticity in the demand for this product as a very large proportion is either wasted or expended on unnecessary activities, but physical and pecuniary elasticity are not identical.

U. S. petroleum consumption will depend on political decisions and economic influences in the world market. The domestic demand which is projected in Figure 12 and all other charts is based on the present growth in the adult population which approximates 1½% per year and will be independent of the birth rate for the next decade. Thus, our projection amounts to zero per capita increase in the immediate future and something close to zero per capita increase after 1985 depending on the U. S. population trend.

FEDERAL ENERGY ADMINISTRATION — PROJECT INDEPENDENCE

The Federal Energy Administration came into existence after the Arab boycott in 1973 and produced its first major prescription for independence from petroleum imports in November of 1974. An econometric, computer model was employed for the projections of potential petroleum production and the inputs or controls of this model were strongly influenced by economic price theory assuming a relatively high elasticity for both the supply of petroleum and the demand for petroleum products.

Figure 15 identifies the 1974 Project Independence petroleum production expectancy under their four stated economic conditions: Business As Usual with two alternative petroleum prices, and Accelerated Development that assumed the complete cooperation of the petroleum production industry with the government, employing the same two levels of price. Prices of $7.00 a barrel and $11.00 a barrel were assumed to stimulate production and curtail demand, but only the accelerated development at a price of $11.00 a barrel at the wellhead came close to reaching the expected domestic consumption, extrapolated on the basis of a reduced growth rate to the target year 1985.

The Federal Energy Administration production expectancies are plotted against our projection as previously described. The F.E.A. anticipations for 1980 and 1985 produced ascending production curves for all but the low priced Business As Usual projection. Obviously, no physical limitations or physical economic considerations entered the Federal Energy Administration's forecast or its prescription for legislative action.

The significance of the 1974 F.E.A. forecast is the identification of the theory which dominates this organization's thinking and petroleum production expectancy. The higher the price the greater the quantity that will be made available. Their computer model goes into great detail matching the funds available for exploration and the expected higher production with each increment in the quantity of money made available by the higher price. There are no limits in economic theory. The computer model is the measure of the reliability of all evidence. The geological evidence with the highest probability of accuracy was rejected because it contradicted traditional economic theory and did not fit the computer formulae.

This dominant philosophy carried into the 1976 forecast despite the admission of physical limits evidence and the acceptance of some influence.

Figure 15

OIL FORECAST COMPARISON WITH 1974 F.E.A. PROJECTION Ref. Tabulations B, D,G,H,I,J,K&L

Sources: American Petroleum Institute Published Data (1976
U. S. Geological Survey, Circular 725 (1975)

Resource Base	Maximum	Minimum
Conterminous U.S.	126.679	81.679
Alaska	66.307	25.307
Natural Gas Liquids	34.350	23.350
(As of 1/1/75)	227.336	130.336

Projections Based On: Consumption At Zero Per Capita Increase
1.5% Annual Population Increase
Alaska Pipeline Capacity
Maximum Probable Annual Production at 2%
of Remaining Recoverable Oil in Place
Minimum Probable Annual Production at 3-1/3%
of Remaining Recoverable Oil in Place

As Compared With Domestic Production Estimated By:
Federal Energy Administration
"Project Independence"
November 1974

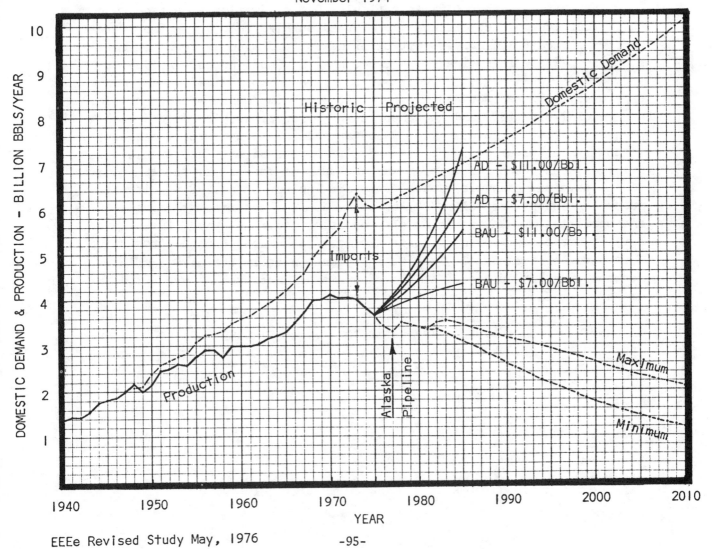

In 1976, the Federal Energy Administration published its current
report. They now had the benefit of the U.S.G.S. inventory of the remaining U. S. petroleum resource (Circular 725) which they had sponsored as
well as the conclusions of the National Academy of Sciences report. Further, the F.E.A. had the benefit of the study of the expected production
from the 59 U. S. oil fields that represented 52% of the proved crude oil
reserves with year by year production estimates by petroleum engineers for
ten years. This is the study that was the principal basis for our Summation of Potential U. S. Petroleum Production (Figure 6). Between 1974 and
1976, the value of the dollar had slipped and the F.E.A. extended its
sights as to the price required to realize its production objectives. A
reference case was maintained at the $8.00 a barrel price but the primary
projections were at $13.00 and $16.00 a barrel with an additional pessimistic short term projection. Political constraints were still in evidence in the F.E.A. projection, but their sanguine expectancy for the
efficacy of the price structure was somewhat diluted.

The Federal Energy Administration's 1976 production expectancy under
their four economic conditions are plotted on Figure 16 against our production forecast and our assumption of domestic demand at zero per capita
increase. There is no longer an expectancy of independence in 1985 or
1990 and the pessimistic forecast comes close to approximating our maximum
expectancy. The effect of this forecast is a compromise between physical
economics limitations and the theories of price elasticity developed by
pecuniary economic theory with a substantial faith in tertiary recovery
methods. The problem is the unresponsive nature of physical problems to
political influence and compromise, and adamant refusal by the F.E.A. to
accept physical economic facts. They did include the U.S.G.S. ultimate
resource finding (Circular 725) as this data was not time denominated
and permitted an assumption of disproportionately high production in the
early years of the forecast. But the most specific petroleum production
forecast was eliminated. The field production estimates of a sample
representing 52% of the U. S. proved crude oil reserves were rejected out
of hand.

We are unable to find any basis for substantiating the conclusion
found in the F.E.A. study of either 1974 or 1976.

OIL FORECAST COMPARISON WITH 1976 F.E.A. PROJECTION

Figure 16
Ref. Tabulations
B,D,G,H,I,J,K,L&M

Sources: American Petroleum Institute Published Data (1976)
U. S. Geological Survey, Circular 725 (1975)

Resource Base	Maximum	Minimum
Conterminous U.S.	126.679	81.679
Alaska	66.307	25.307
Natural Gas Liquids	34.350	23.350
(As of 1/1/75)	227.336	130.336

Projections Based On: Consumption At Zero Per Capita Increase
1.5% Annual Population Increase
Alaska Pipeline Capacity
Maximum Probable Annual Production at 2% of
Remaining Recoverable Oil In Place
Minimum Probable Annual Production at 3-1/3% of
Remaining Recoverable Oil In Place

As Compared With Domestic Production Estimated By:

Federal Energy Administration
"1976 National Energy Outlook"
February 1976

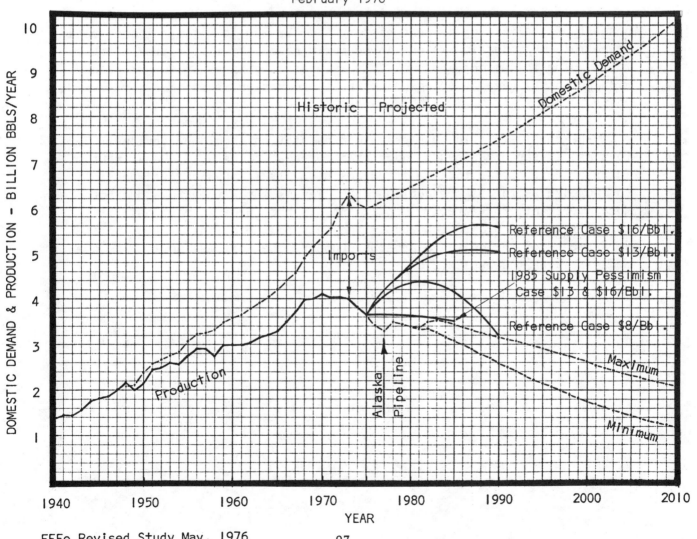

EEEe Revised Study May, 1976

U. S. DEPARTMENT OF THE INTERIOR AND M. KING HUBBERT PETROLEUM PRODUCTION
EXPECTANCY

Figure 17 compares our projection with the U. S. Department of Interior,
Bureau of Mines anticipation of petroleum production in their publication,
"United States Energy Through the Year 2000," which was released in December
1975. The publication includes projections of coal, gas, liquid synthetics,
and electrical energy and breaks down the market between household, commercial, and industrial sectors as well as providing versions from physical
measure to electrical and heat units; but the publication does not identify
the methodology or basis for its estimates of petroleum production. The
conclusions appear to be totally unsupportable indicating a dependence on
the F.E.A. conclusions that we were unable to confirm.

Figure 17 also positions the forecast of Dr. Hubbert taken from the
July 1974 publication of the 1971 updating of his 1956 projection. All
forecasts were tied to the historic record at the end of 1975 and the
short term extrapolation of current production including the anticipated
increase with the first flow from the Alaska pipeline. Also, each begins
at a common point at the end of 1976, assuming that each forecast had the
benefit of the fact of current history and the inevitability of the trend
in petroleum production which can be influenced very little from month to
month. The lead times are such that even great changes in future production potential have no effect on current production, sometimes for several
years.

The conclusions in this graphic presentation should be obvious. Our
forecast is supported by Dr. Hubbert's forecast. The U. S. Department of
Interior forecast is totally irresponsible. It is physically impossible
to increase petroleum production to the levels which they have projected.
More important, the Interior Department has the specific responsibility
for this kind of projection and is the only source of information to the
departments of the United States Government, the business world, and the
media serving the public.

OIL FORECAST COMPARISON WITH U. S. DEPARTMENT OF
INTERIOR & DR. M. KING HUBBERT'S FORECAST

Figure 17
Ref. Tabulations B,
D,G,H,I,J,K & L

Sources: American Petroleum Institute Published Data (1976)
U. S. Geological Survey, Circular 725 (1975)

Resource Base	Maximum	Minimum
Conterminous U.S.	126.679	81.679
Alaska	66.307	25.307
Natural Gas Liquids	34.350	23.350
(As of 1/1/75)	227.336	130.336

Projections Based On: Consumption At Zero Per Capita Increase
1.5% Annual Population Increase
Alaska Pipeline Capacity
Maximum Probable Annual Production at 2% of
Remaining Recoverable Oil In Place
Minimum Probable Annual Production at 3-1/3% of
Remaining Recoverable Oil In Place

As Compared With Domestic Production Estimated By:
Bureau of Mines, U.S. Dept. of Interior – December 1975
and
Dr. M. King Hubbert – Printed July 1974

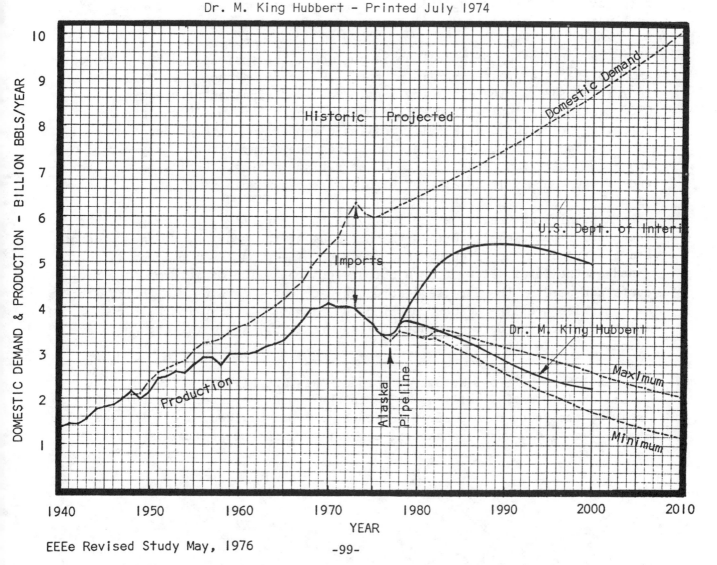

HISTORIC PERSPECTIVE ON WORLD PETROLEUM SUPPLY

Estimates of the world petroleum reserve were included in the National Academy of Sciences 1975 study. Figure 18 was prepared in April of 1974, based on 1972 and 1973 statistics. When Figure 18 was prepared, the recession of 1974-75 had not yet been anticipated and U. S. demand was projected at a 3% growth recognizing only the potential influence of the Arab boycott. The petroleum price range at that time had been established between $8 and $12 a barrel with most conservative economists anticipating that the lower limit would be penetrated. The inflationary trend contributed to raising the expectancy to the $8 and $12 conclusion. An optimistic slow decline in the U. S. supply with a boost from the Alaska pipeline was reasonably conservative in 1974.

With 1976 perspective, U. S. demand is three years late but catching up rapidly. However, U. S. production is 10% below the optimistic anticipation only two years ago and is now falling just as fast. As a consequence, the foreign imports are larger in 1975 than anticipated and the foreign imports will exceed the seven year projection if U. S. consumption continues to increase anywhere near the present rate.

The world price of petroleum is now above the anticipated $12 a barrel and represents a greater strain on the U. S. trade balance when delivered in foreign ships. There is very little real anticipation of breaking the OPEC control. Actually, there is economic reason for an $18 and higher petroleum price based on a fully realistic comparison with the cost of coal liquefaction or shale oil conversion. Even the transportation segment of the U. S. petroleum demand could not be satisfied by synthetics before the end of the century if an all-out effort were begun now.

A significant relationship indicated on Figure 18 is the comparison of the cost of petroleum imports with the value of the gross U. S. farm product, and the trend in the value of this product. The gross farm product is defined as the total value of farm output less the value of intermediate products consumed in the farm segment of the economy — grains fed to livestock or otherwise consumed before reaching the market. It compares with the value of petroleum before transportation, refining, and marketing costs are added.

In 1950, the gross U. S. farm product was $20 billion. The corrected value for 1972 is $35 billion, close to the amount reported on Figure 18. In 1973, the gross farm product represented $56.5 billion, a 60% increase in one year and a very substantial correction from the preliminary figure

Figure 18

1974

SEVEN YEAR PETROLEUM IMPORTS PROJECTION

1974 THROUGH 1980

| | U. S. Supply and Demand Billion Bbl. per Year | | | | Cost of Foreign Supply $ Billion per Year | |
	U.S. Demand @ +3%/yr.	U.S. Supply**	Foreign Supply*	% Import	$8 per Bbl.	$12 per Bbl.
1973 Actual	6.30	4.04	2.26		18.08	27.12
1974	6.49	4.03	2.46	37.9	19.68	29.52
1975	6.68	4.02	2.66	39.8	21.28	31.92
1976	6.88	4.01	2.87	41.7	22.96	34.44
1977	7.09	4.00	3.09	43.5	24.72	37.08
1978***	7.30	4.18	3.12	42.7	24.96	37.44
1979***	7.52	4.36	3.16	42.0	25.28	37.92
1980***	7.75	4.71	3.04	39.2	24.32	36.48
	Total Costs to 1980				163.20	244.80

VALUE OF GROSS U.S. FARM PRODUCT   1971   30.4
(U.S.D.A. Economic Research Serv.)   1972   34.4
                                                1973   47.7

Prepared from 1973 data available in April 1974.
*As reported. U. S. Dept. of the Interior, Year 1973.
**Includes hydrogen, N.G.L., L.C., and refinery and reporting gain or loss.
***With Alaskan pipeline supply @ 2$\overline{M}$ bbl/day in 1980, ½$\overline{M}$ '78, 1$\overline{M}$ '79

reported on Figure 18. With the recession, there was no increase in the 1974 farm product value, but at $18 a barrel, and no substantial increase in the per capita consumption of petroleum, the cost of petroleum imports could exceed the present value of the gross U. S. farm product by 1980, maintaining pressure on increases in the value of this commodity and the inflationary cycle.

As U. S. agriculture is both petroleum dependent and energy intensive, and as agriculture produces our most reliable trading commodity, our primary influence in the world market will be affected by the level of the U. S. petroleum imports on the one hand and the quantity of our agricultural surplus on the other. Unless this balance is maintained, the imbalance will accentuate world inflation. Unless the decline in U. S. production of petroleum is met with either an increase in energy production from alternative sources or reduced net energy consumption, the continued inflationary pressure will be maintained. The gimmickry of credit transfers and the temporary trade balance realized by weapons sale are expediencies, not solutions.

The controlling facts are physical rather than pecuniary. The world supply of petroleum is inadequate to meet projectable U. S. demand in an expanding economy. Even the abundance of coal and oil shale resources of the United States are inadequate in net energy availability. We cannot build the coal liquefaction facilities fast enough to offset the decline in the U. S. petroleum production and at the same time reduce petroleum imports. A break must occur in the increasing consumption of petroleum products.

Figure 19 advances the perspective one year to 1975 when the National Academy of Sciences released their estimates of U. S. and world petroleum reserves. The year-by-year records of world crude oil production are kept by the U. S. Department of the Interior with a two year lag for compilation. The most significant fact in this observation is the rapid increase in the world production which matches world consumption. In ten years, the annual production increase moved from 7.3% to 9.3%, almost double the U. S. annual increase.

The significance of these figures is the rapid increase in the world consumption of petroleum and the limited world reserves. The ratios of annual consumption to the ultimate reserve are the only comprehensible numbers, but they only indicate the relative problem. The significant fact will be the peaking in world production, after which there will be less and less each year. This peaking is anticipated before the end of the century.

Figure 19

SIGNIFICANT WORLD PETROLEUM STATISTICS

World Crude Oil Production in Billions of Barrels: (Source U.S.D.I. 1961 - 1973)

	1973	1972	1963	1962	Ten Year Increase 1963 to 1973
North America	4.2	4.2	3.1	3.0	35%
South America	1.7	1.6	1.5	1.4	13%
Middle East	7.9	6.6	2.5	2.3	216%
Africa	2.2	2.1	.4	.3	450%
Asia & Pacific	.8	.7	.2	.2	300%
Communist World	3.6	3.3	1.7	1.5	112%
Total World	20.6	18.6	9.5	8.9	117%
World Increase/Year	+9.3%		+7.3%		

Eleven year compound annual
increase in world production   7.9%
$s = p \cdot (1+i)^n$

U. S. and World Petroleum Recoverable Reserves - Billions of Barrels
    1975 Estimate by National Academy of Sciences (Source NAS 1975)*

	United States	World
Proved Reserves	37.5	600
Undiscovered Reserves	113.0	1,130
Total Recoverable Petroleum	150.5	1,730

Ratio Total Recoverable Petroleum to 1973 Annual Consumption (Years Supply)

	United States	World
@ static consumption	24	84
@ past consumption increase (compound annual rate 7.9%)		27
@ 5.0% increase per year	16	34
@ 3.0% increase per year	18	43

  Prepared from data available in April, 1975, 1972 + 1973 statistics.
* National Academy of Sciences "Mineral Resources and the Environment"
  LCCN 75-4176, ISNB 0-309-02343-2.

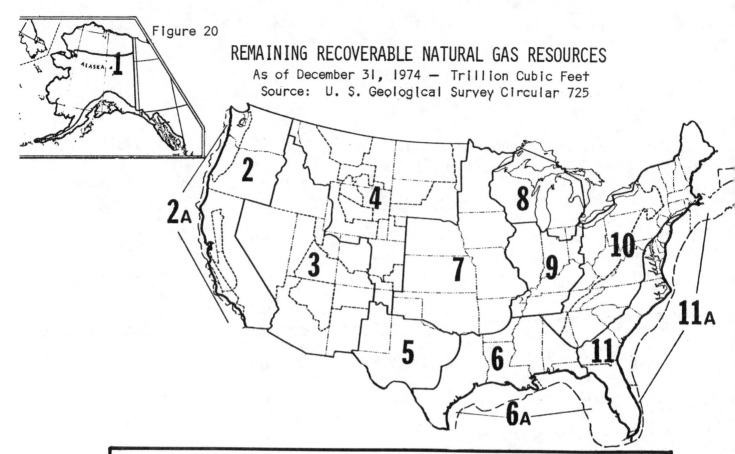

Figure 20

REMAINING RECOVERABLE NATURAL GAS RESOURCES
As of December 31, 1974 — Trillion Cubic Feet
Source: U. S. Geological Survey Circular 725

Regions	Cumulative Production	Demonstrated Reserves Measured	Total Cumulative Production + Demonstrated Reserves	Inferred Reserves [1]	Undiscovered Recoverable Resources	
					Statistical Mean	Estimated Range [2] (95%-5%)
ONSHORE						
1. Alaska-------------------	0.482	31.722	32.204	[3]14.7	32	16 - 57
2. Pacific Coastal States----	25.455	4.732	30.187	4.0	13	8 - 20
3. Western Rocky Mountains---	10.728	9.081	19.809	2.9	14	6 - 25
4. Northern Rocky Mountains--	11.485	6.754	18.240	5.3	29	18 - 47
5. West Texas and Eastern New Mexico--------------	58.686	24.624	83.310	23.3	70	35 - 101
6. Western Gulf Basin-------	197.899	81.903	279.802	58.7	133	85 - 196
7. Mid-Continent------------	107.700	34.150	141.850	20.6	72	50 - 101
8. Michigan Basin-----------	0.558	1.458	2.016	0.8	1	0.8 - 2
9. Eastern Interior---------	2.797	0.766	3.563	0.5	2	0.7 - 4
10. Appalachians-------------	31.057	5.985	37.042	3.3	10	5 - 17
11. Eastern Gulf and Atlantic Coastal Plain-----------	0.001	0.001	0.002	[4]Negl.	1	0.4 - 2
OFFSHORE (0-200 metres)						
1A. Alaska-------------------	0.423	0.145	0.568	[3] 0.1	44	8 - 50*(8)
2A. Pacific Coastal States---	1.415	0.463	1.878	0.4	3	2 - 6
6A. Gulf of Mexico----------	32.138	35.348	67.486	67.0	50	18 - 91
11A. Atlantic Coastal States--	0.000	0.000	0.000	0.0	10	[5]5 - 14
Totals:		237.132		201.6		257.9 - 691.0

TABLE 5.—*Production, reserves, and undiscovered recoverable gas resources for the United States, December 31, 1974 (trillion cubic feet)*

*Realistic Maximum

Maximum Remaining Recoverable Natural Gas = 1,130 TCF
Minimum Remaining Recoverable Natural Gas = 697 TCF

NATURAL GAS AND ITS SUBSTITUTES

Our forecast for gas employs the methodology described for oil except that individual projections were made for each of the major regions. Only the four regions in the eastern half of the U. S. could be combined without losing precision in the forecast conclusion.

This introduces a substantial statistical difference in our use of U.S.G.S. Circular 725. In the oil forecast, we accepted the statistical conclusion for the total U. S. undiscovered recoverable resource on the maximum and minimum basis. This conclusion varies from the summation of the independent regions because of the mathematical methods employed by U.S.G.S.

We found the regional forecast necessary because of the wide variation in the production histories and the relationship between the size of the resource and production capacity from region to region. Thus, my forecast used the summation of the demonstrated reserve, the inferred reserve, and the estimated undiscovered recoverable resource, first for the maximum estimate and second for the minimum estimate. The ten year history of the ratio of production to the ultimate resource was computed and a stabilized withdrawal rate was employed in the forecast. The rates represent an extrapolation considering all economic and physical information bearing on the probable future development of the regional resource. The tabulation identifying this mathematical process for the maximum and minimum forecast of each region is reproduced in the Appendix, Tabulations N and P.

Figure 20 identifies the U.S.G.S. Circular 725 conclusions of remaining resource together with past cumulative production and reserve breakdowns. The map at the top of Figure 20 identifies the regions. The tabulation includes the notation of our interpretation of the offshore Alaskan undiscovered recoverable resource. In the U.S.G.S. Circular 725 footnotes, this resource is identified as outside the geological evidence and statistically not supportable. For this reason, we have reduced the maximum estimate to their minimum which is within reason. Finally, the summations shown at the bottom of the tabulation have only relative significance as they do not represent a statistical conclusion and this total was not employed in our forecast. The statistical summation in U. S. Geological Survey Circular 725 produced a more restrictive range than the totals indicated. Thus, our forecast base is relatively broader - a larger maximum and a smaller minimum resource estimate - even though we reduced the Alaskan maximum estimate.

The distribution of the remaining gas resource in the U. S. is not even. The great majority of the resource is located in the Gulf area. There is gas in the Great Plains and on the West Coast, but there is very little in the eastern one-third. The Atlantic offshore gas potential has not been proved and could very well be totally discounted, but the U.S.G.S. estimate is small and this estimate has been included in our summation.

Figure 21 graphically presents our conclusion as to the probable year-by-year production of natural gas. Tabulation N summarizes the maximum estimate identifying each of the ten regions which were separately computed in the forecast procedure year-by-year from 1976 through the year 2000. Tabulation P summarizes the minimum production expectancy with the same backup derivation. Each of the supporting tabulations identify the ten year history of production from the region, developing the withdrawal rate which was employed in the forecast. Additionally, all information available as to the age of the field, the availability of the identified resource for exploration and production, and the availability of pipeline transportation year-by-year was considered in establishing the withdrawal rate. A separate analysis was made of the 56 selected major oil fields that were covered in the ten year forecast completed by the Federal Energy Administration under Public Law 93-275. This sample is primarily concerned with associated gas and is not directly usable in forecasting future gas production as the great majority is non-associated. However, this sample was specific in our projection of Alaskan gas production as the Prudhoe Bay field is included in the sample.

Environmental restraints and cost advantage put pressure on a rapid development of the gas industry over a short time span. Release from price control could result in rapid production increases, covering the current shortage in the gas required to fill pipeline commitments, but this increase cannot continue for long as the physical resource is rapidly being exhausted. The short term forecast is vulnerable, but the long term forecast cannot be exceeded by very much. On balance, our minimum estimate appears to be the most realistic and the maximum estimate should cover most short term spurts, excepting only a possible quick release of shut-in gas when price control restraints are removed or substantially relaxed.

Figure 21   Ref. Tabulation N-I & P-I

SUMMATION OF U. S. NATURAL GAS
PRODUCTION & DEMAND

Sources: American Gas Association Published Data - 1976
U. S. Geological Survey Circular 725 - 1975

Remaining Recoverable Resource	Maximum	Minimum
Lower 48 States	1018.065	625.965
Alaska	111.667	70.667
(As of 1/1/75)	1129.732 TCF	696.632 TCF

Production projection based on maximum and minimum probable
annual regional production at variable rates of withdrawal
as related to the fields in question and the alternative
transmission systems proposed.

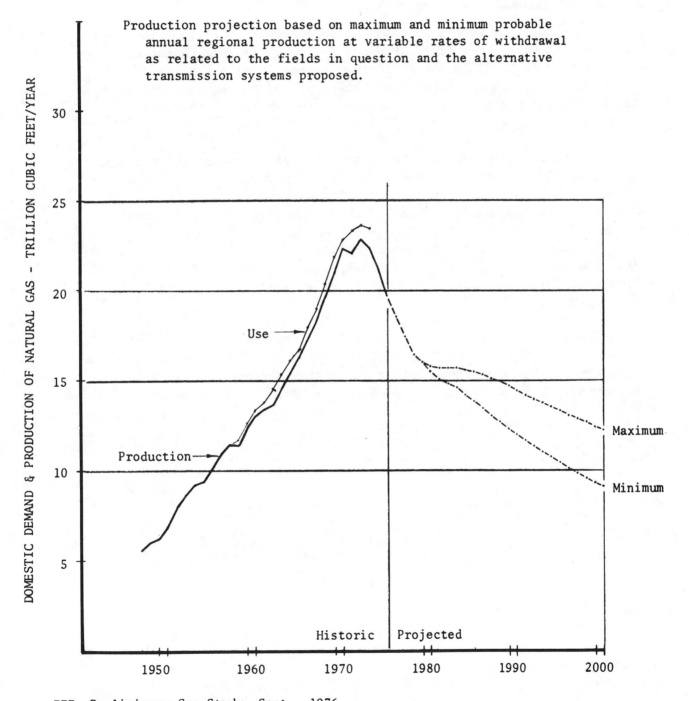

EEEe Preliminary Gas Study, Sept., 1976

GAS PRODUCTION AND DISCOVERY HISTORY

A critical fact in the gas history is the relationship between the rate of discovery and the rate of production. As with petroleum, past discoveries have produced a substantial reserve which is the shelf inventory of this industry and the current ratio of proved reserves to annual production indicates a comfortable margin of eleven times. But this margin is most deceptive when the reserves are identified by the date of their discovery.

The two graphs were prepared by Gordon Zareski, chief of the gas planning responsibility of the Federal Power Commission. Both charts are based on the most recent estimates of the ultimate gas reserves, basin by basin. In this analysis, the amount of gas in each basin is identified for the year of its discovery, thus relating this reserve to the proper time sequence.

In the top graph, a profile of the discovery history is indicated by the solid line, complemented by the three year moving average dotted line. This history clearly indicates the peaking of U. S. natural gas discovery between 1957 and 1958 and the precipitous decline since then.

The bar chart at the bottom of Figure 22 employs the same data but groups discoveries in five year blocks, carrying the discovery history back to 1920. This profile identifies a discovery peak before World War II (dark bars).

The light bars identify production for the same five year intervals. It was not until a period from 1960 to 1964 that production eclipsed new discoveries, but then the acceleration in the differential is clearly indicated. When the ratio of discovery to production is computed on this five year basis, the critical period in the peaking of the discovery ratio moves back to the time interval 1920 to 1924.

Figure 22

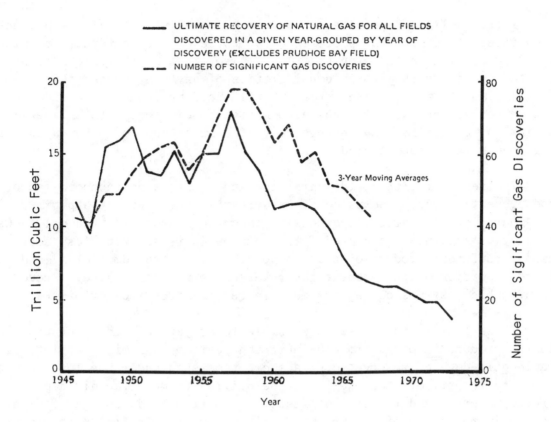

COMPARISON OF SIGNIFICANT DISCOVERIES AND ULTIMATE GAS RESERVES
BY YEAR OF DISCOVERY

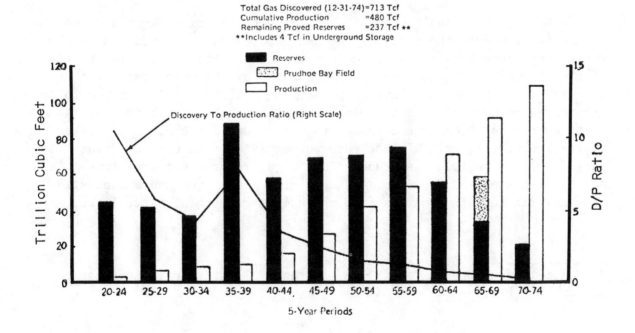

ULTIMATE GAS RESERVES BY YEAR OF DISCOVERY VS. ANNUAL GAS PRODUCTION
5-YEAR PERIODS (1920-1974)

Source: Gordon K. Zareski, Chief, Planning & Development Division,
Bureau of Natural Gas, Federal Power Commission, Jan. 1976

COMPARATIVE GAS FORECAST

There is little consistency between comparative natural gas production forecasts except the preference for three or more alternatives with a wide variation in the probabilities. Also, most of the forecasts are limited to ten years with no consideration of anything beyond this time. Finally, most forecasts are strongly influenced by economic considerations introduced as the basis for the alternative conclusions with a liberal sprinkling of optimism and deference to the high hopes of other agencies engaged in the forecast trade.

The reason for this wide variation and emphasis on economic factors is the presently controlled price of interstate natural gas at approximately one-fourth of its value compared with imported gas or imported oil.* Gas production from non-associated fields can be increased with less cost and danger to future production than is possible in petroleum fields, and the largest portion of the present gas reserves is non-associated. Proved recoverable reserves of gas are much larger than reserves of oil.

These four factors make it possible to project a holding of the line in the production of gas for the next ten years by assuming a relatively rapid pull-down of reserves over a short time span under the influence of economic incentive. More wells can be drilled to more rapidly deplete proved reserves and the size of feeder lines from producing gas fields can be increased to offset the production decreases in fields that have been depleted. Thus, there is more elasticity in the immediate natural gas production than in petroleum.

Finally, the casual forecasts have ignored the significance of the long range trend in the discovery of new gas basins. We referred to the F.E.C. development of these trends, reproduced in Figure 22. The source of the confusion is more clearly demonstrated by the comparison of the two graphs on Figure 23. Current production appears small compared to the proved recoverable reserves in the left hand chart. It is only when reserve additions are compared to net production that the failure of the industry to maintain the reserve supply becomes evident. The large addition in 1970 was Prudhoe Bay, a gas reserve not available at the present time, and representing a geological area and a statistical universe totally separate from the primary source of natural gas.

---

* Refer to footnote on Page 51 for current interstate price regulation action by F.P.C.

Figure 23

THE TWO FACES OF THE FUTURE OF U. S. GAS PRODUCTION

Source: American Gas Association

The Large Reserves

The Small Additions Since 1967

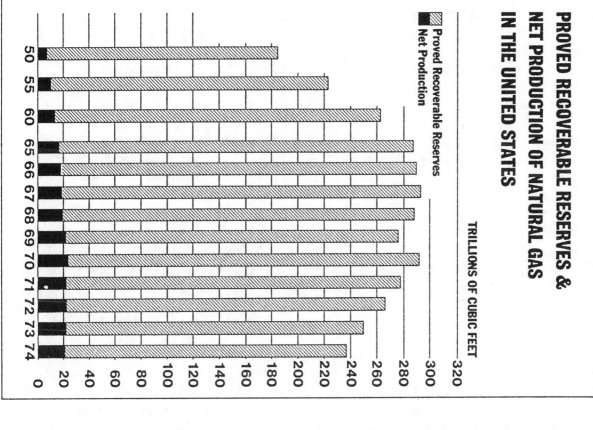

PROVED RECOVERABLE RESERVES &
NET PRODUCTION OF NATURAL GAS
IN THE UNITED STATES

▨ Proved Recoverable Reserves
■ Net Production

TRILLIONS OF CUBIC FEET

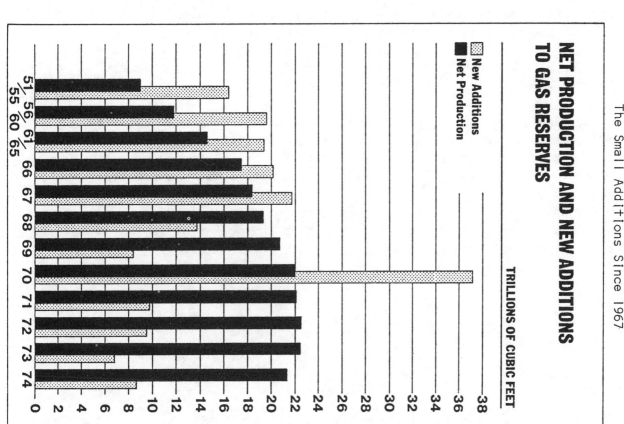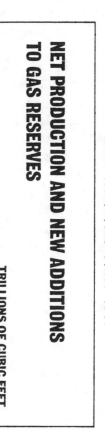

NET PRODUCTION AND NEW ADDITIONS
TO GAS RESERVES

▨ New Additions
■ Net Production

TRILLIONS OF CUBIC FEET

These facts make it necessary to qualify all forecasts, including my own, in their short term perspective. Our estimates of future production are based on the orderly production of existing gas fields and maximum consistent exploration and production of new fields or the extensions of existing basins or new basins. We must recognize the possibility of what would be an uneconomical short term development of natural gas under economic or political pressures. Our forecast methodology precludes adjustments for these potential short term stimulations, but the possibility must be accepted. This recognition is the principal explanation for the wide variation in comparative forecasts, but the trend from year to year in the comparison of these forecasts indicates a substantial reduction in the extremes and a more conservative conclusion. There are physical limits to the capability of producing basins and it is expensive to enlarge feeder transmission lines. Also, gas production has not been reduced to the extent that the lack of economic stimulation has suggested, thus dampening anticipations for the reverse situation if price restrictions are removed.

Figure 24 compares our long range forecasts with the published forecasts of the Federal Power Commission from 1974 to January 27, 1976. The derivation and full scale of our forecast is Figure 21.

The lower graph is the Federal Power Commission technical staff's most recent and most unequivocable conclusion. It includes their estimate of the curtailment of gas production resulting from the present price restrictions and their anticipation of the production which would have occurred if these restrictions had been removed. This F.P.C. estimate closely parallels our projections and it is identified as "reasonably optimistic."

The middle graph presents the F.P.C. estimate made a year earlier with proper qualifications to satisfy political reality. Only the middle projection has significance. The lower projection assumes no further gas discoveries, providing a complement to the optimistic upper projection.

The upper graph is the F.P.C. projection of 1974 and indicates political dictates and constraints. Both the high and medium estimates fall outside the evidence now available.

Figure 24

U. S. GAS FORECAST COMPARISON WITH FEDERAL POWER COMMISSION FORECASTS

1974, 1975, and 1976

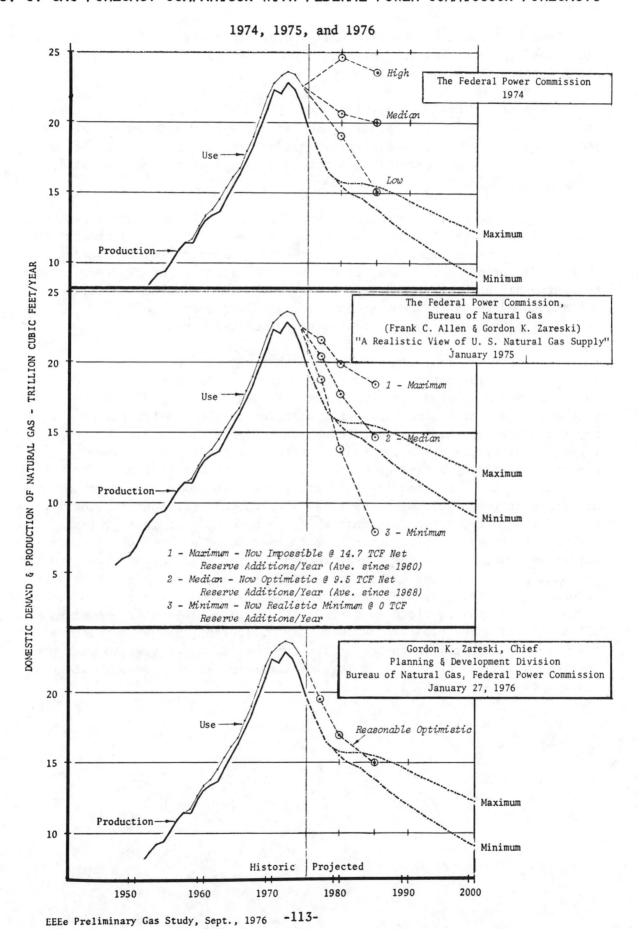

Figure 25 compares three Federal Energy forecasts, the first in 1974, the second in 1976, and the third after a compromise with the Federal Power Commission in their testimony to Congress.

There is virtually no physical economic basis for the F.E.A. conclusion. I have previously discussed the lack of evidence to support their economic theory of an increase in oil production as a consequence of an increase in price. Their 1974 gas forecast is a little more defensible but not much.

The 1976 forecast - middle graph of Figure 25 - is an improvement over 1974 but it has little relationship to the reality of gas production. Even the most pessimistic profile anticipates a substantial production increase at prices which have already been realized or anticipated in the international market and in intra-state contracts. This position was abandoned in conferences with F.P.C. as a consequence of the necessity of supporting their testimony. (see lowest graph)

These comparisons seem to indicate that our gas forecast is slightly low. Only the low estimate of the Federal Energy Administration in 1974 falls below our minimum estimate. But this conclusion should not be reached, as all of the comparisons are influenced to some extent by political considerations. John Duane, an independent analyst for whom I have considerable respect, projects production below our minimum employing a totally different methodology. Dr. Hubbert's forecast of the complete gas cycle for the lower 48 states falls below our minimum in 1995. His range is comparable with our range when the Alaskan contribution is added. In reviewing the judgments which we have made in interpreting the historic data region by region, there appears to be as much chance of our forecasts being high as low. Even though the gas industry has opportunities to boost production over a short range, and even though there may be considerable amounts of gas which have been shut in for economic reasons, the industry is operating close to a production rate of 10% of its reserves which is considered close to maximum. My projections assume a political climate which recognizes the necessity for more than the year to year production potential, and by the nature of the forecast methodology, the primary concern is with the long term.

Figure 25

U. S. GAS FORECAST COMPARISON WITH FEDERAL ENERGY ADMINISTRATION FORECAST

1974, 1976 and Compromise Conclusion 1976

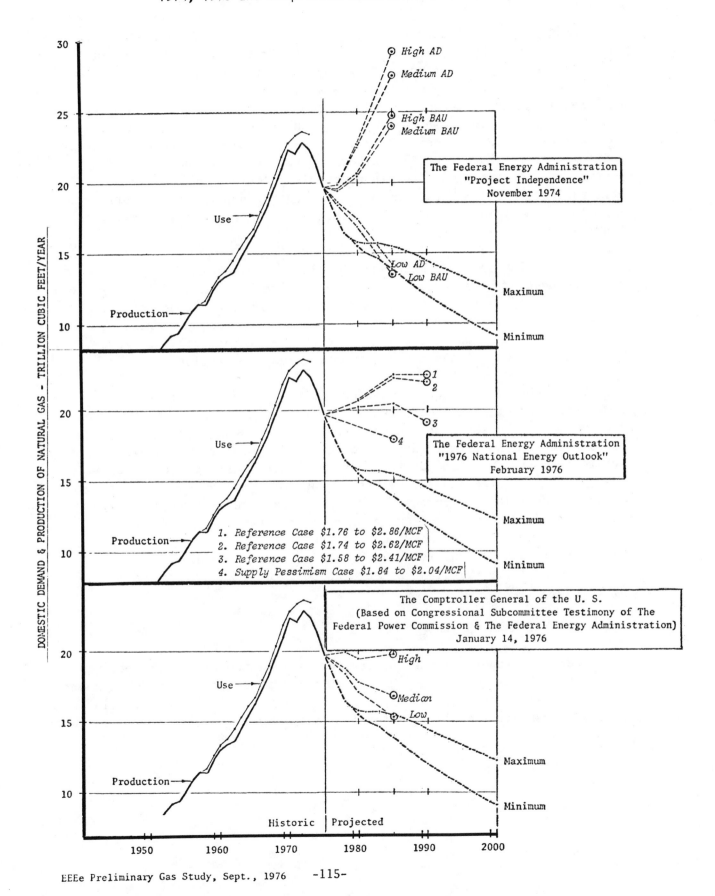

THE FIRST ALTERNATIVE TO NATURAL GAS, PETROLEUM SUBSTITUTION

Petroleum substitution will become the obvious alternative for the small industrial and commercial user cut off from his supply of natural gas. Oil burning conversion units are generally available. Liquid petroleum tanks require a minimum of space. The increase in air pollution resulting from burning petroleum need not exceed the limit of federal, state, and local laws. The alternative conversion to coal would involve substantial capital expenditure including almost prohibitive air pollution control costs. Thus, the free market and the laws and administrative posture of the government encourage petroleum conversion despite the obvious long range implications of an increasing dependence on petroleum imports, threatening the national security and economic stability of the country.

A variation on the simple substitution of petroleum for gas is its use to produce synthetic gas. The light ends of liquid petroleum (naptha) can be employed by the gas utility to produce pipeline grade gas for distribution to its customers. This process is currently economical even in the present unnatural mix of controlled interstate gas prices with uncontrolled intra-state and imported gas competition.

Quite obviously, liquid petroleum is available to replace gas in the production of electricity by the major utilities with identical consequences for the long run national interest. One-half of the total gas consumption in the recent past is represented by interruptible gas service to industry, gas used by the major utilities for the generation of electricity, and the industrial use of gas for heat and power. Most of the interruptible service has already been forfeited. Most probably it is already too late to avoid conversion to petroleum in much of the industrial sector. The question is whether the utilities will be permitted to make this conversion and whether industry will be encouraged by the economic restrictions on burning coal to first convert to liquid petroleum.

LIQUEFIED NATURAL GAS, LNG

The most economical alternative to the replacement of the declining U. S. natural gas supply and the scheduled termination of Canadian imports is the overseas importation of liquefied natural gas. The process is capital intensive, requiring extensive cyrogenic facilities to reduce the temperature of the gas to the required negative 250°F. and maintain this temperature in ocean transit, delivery, and storage.

The process is dangerous. Gas released for any reason will flow on the land or water surface, absorbing heat from all adjacent bodies with a resultant quick freeze, and the combined gas and air is highly explosive in any confinement if ignited. A harbor collision in a populated area could have almost unimaginable consequences. The practical implementation of an LNG replacement of natural gas in even moderate quantities requires a special port facility properly located for economical distribution to the east coast market and properly isolated from population centers. This is not impossible, but it will require a reorientation of national priorities, legal prerogatives, and a compatible federal energy policy. Liquefied natural gas will be substantially more expensive to deliver than the presently available alternative of intensified exploration for the remaining U. S. resource. The free market response would increase the present cost of interstate gas by five times or more. The alternative is federal financing of the liquefied natural gas program with or without federal control.

Liquid natural gas importation is much more complicated and expensive than petroleum importation, and the United States is not even efficient in this function. We have no east coast ports able to accommodate the 80' draft supertankers. They must unload offshore or in Caribbean harbors to barges or small tankers able to enter the east coast ports. Ocean harbors planned in the last decade are only now being built and none have been authorized in the critical east coast area. The continental shelf of the east coast limits the easy solution to a close-in ocean port in most locations. The few locations available would have to come under federal jurisdiction to overcome the almost certain local objection to a cyrogenic ocean port. Initially, LNG could be imported in economically operational small ships. This limits the source of supply to the North African countries and this source is subject to potential direct competition with the European countries across the Mediterranean.

This potential international competition in the demand for liquefied natural gas cannot be ignored. The U. S. developed the natural gas industry because of the proximity of this raw material to its ultimate users, assisted by the existence of pipelines in the early stages of the marketing development. At that time, there was no world shortage of alternative energy or price doubling every few years or danger of a total failure in the energy supply. Europe and Japan did not have great

quantities of available natural gas. Today that is all changed and both
Europe and Japan can afford to build a gas economy based on imported
liquid natural gas. They could very well lay claim to the supplies in
their geographic area. Thus, looking ahead, a liquefied natural gas industry must recognize the probable source of natural gas to be the Arabian
Peninsula. There will be very little enthusiasm on the part of the world's
shipping industry for sharing the ocean or port facilities or canals with LNG
transport tankers. Finally, liquefied natural gas will depend on a foreign
supplier. Still, with all these disadvantages, liquefied natural gas has
economic, national security, and environmental advantages over an increase
in petroleum dependence or a dependence on substitute natural gas from
other sources.

SNG, SYNTHETIC OR SUBSTITUTE NATURAL GAS

The third alternative for a replacement of the source of natural gas
is coal. SNG can be produced from coal by a number of processes with a
relatively wide spectrum of costs and end product quality. Pipeline grade
gas with approximately 1,000 Btu per cubic foot is directly comparable to
natural gas and thus can utilize the transportation system and can be used
in all existing energy conversion installations. Although the low Btu gas
which is much more economical to produce has its specific applications,
only the pipeline grade process needs to be considered to satisfy the requirements of our overall energy perspective.

There are no theoretical problems with the production of synthetic
natural gas of pipeline grade. The process is available and the plants
can be built. The problem is economic and political. SNG will cost
nearly ten times the present 52¢ interstate price established by the
federal government, and it is very difficult to conceive of a free
price SNG economy in the present political climate.

Synthetic natural gas also raises many environmental questions which
are part of its political vulnerability. As with all alternatives to petroleum and natural gas, the product results from an industrial process which
disturbs the earth, pollutes the air, requires substantial quantities of
scarce water every day, and requires the construction of a plant using
materials that will become scarce if all the required plants are built.

The physical parameters of a synthetic natural gas plant have been established. The elements critical to our overview include: a daily capacity of
250 million cu. ft. of pipeline grade gas at 60% overall efficiency, a daily
requirement of a little more than 10,000 tons of relatively high grade coal,
and a plant investment which was originally estimated at $1 billion. This

last year, that original estimate was increased to $1.3 billion. Recognizing the time required to build a plant of this size, it is doubtful that the described plant could be made available for operation if it were begun today for less than $1.5 billion.

In economic terms, the financial carrying cost of the plant at 8% will represent $329,000 per day or $1.32 per thousand cu. ft. at capacity. A coal cost of $20 per ton would represent an additional 80¢ per thousand cu. ft. This adds to over $2 per thousand cu. ft. before considering labor costs, management costs, distribution costs, return on the equity capital invested, and a reserve for maintenance and replacement of the plant. Three dollars a cu. ft. would be optimistic and $5 would be more realistic.

The environmental impact can be judged by the number of these plants that would be required. To produce one trillion cu. ft. per year the country would need eleven plants, each supplied with more than 10,000 tons of coal per day. In 1973 the United States used 22.6 trillion cu. ft. and more adjustments will be required in eliminating non-economical use of natural gas to bring the U. S. requirement down to 20 trillion cu. ft. As less than 10 trillion cu. ft. can be expected from U. S. natural gas sources by the end of the century, 10 trillion cu. ft. of substitute natural gas will be required for a stabilized economy and twice that amount will be needed for a 3% growth — less than the projected growth requirement to reduce unemployment and "get the economy going."

We will be fortunate to have full scale SNG plants in operation, proving the process and the engineering and the economics of their operation by 1980. This would leave twenty years to build the 220 plants required to keep the economy going and to keep up with the decline in natural gas availability. One plant would have to be completed every thirty-three days. The $300 billion cost of these plants is quite incidental to the reality of this projection, and the coal requirement would approach one billion tons per year, just for the replacement of the declining natural gas resource.

THE GAS ECONOMY SQUEEZE

Figure 26 brings together in tabular and graphic form the information required for an overview of the gas consumption situation at the end of 1975. There is little question about the general priority of the primary economic sectors in their claims on the remaining gas supply. The natural gas industry has the first claim for obvious reasons. Only the gas that is left over after counting the transmission loss, field use, refinery use, and the fuel used in the pipeline system can be available to the general economy. Each of these industry uses is identified in Figure 26 and the twenty-five year history is extrapolated for the ten year projection.

We have considered all available information which will affect each
of these contributors. With the Alaskan source, gas will be coming from
farther and farther away and transmission losses will increase. For the
same reasons, field use will probably increase with gas supplying the primary fuel source for the Alaskan oil production. On the other hand, vent-
ing and flaring will decrease. With smaller amounts of total gas and oil
production, refinery use should decrease and we have assumed the same influence on the pipeline fuel requirement. The net effect of these five
employments by the gas industry projects an almost constant requirement
for the next ten years.

The residential sector has declined the last three years with the
slow-down in gas available for new construction, the turning-down of
thermostats, and the economic effect of higher costs. This trend may continue but it can be assumed that residential use will be given priority
treatment and there may be an expanding trend in residential use if oil
becomes less available and the environmental interests maintain their influence. The residential sector cannot burn coal without substantial pollution.

The commercial sector follows the same pattern as the residential.
The influences on this sector are approximately equal for increases and
decreases during the next ten years. At the same time, in any given community, both the residential and commercial sectors may be substantially
squeezed by the unavailability of gas and the necessity for protecting the
industry serving that community or the utility company unable to make the
transition. Electricity and gas will continue to be of equal importance
to the consumer and both will have to be curtailed when the total energy
availability is reduced.

Industry increased its consumption of gas as it became available. By
1985, the industrial claim may very well be back to the level of 1950 even
though total gas production is expected to be approximately double the production in 1950. However, we have not projected this substantial reduction
in industrial use of gas. I do not know how fast industry can convert to
another source of fuel. We can only assume that industry will make the conversion and that the industrial sector is able to move the fastest.

The utility sector of the economy is the most obvious waster of natural
gas. However, this industry is not able to move as rapidly as it should.
Public restraints on the utility industry limit its ability to obtain the
financing for the necessary transition through the price structure. This is
the most obvious area where the market clearing principle of supply and

Figure 26

U. S. GAS CONSUMPTION BY SECTORS OF THE ECONOMY

Sector Consumption:	1950	1955	1960	1965	1970	1971	1972	1973	1974	1980	1985
Electric Utility	.63	1.15	1.73	2.32	3.88	3.99	3.98	3.61	3.43	1.81	1.07
Industrial	2.04	2.78	3.76	5.12	7.20	7.44	7.42	7.98	7.56	7.50	7.50
Commercial	.39	.63	1.02	1.44	2.06	2.17	2.29	2.29	2.26	2.25	2.25
Residential	1.20	2.12	3.10	3.90	4.84	4.97	5.13	4.88	4.78	4.75	4.75
Gas Industry Use:	-	-	-	-	-	-	-	-	-	-	-
Transmission Loss	.18	.25	.27	.32	.23	.34	.33	.20	.29	.32	.30
Venting & Flaring	.80	.77	.56	.32	.49	.28	.25	.25	.17	.20	.10
Field Use	1.19	1.51	1.78	1.91	2.31	2.30	2.36	2.41	2.36	2.50	2.75
Refinery Use	.46	.63	.78	.86	1.03	1.06	1.07	1.07	1.04	.90	.85
Pipeline Fuel	.13	.25	.35	.50	.72	.74	.77	.73	.67	.60	.55
TOTAL CONSUMPTION:	7.02	10.09	13.35	16.69	22.76	23.29	23.60	23.42	22.56	20.83	20.12

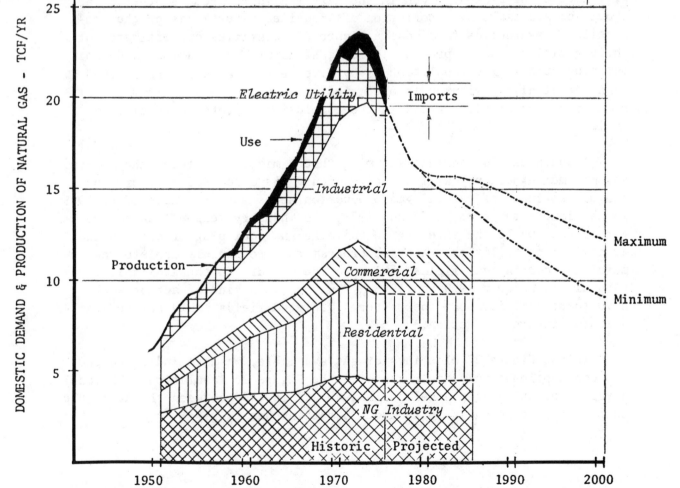

EEEe Preliminary Gas Study, Sept., 1976

demand economics would be effective. Relieved from restraints, the utility industry could very rapidly reduce the consumption of electricity, raise the funds for alternative sources of fuel, and maintain the balance in available electricity at its cost. However, the political probability of this independent economic action is remote. The utility response to the gas availability crunch becomes a function of the political process and is predictable only on these terms.

Imports are indicated on Figure 26 as the dark section on top of the identified consumption sectors. For practical purposes imports represent Canadian natural gas which will be terminated after 1985 by decision of the Canadians. This fact accelerates the decline in the available resource very substantially. Imports are a part of the electric utility use in the graphics.

POTENTIAL FUTURE GAS

By the end of the century, the stalemate in governmental decision will have to be broken. Even in the next ten years, some synthetic gas should be available by importation of liquefied natural gas or the production of synthetics from coal. Figure 27 identifies our estimates of these additions to our previously forecast natural gas maximum and minimum production. The tabulation is by five year intervals through 1995. Each potential contributor is estimated on a maximum and minimum basis resulting in a broader spread in the conclusion of total potential gas available.

I would caution against assuming that a midpoint between the maximum and minimum expectancy will actually occur. As discussed earlier, the minimum estimate of natural gas production seems more probable after 1985. In the immediate years, 1977 and 1978, the industry response cannot be very great due to the time lag in building and equipping production and transmission facilities. A crash program to more rapidly deplete the remaining producing gas fields could provide a spurt in the availability of natural gas between 1979 and 1985. However, this kind of action would have to be paid for soon thereafter. Depleted fields would not be available for future production.

In the Figure 27 plottings of gas available, we have indicated the gas consumption conclusion reached in the Figure 26 tabulation. Obviously, a very substantial gap develops in 1980 and in 1985 between the available supply and the demand as extended. Something has to give.

Figure 27

SUMMATION OF U. S. NATURAL GAS
PRODUCTION & DEMAND

Sources: American Gas Association Published Data - 1976
U. S. Geological Survey Circular 725 - 1975

Remaining Recoverable Resource	Maximum	Minimum
Lower 48 States	1018.065	625.965
Alaska	111.667	70.667
(As of 1/1/75)	1129.732 TCF	696.632 TCF

Projected Gas Supply	1975 Actual	1980 Max.	1980 Min.	1985 Max.	1985 Min.	1990 Max.	1990 Min.	1995 Max.	1995 Min.
Domestic NG Production	19.72	15.75	15.48	15.47	13.81	14.43	11.99	13.30	10.42
Canadian NG Imports	1.00	.50	.30	.20	0	0	0	0	0
LNG Imports	0	.60	.20	1.00	.50	1.50	1.00	2.00	1.00
Coal Gasification	0	.30	.20	1.10	.70	2.20	1.20	3.00	2.00
Naptha (NGL's)	.40	.40	.30	.40	.20	.30	0	.20	0
Storage Losses	-.09	-.15	-.10	-.15	-.10	-.15	-.10	-.15	-.10
U. S. Exports	-.07	-.04	-.02	-.01	0	0	0	0	0
Total Supply (TCF/Yr)	20.96	17.36	16.36	18.01	15.11	18.28	14.09	18.35	13.32

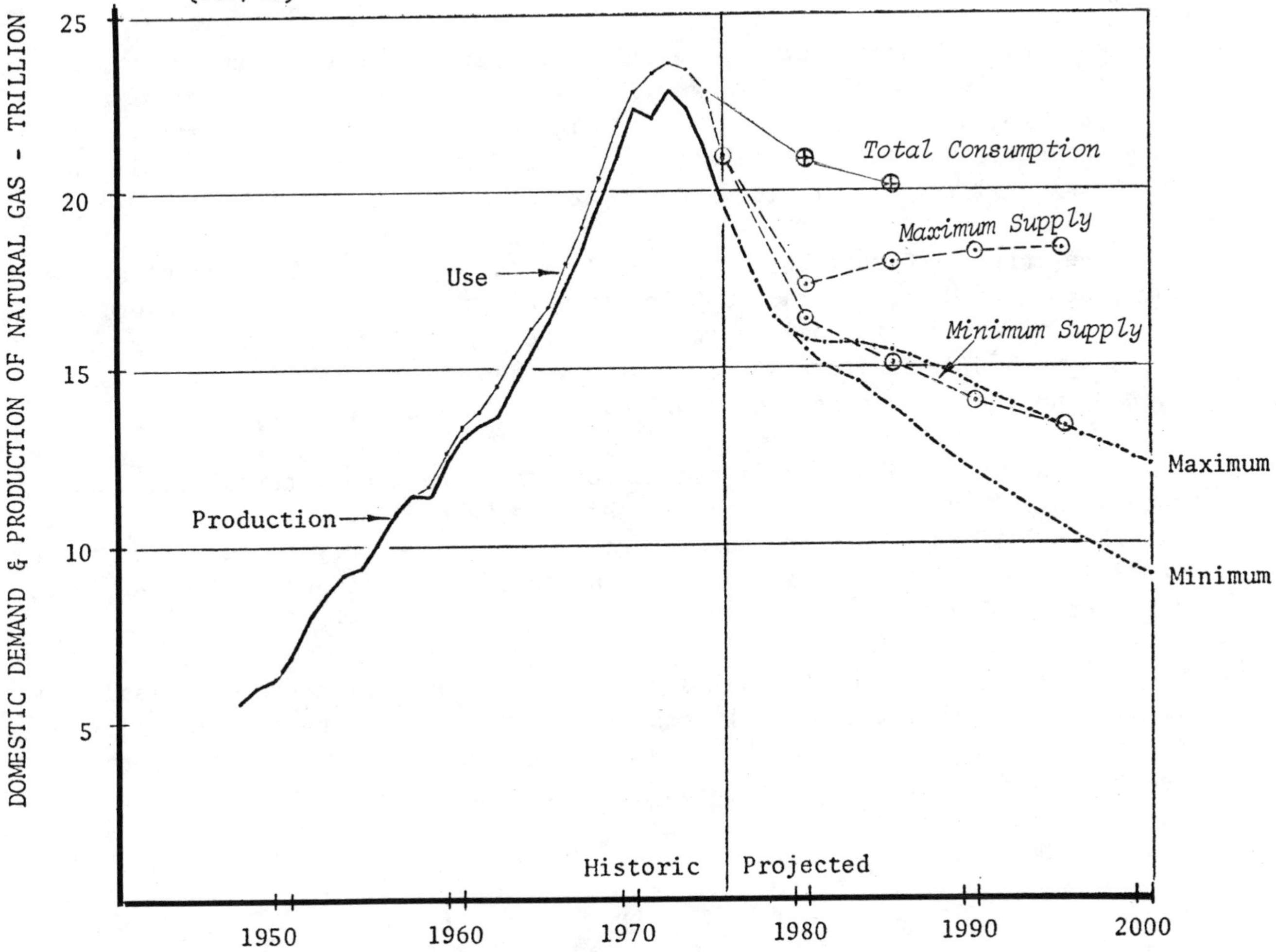

EEEe Preliminary Gas Study, Sept., 1976

X I

C O N C L U S I O N

The United States does not have an energy policy and without an energy policy, there cannot be an energy plan or effective legislation and administration. An energy policy can develop only with public participation in the debate. The conspiracy to deny physical facts in the protection of outmoded idealogies must give way to comprehension of the real problem.

The Federal Energy Administration was organized with the promise of providing energy independence, a promise that was not possible when the Agency was created and that impossibility is now generally recognized. This Agency has acquired instructions from the Administration and from the Congress through legislation to maintain petroleum prices at levels that encourage the continued expansion in petroleum consumption and discourage effective conservation. The Federal Energy Administration's plan and forecast are based on inappropriate economic theory and short term political objectives.

The Energy Research Development Administration set forth energy goals in the 1976, *National Plan for Energy Research, Development and Demonstration,* but these goals are not all possible and they include conflicts, one with another. We could not identify their origin. They represent only the political reality of confusion and the denial of reason.

The Interior Department is primarily responsible for the control and forecasting of U. S. mineral supplies but only the current U. S. Geological Survey estimates of the oil and gas resource are reliable. Previous forecasts by U.S.G.S. and current forecasts by the Bureau of Mines are not supported and there is no reason to believe that they are supportable.

Virtually all departments of the government have an interest and a concern with the availability of energy and some have direct responsibility for finding solutions to the probable unavailability of energy in their own field of responsibility. There is no coordination of these efforts below the level of superficial administrative organization.

The energy problem will build year-by-year, even with the increased flow of Alaskan oil that will make its maximum contribution between 1978 and 1980. There is no clearly identifiable sequence of events that will relieve the energy supply problem. The present generation of light water nuclear reactors

face the problem of the limits of uranium supply which exceed the availability of petroleum in the United States by only a few years. Breeder
reactors have not yet been proved technically or sociologically, although
it can be assumed that the environmental problems will be resolved.

There is no current assurance of a technical breakthrough for controlled
nuclear fusion within the limits of the political time restraints and the
necessity for its availability. Approximately twenty years will be required
from the time of the solution of the technical and sociological problems to
the delivery of power to the U. S. economy in the quantities required. Cost-
wise, the alternatives to the petroleum supply required to maintain our
present dependance on automotive and truck transportation represent multiples
of approximately ten times the present costs of the basic petroleum.

Applying these parameters to the projection of the growth of the U. S.
economy requires specific attention to the transportation segment. Transportation is almost totally dependent on liquid petroleum and accounts for
more than half the U. S. petroleum consumption. The greatest economy potential
and the most significant contribution to the long-term solution of an energy
balance in the U. S. economy requires immediate concentration on this segment,
first employing the obvious and available solutions, the reduction of the
necessity for transportation by concentration of the population in efficient
production centers and the development of available mass transit between
centers. The theoretical five to one energy advantage of rail transit over
trucks can no longer be ignored.

Time is the ultimate resource for man, and the balancing of the energy
equation requires perspective on time, time in terms of physical resource
availability and time to adjust our idealogies - religious, legal, economic,
and social. The remaining petroleum resource represents time to realize
the transition and break with the inherited concept of what is private and
what is public, what is human, when life begins and ends, what is in the
national and world interest, what is real and what is illusion.

The technological and philosophical competence is available. The
question and problem that remains is the acceptance of the evidence: how
to break the barriers of the defense of impossible idealogies, how to
penetrate the conspiracy to deny the reality of limits, how to gain
recognition of physical economics. There is no real enemy. There are no
problems that cannot be resolved. But it could take a world depression or
worse to open the mind of every man and separate him from his current loves
and inherited fears. In this perspective, the reality of the petroleum and
gas figures should be palatable medicine. It might even be effective.

POSTSCRIPT

A book omitted from our bibliography and discussion is *The Hunting of the Snark* by Lewis Carroll, the Victorian age mathematician whose insights have intrigued the young and the old. There is danger in the hunting of the snark as the snark may turn out to be a boojum and then the hunter will fade away.

The energy problem is more serious than generally recognized, and the problem is compounded by the uncertainty of potential technological and sociological solutions that cannot be put in a time frame. Modern society is faced with a second revolution and the characteristics of revolution are not so much the violence as the absence of a middle ground, the opportunity to compromise.

The revolution that set the stage for the energy problem occurred two hundred years ago. The economic revolution credited to Adam Smith and the American Revolution both date from 1776. The religious revolution was earlier, but all three had roots deeper in time. Seers of our current problem surfaced in the last century and the resistance to their prophecies has been building since then without accommodation or compromise, confirming the absence of middle ground. The economy as we know it cannot grow without energy. Other materials can be recycled but energy cannot. This new problem faces our entire social structure with an obsolescence of the values and the skills that are the basis of power and the source of confidence. The dilemma is moral. It attacks the foundations of the individual *and* his society. The challenge is first to the educators and the religious leaders who must now learn physical economics.

PART THREE

THE SHAPE OF THE FUTURE

The rapidly developing energy crisis will face western civilization with
the specter of its demise, its history passing in rapid review: the Cru-
sades, the slaughter of the native populations in the New World, the economic subjugation of earlier civilizations and primitive peoples, the ex-
portation of inappropriate law and religion to human communities at peace
with their environment, the creation of a world dependent on an infinite
increase in energy consumption, the production of people, people, people
crowding their own dung hills.

The future is comprehensible only through the numbers, but the numbers
are too many. The perspective must be narrowed. Perhaps two numbers
will do: four and one, the fingers and the thumb of one hand. The one
stands for a single decade. The four, for the percent of our energy
that will be atomic. The one, for one-tenth of one percent that may be
solar at the end of the decade. Most of our energy comes from four
giants: U. S. produced oil, imported oil, natural gas, and coal. All
the other sources, hydro, atomic, solar, wind, geophysic power, will not
add together to exceed the error in estimating the energy supply at the
end of the next ten years.

There will not be time for argument in Part Three. It will be an outline,
figures on the horizon.

XII

THE GENERALS

Generalities are less dangerous than specifics At some time, their origins must be disclosed, but the conclusions are at least temporarily acceptable when nothing has to be done right away.

The subsidy of cheap energy must end.   When the end is in sight, it will be much less difficult to recognize that neither the government nor the laissez-faire economic system can serve a continuously expanding humanity from nature's limited abundance. Unlike the fertile lands of the New World, the oil and gas resource required only discovery and relatively minor costs to produce and distribute. No matter how great the desire, the government cannot guarantee the continued flow. Price ceilings can now be viewed as a tragic mistake and must be replaced by taxes to discourage and space out the availability of the remaining resource through the time required for the development of a less energy dependent social structure. There will be no precedent for the size of the tax discouragement required and the revenue will be needed.

The political hypocrisy of great concern for the poor must be recognized. The poor have always been with us and always will be. How much we have done for them is a question, but they have not been served by false promises of infinitely available, inexpensive energy. The reduction in consumption will require painful conservation by all. The subsidy must end for all. The political consequences will become secondary when survival is recognized as the primary consideration for society.

Effective government requires a respected and responsible bureaucracy. The bureaucracy is the government and has been the government in most civilizations that have reached maturity. The bureaucracy can be improved, but its replacement by political government would introduce only a short period of chaos. Solution to the energy problem requires the focusing of governmental responsibility not its elimination.

Reason must replace commodities as the cornerstone of government. Government based on reason is fragile, but we have no alternative. The illusion of a currency based on gold, of religion based on infallible persons or writings, and an economic system based on unrestricted material capture is no longer feasible. The transition has already begun in financial economics and it must be started in physical economics.

The confrontation between expansionist economic theory and the fact of resource limits will have to be resolved. There is no basis for believing that the economy can expand without limit. The contrary evidence has been building for more than one hundred years and the only reason for discarding this evidence is the past success of our economic development. Economics, as a discipline, has failed to develop beyond the monetary control mechanism and the summation of deprecatory activities. Energy will force a recognition of limits.

War is not a solution to the energy problem, but the psychology of war will be needed. When our petroleum supply peaked and began to decline, we recognized our Viet Nam defeat. This is not an unrelated coincidence. Oil was the principal material resource responsible for the United States world supremacy which was realized at the end of World War II. Although a war to win the petroleum resources of another country is not feasible today, the willingness to sacrifice, which is the hallmark of a nation mobilized for war, will be required for the needed political and economic adjustments.

The free economy and the free society are not endangered. Rhetoric which equates freedom with the fading away of government is anarchist. Even the Communists have abandoned that music. The importance of oil and gas in the development of the American economy during the last hundred years can hardly be overstated, but the oil and gas wealth has been relatively widely distributed. Future control of the energy segment of the economy is compatible with a continued freedom in the economic lives of the vast majority of the populace and the continued freedom of the social and economic structure. The form of control which proves to be most desirable over the energy producing segment of the economy is not critical to the survival of the free society, but the failure to realize a control and a supply of energy could very well spell the demise of democratic institutions.

Population must be limited. Societies either control their populations or they are controlled by the consequences of population increase. Unlimited reproduction, starvation, and plague have been the most common and the most undesirable methods. Sudden death in war and the slaughter of rival populations are very slight improvements. The absence of population control is the principal reason for the failure of individual life improvement in the developing world. The discouragement of available voluntary population control is an anachronism in our social structure today and the positive control of population cannot be avoided in the future.

XIII

THE INDUSTRY SPECIFICS

There are fairly obvious solutions to the energy problem if each
segment of the energy industry is individually analyzed and the solution
methodology is not limited. This approach has the advantage of establishing a feasible objective before dealing with ideological conflicts.

ELECTRIC POWER

The electric utility industry is considered to be endangered, the sick
corporations unable to find public financing, unable to plan, unable to
meet demands for their services, facing potential takeover by local and state
governments who fear the strangulation of their economies.

The sickness of the utilities is contrived. There is no problem with
the physical economics of the manufacture and distribution of electric power.
The problem is with the political institutions which govern and control this
industry. The problem is with the illusion of the feasibility of cheap energy,
the illusion of the protection of the poor people, the reality of practical
politics in conflict with the hard facts of limited energy fuel and the high
cost of that fuel.

The electric utility industry is in the best position to employ the economic principles of price clearing with a minimum of social and economic disruption. The industry is very large proportional to its expansion requirement and the expansion necessity will become smaller as the total society
adjusts to a less energy intensive mode. The increase in the price of electric
power needed to finance the continued production of electric power from resources which will be available in the future is natural and necessary.

The regulatory agencies for the protection of the consumer are in place
and able to function at the state and local level and at the federal level.
However, substantial streamlining is indicated. Competition between states
and regions of the country is not in the best interest of the nation, and
the balance of power in the exercise of controls over the utility industry
should shift to the federal level. The industry could function with a net
reduction in governmental control and interference.

GAS

The situation in the natural gas industry is completely different. This is a young industry, split between gas finders, gas producers, pipeline operators, and retail distributors. The nation's gas is rapidly running out and the nation's dependence on gas for life support in home heating is complete for practical purposes. A free enterprise increase in gas prices would benefit only the finders who hold title to the inventory and who would contribute little to the financing of a synthetic gas industry. Conversion to oil is too temporary a solution to be considered. Conversion to coal would return the nation to an unacceptable level of air pollution.

The gas distribution system is in place and the synthetic production of gas from coal is practical and relatively efficient. The only physical economic problem with the conversion of the gas industry to a coal-based supply is time. However, the political and pecuniary economic problems are severe.

There is no synthetic natural gas industry and the private sector is unable to generate such an industry. The political control of gas prices at approximately one-tenth the economic cost of the synthetic product effectively blocks the free market function. The same price differential creates problems in a controlled economy. The ten times price increase would not be politically acceptable.

The gas industry presently has approximately an eleven year inventory in the ground including the Alaskan reserves, ten years in the lower 48 states. A ten times increase in the value of this inventory would represent an unconscionable windfall and there is no reason to believe that this increased value would be funneled into the financing of the synthetic industry. The ownership is divided and the free economy has already lost its momentum under governmental control. Only a small part of the windfall to the owners of the gas inventories would find its way into the financing of a new synthetic gas industry. Most would simply inflate the general economy. As the gas industry may require $300 billion in capital before the end of the century, the slippage does not appear to be tolerable.

It could be more surely financed under total government control. The new synthetic gas industry will include both the production of pipeline grade gas from coal and the importation of liquefied natural gas from the African and Arabian producers. This industry will not develop without government financing and carefully orchestrated price increases that balance political reality with economic necessity. It will develop much more rapidly if the planning, financing, and direction are integrally controlled.

The natural source of financing is the taxation of the existing gas industry, the inventories in the ground. This administrative function can be performed by an independent power authority which is substantially insulated from political control and influence. The mixture of public and private administration below this level of decision and planning can be varied. The price of gas must be high to discourage use. There simply will not be enough of it and it cannot be imported or manufactured fast enough to keep up with the retreating supply of the natural material without introducing substantial restraints on the economy.

With a responsible and independent gas administrative authority, the problems of the gas industry can be resolved. The price must increase by more than $1 a thousand cubic feet. That amount of increase has already been authorized by the Federal Power Commission in pricing new gas and there are very good reasons for rejecting the concept of a dual price system. A $2 tax on the demonstrated reserves as they are used would not burden the industry and this tax would eventually produce $475 billion. These are the nation's reserves within the nation's borders and the tax would in no way be confiscatory. In actual practice, the act of confiscation was the decision to control the price of gas, and this decision has already been upheld by the Supreme Court. If the proposed tax is not imposed and if the price of gas is released from control, the gas price can be expected to increase by a greater amount than the suggested $2 tax. The windfall profit to the owners of these reserves would increase by the same amount. A second doubling of the gas price would put the windfall close to $1 trillion. The implications of this effect on inflation should be obvious.

TRANSPORTATION AND OIL

The oil economy is substantially different from that of gas. It is much more complex and the easy solution of replacing the present oil flow — diminishing only a little the daily consumption — is not practical. It is the oil problem that will motivate economists and politicians to develop energy policies.

Oil is first and last the necessary support of transportation in the United States and most of the developed world. There is no practical replacement for oil in this function for the remainder of the century, and the world oil reserve is inadequate to maintain even a substantially reduced rate of growth.

Oil used for purposes other than transportation - excepting chemical feed stocks which represent a more beneficial use of oil - must be discouraged to reserve as much of the remaining oil supply as possible for the primary transportation employment. The burning of oil for heat must be almost totally discouraged, and more than the economic restraints of price will probably be required to accomplish this discouragement.

As with gas, there is no actual financial problem. A minimum increase of one dollar per gallon is indicated just to begin discouraging consumption and two dollars must be recognized as within the range of probable necessity to accomplish this discouragement. In the form of a one dollar tax to the federal treasury, the measured oil reserve at the end of 1974 represents $1,436 billion with an additional $193 billion in the indicated reserve. This is the oil in the ground that has been identified. The exploratory costs have been paid. A substantial proportion of the producing costs and the capital investment in the distribution system have been paid. As with gas, a one dollar per gallon increase in the value of this inventory - the basis of these calculations - would represent a windfall to the industry if no tax were applied and if the natural market forces were allowed to operate. The minimum undiscovered resource which we have employed in our estimates of the probable quantity of producible oil that will be available more than doubles these figures. The fifty billion barrel undiscovered producible resource represents $2,100 billion at one dollar a gallon.

On the basis of the annual flow of petroleum produced and consumed in the U. S. market, a one dollar per gallon tax would produce $150 billion on the domestic production and $100 billion on the imported production, assuming that all fractions of the barrel were taxed. Obviously, this is not practical and approximately half this amount would be represented in available tax on the distilled fraction. We would assume that the suggested tax was in addition to all other currently applied federal and state taxes on this industry and its products. Recognizing that more than one dollar a gallon is required to satisfy the needed discouragement in consumption, a tax revenue between $100 and $200 billion per year is available - a non-inflationary source of revenue to accomplish the transition to a less petroleum-dependent economy.

This is not enough. The transition away from oil will affect the total economy in some aspects and the cost of the transition must be recognized in its totality. There will be a problem in financing the transition and a failure to resolve this financial problem could result in inflationary pressures, but our physical economic concern is less with the financial problem than the physical and social problem.

A reduction in the flow of oil to the transportation system of the
country will affect every citizen. If a one dollar tax per gallon is not
effective, the tax must be increased. Recognizing the reality of the
political and social problem, the tax must be accompanied with a rationing system — the rationing coupons already printed and anticipated to be
negotiable. Those who can afford high priced gas will not be inconve-
nienced and those not needing their coupons can sell them. The actual
transition must occur in the reduction of private automotive consumption.
Passenger travel must be provided by a replacement bus and train service.
Similarly, wasteful long distance trucking must be replaced by the three
to five times more fuel efficient rail system. Finally, the cities must
be reestablished to reduce the travel radius required for a functioning
economy independent of unnecessary transportation.

The mix between the public and private sectors of the economy are too
complex to analyze at this stage of our discussion. It would seem obvious
that the government must take over the rail right-of-way problem making it
possible for the railroads to compete and rebuild their service capacity.
It is also obvious that public transportation must be very substantially
increased, to the limits of the industrial capacity, to produce the buses,
the terminals, and the right-of-way alterations. There is no time to substitute new railway systems, new subway systems, or new innovative people
and material movers.

We do not know the price elasticity of the transportation system as
it exists today and we cannot know the elasticity in the price of a transportation system in transition. If nothing else, the Federal Energy Administration has demonstrated the poverty of economic scenarios of this sort.
Three years have been wasted in this exercise and that should be enough.

There is no possibility of "fine tuning" a transportation system
transition in the private economy under political direction. This has
also been demonstrated in the last few years.

At the same time, no substantial curtailment of the free economy or
the free society needs to result from the radical alteration in the economy
which is implicit in the solution to the transportation problem. Transportation is a necessity to the economy comparable to the postal service and
the national defense. As with the postal service, its management can be
either contracted or directed and there may be no great significance in the
difference, but the management of the transportation system must be insulated from day to day political control.

Earlier, I discussed the comparability of the Federal Reserve Board's independence in controlling the monetary system with the desired independence of an energy authority. The Executive and Legislative branches of the government delegated substantial authority in setting up the Federal Reserve Board and despite periodic rumblings, it is improbable that Congress will wish to abrogate this delegation. An energy authority would be primarily concerned with the transportation system and the energy authority would have to include all necessary prerogatives to restrain the existing bureaucracy in the transportation segment. Again, the net result of a properly established energy and transportation authority would be a reduction in the bureaucratic functions and costs.

The resolution of the transportation problem will very substantially disrupt the economy. Industries must shift to new markets and new products. The transition *should* be accompanied with broad changes in the economy reducing the consumption of all materials and unnecessary waste. The economic incentive to reduce labor costs was always an oversimplification of the social objective — a failure of the social science disciplines to develop beyond segmented and often sterile inquiries and prescriptions. Energy economy will require more than a new emphasis in the economic equations. Future planning must be introduced, long range planning.

ATOMIC POWER

Atomic power is a source of energy for the generation of electricity in relatively large quantities. It has been the darling of expansion economists and the hope of the future with the advent of the fusion reactor. Atomic power is the nemesis of the environmentalists. Atomic fission reactors employing the elementary light water system account for between two and three percent of the U. S. energy supply and can be considered essential to the electric power generation in the northeast region and in other local markets which have come to depend on this source of electric power.

Atomic power cannot resolve the U. S. energy problem during this century and appears to be improbable as a primary source of power in the next century. The expansion of atomic power generation is not essential if air pollution problems connected with the burning of coal are either resolved or reduced by relaxation of the required standards. There is no technical problem with the clean-up of coal emissions but there are still substantial economic problems, most of which would find their natural solution under an energy authority constituted with adequate latitude.

The atomic industry has both a public and private basis. The generating plants are owned and operated by the privately owned public utilities, but the design of these plants was pioneered under federal financing and private industry has not been able to proceed beyond the light water system. Research and development of the more efficient gas reactor was abandoned after several hundred million dollars of losses by the developer and the utility.

Supply and processing of atomic fuel has been federally financed and directed. Attempts to move this processing into the private sector have required federal loan guarantees that compromise the realistic viability of the industry in the private sector.

There is no reliable inventory of the discovered and undiscovered uranium reserve, and future price guarantees can no longer be provided to underwrite the economic viability of new plants.

On balance, the atomic power industry has been subsidized, is subsidized, and probably will remain primarily subsidized by the public sector of the economy. The resolution of the conflicts concerning the future of atomic power are not essential to the current discussion of the U. S. energy resource in the next twenty to thirty years. However, positive decision is required to reach this conclusion. The discussion of future atomic power is the primary cover for avoiding the critical decisions which will determine the actual availability of energy in the U. S. economy and the social and political structure of the country for the next thirty years.

SOLAR, WIND, SHALE, AND GEOPHYSICAL

The specifics of energy from the sun, derivations of solar power, geophysic heat and tidal power are all very similar. There has been little advancement of the industry in the private sector and no significant amount of energy is being produced. Solar power and wind power cannot compete with cheap fossil fuel in the free economy. Conservation of energy employing the practical principle of insulation, shade, design to facilitate solar radiant receipt, heat transfer within the structure, temperature control, and temperature time control requires small expenditures and produces substantial return on the investment at present primary energy costs. These efforts will be more rewarding as energy costs increase.

Solar energy considerations can contribute substantially in the design of new building structures and low temperature solar energy can become a primary source of heat in the southern third of the country, particularly the southwest. Terrestially based high temperature solar generators can develop auxiliary sources of energy in the southwest and these energy sources can become primary although not independent at the end of this century.

Discussions of the future contribution of solar energy to the resolution of the U. S. energy problem in this century is premature and potentially dangerous in contributing to the avoidance of critical decisions. Solar energy proponents have demonstrated a lack of candor and responsibility in this respect. Wind energy is very similar to solar energy in its time limitation. Winds of less than eight miles per hour have little value as a source of power and high winds are destructive of wind generators. In open country and on shoreline ridges wind is available for a substantial contribution to the power resource. This contribution will become economically viable as alternative energy costs increase. Wind energy has to be combined with other sources of energy to deliver acceptable power to our present economy. The home generator with its battery backup is not objectively economical in competition with available utility service.

Geophysical power is now being produced on the west coast in areas where the earth's crust is thin, hot springs are in evidence, and volcanic action is part of recent history. These conditions apply to much of the world Pacific basin but to limited areas of the United States as a whole. Energy will have to become much more expensive than is anticipated in the next thirty years to justify resolution of the engineering problems of harnessing heat five miles below the earth's surface.

Shale oil is being produced in situ in small quantities. Ambitious recovery programs and expensive leases have been abandoned. The tremendous shale resource in this country is no longer considered immediately available as a source of energy. It may become a source of energy with improvements in processing methods or very substantial increases in the competitive cost of crude oil and natural gas.

AGRICULTURE

Agriculture is a source of energy. The natural photosynthesis of growing plants is approximately 1% efficient in gathering the solar energy to produce combustible fibers and carbohydrates which can be turned into an energy resource either by direct burning or conversion to alcohol, methyl or ethyl. Agriculture is also the darling of the economy in producing the food and fiber trading resource for petroleum products in the world market. Secondarily, agriculture is the primary source of garbage and sewage capable of producing energy. However, all of these energy sources are disappointing.

Primary agriculture is energy intensive in a caloric balance. The units of heat required for the production of fertilizer, the power for cultivation and harvesting, and the directly related transportation and drying of the American agricultural crop exceed the heat value of the total crop. Agriculture is a net user of energy in substantial quantities and almost all of the heat input is represented by oil and gas.

In the specifics of the energy balance for the remainder of this century, the energy contribution of agriculture is negative. All of the garbage and all of the sewage is needed for composting in the production of fertilizer to relieve the economy of the present oil and gas cost in supplying this industry. As it is improbable that any substantial action will occur in this direction for the remainder of this century, the decision concerning agriculture is the treatment of its anticipated claim for priority consideration in the physical and economic rationing of oil and gas. As U. S. agriculture must eventually learn to be less dependent on these sources of energy, permanent subsidy is inadvisable, but rationing priorities will be necessary to maintain the immediate U. S. trade balance and world food balance.

Exotic sources of energy in food based on the controlled development of algae in tropical climates does not appear to be a specific for the remainder of this century as the costs are still marginal and the product has not developed to the point of acceptance. This is essentially a solar power gathering process that can be important in the future as competing energy resources decline in availability and increase in their cost.

XIV

THE FUTURE FOR THE INDIVIDUAL

Every material thing and most of the services that make up the cost-of-living require substantial quantities of energy, and three-quarters of this energy is oil and gas today. The replacement of the oil and gas resources will require a whole new industry: labor and materials and investment in operations to mine coal and convert the coal to gas or liquid hydrocarbon; more labor and materials and investment to liquefy foreign natural gas and transport it to this country; and the same to find uranium ore, process the ore, produce the nuclear power, and process the waste. In combination, this new energy industry will have the characteristics of a war, great expenditures of manpower and material wealth with no gain. All that we will accomplish will be to replace the oil and gas that flowed freely from the earth and used to require only a small cost paid to the finders and producers of that oil and gas. In monetary terms, the new sources of energy will represent ten times the cost if this new industry does not trigger an inflationary spiral. As in wartimes, controls can be expected to avert this consequence.

More important than the relative cost of new energy resources, this great effort will not produce as much oil and gas as we have been using, and it will produce only a little more electricity. How much less will depend on environmental considerations which will certainly restrict the whole activity. We may produce only a fraction of the energy which has been available in the recent past.

The impact will be on the individual consumer and producer. He will have much less gas and oil and only a little more electricity. As a society, much more of our time will have to be spent in building the plants, digging the coal, and processing the new primary energy. This new time expenditure must come out of what has been society's profit taken from nature's gift, the oil and gas endowment. The production of energy will now require human effort and a major portion of society's total economic commitment. The commitment relates to resources and time, physical things. In pecuniary economic terms, energy will cost much more and the individual income available for other employments will be much less. This fact and these relationships are independent of any consideration for inflation. Unit energy costs will increase and this portion of the cost-of-living will increase before there is any actual inflation. If there is actual inflation, it will be in addition to this energy cost increase. The problem with present measures of inflation is the employment of indices which fail to maintain this differential. In the past, it has been relatively unimportant.

A secondary reaction to the increased costs of energy to replace gas is the effect of these increased costs on competing sources of energy. As coal will be the primary resource used for the production of replacement oil and gas, the easily mined, close to market coal will be used up more rapidly and the coal which requires more labor and material costs to produce will have to be substituted. A real increase in the cost of producing coal will occur in addition to the potentially inflationary effect of competing demands on the resource. The higher cost of coal will automatically translate to a higher cost of electricity.

Hydroelectric power will not be directly affected by increased costs, but its price can be expected to increase for competitive market reasons. Nuclear energy will be affected by the same combination of higher mining costs and higher processing costs for the primary fuel and the influence of higher competitive costs for electricity produced from coal.

CONSUMER ATTITUDES AND EXPECTANCIES

Higher energy costs and a lesser quantity of available energy will affect the total economy, but the effect will be most severe on the individual as a consumer. In this role, he will be the primary casualty in the adjustment to a less energy intensive way of life. However, the physical deprivation will not be the initial, principal stress on the individual.

The United States has a relative abundance of energy resources. We can continue to feed and house and clothe and entertain our citizenry beyond the expectations of any other country in the world and beyond the expectations of any people in former periods of history excepting only the last twenty-five years in this country. But the expectancy cannot continue to increase. It must decrease, and some individuals will have great difficulty in adjusting to the more limited expectations.

Necessities will have to be redefined. Every man cannot expect to live as a king, lighting a thousand candles and maintaining a castle to entertain his friends. Reduced expectancies can be devastating to an upward motivated society. It will appear to attack basic moral concepts of what is right and the rewards that are due. Progress will appear to run in reverse.

Unrestrained competition will be a casualty of the less energy intensive society. *Bigger* and *farther* and *more* require a frontier and infinite resources. Conspicuous consumption will not be encouraged, and the reversal of priorities will raise questions as to man's nature and his ability to adjust.

The throttling down of economic expectancy strikes at the heart of the incentives which motivate the free economy. Restrained exploitation will be equated with a loss of freedom, even though these restraints are confined to the energy resources. Energy cannot be conserved without restricting in some measure all economic and personal activities. Expansionist economics has provided the cover for gross distribution inequalities. Unlimited acquisition and unlimited distribution rewards will become a casualty. The extensions of income protection will be interpreted as further restraints on individual freedom. There will be an inevitable extension of welfare and its affront to both the grantor and the grantee.

But man can adjust his attitudes. He can learn to accept more limited expectancies. Adaptation has been the secret of his survival and his adjustment to the universal problem of a more limited energy resource could proceed very rapidly with the right kind of music.

HOME HEATING

A warm shelter in winter is the first concern of most individuals living in the northern one-third of the United States. Home heating costs per unit of energy may increase by four times. From the present level of approximately $1.50 per thousand cu. ft. of natural gas, $6.00 will be the expected home delivery cost of gas produced from coal. Other energy sources can be expected to reflect the same costs, but the price to the consumer could be substantially greater.

The price must reflect either the economic or the political method of controlling the supply. In the free economy, consumption will be encouraged until the supply is depleted and then the price will increase. The probability of an unlimited price increase and/or a net supply failure eliminates any serious consideration to a free price structure for the ultimate energy resource available for home heating. Death by freezing is not politically acceptable.

It must be assumed that the price of home heating energy will remain controlled or will be freed for a very short period of time. Both price and rationing methods will be needed. This will not be difficult for gas and electricity and there is a natural solution. The minimum energy need can be priced at an affordable rate. Beyond the minimum quantity, the price structure can be steeply graded. Conservation objectives in the utility administered segment of the home heating industry could be finely tuned with almost no cost. Controls on oil, bottle gas, and coal will be much more difficult.

The individual will have to decrease his home heating fuel requirements. The rationing and price mechanism will be employed with smaller
and smaller quotas and higher and higher costs until the supply and demand are brought into balance. Methods are available to accomplish the
reduction to the required quantities of fuel. The individual will have
the opportunity to reduce his home heating costs at the same time that
the cost per unit of energy increases by as much as four times.

First, home insulation provides the opportunity to reduce cost by
one-half or more. The average home in Michigan during the five month
heating season requires 828,000 Btu's per day. The same size home built
to minimum electric heating standards requires only 387,000 Btu's per
day, and these standards can be improved. Triple storm windows, more
ceiling insulation, and fiberbacked aluminum siding over additional
insulation will produce a higher insulation barrier than the minimum
electric standard for most existing housing units.

Precise thermostatic control of temperature, automatic time control
of temperature, raising the temperatures to required expectancy only during times of occupancy, can reduce energy requirements by five to twenty-
five percent. The efficiency of furnaces can be substantially improved
by installing smaller units and controlling flue losses. A potential one-
third reduction in required fuel is indicated.

A reduction in the heated living space can result in the greatest
economies and the architectural changes may not be very expensive. In
New England, the part of the country most sensitive to the home heating
problem, colonial architecture was based on the contraction of living
space during the winter months. Bedrooms were not heated. The entertainment areas were heated only for specific occasions, and the kitchens
served the total living purpose. Many modern, contemporary homes are
designed around this early concept with the family room able to be isolated and separately heated to serve as the total winter living area.

Although solar heat can make a very small contribution to the heating
of existing homes in the areas of the country where winter heat is most
critical, solar heat in combination with insulation, improvements in
radiant capture through windows, and in sophisticated combinations with
the storage of relatively low temperature heat and the use of an electric
powered heat pump can contribute to the reduction in the required fossil
fuel energy. At the level of a four times increase in the cost of this
energy, these installations will become economical.

The fireplace can be improved as a source of heat with its added contribution to morale. A small cost in electric energy for a blower can move air through pipes under the fireplace grate, increasing the convection efficiency. An atmospheric source of air for the fireplace combustion itself can eliminate the drainage of warm air out of the living area. Flue controls can further improve the efficiency of this source of heat with its versatility in burning available wood waste, including the family garbage that is not composted.

A properly designed cast iron stove can be even more efficient in a kitchen area or other living space architectually suited.

Offpeak electrical heating can make a contribution to the total efficiency of the electric power utility and serve a small but significant portion of the home heating load. Electric power can be converted to hot water heat and stored in heavily insulated tanks for use over a twenty-four hour cycle with very little heat loss. The technology is available for controlling the release of this power at the utility station, thus permitting a precise balancing of the electric load. Under these conditions, offpeak power could be sold at a much lower rate. A heat pump would multiply the effective use of this electrical source, and it would be possible to combine the heating system with solar heated medium temperature water for the cold leg of the heat pump.

The tremendous quantities of low temperature heat discharged by the electric power utilities could be harnessed if these utilities were located within a reasonable distance of the homes or industries to be heated. Low pressure steam can be delivered in heavily insulated pipes relatively long distances. Many central steam supply systems were abandoned because of the availability of cheap gas. With its higher cost, this industry could be greatly expanded, and new communities could be planned around electric power generating plants.

TRANSPORTATION

No significant progress can be made in the reduction of oil and gas consumption without effecting relatively radical changes in the transportation segment of the economy. A 50% reduction in the quantities of fuel used for transportation is the minimum requirement. Substantially more than a 50% reduction will be needed if economies in other segments, including reduction in population, are not successful.

A four times increase in the retail cost of transportation fuel is a reasonable starting point for consideration of ways and means to discourage demand. Voluntary methods of reducing the consumption of any energy form in any segment must be recognized as unrealistic. Voluntary restraints can be effective only for a short war and there is no foreseeable limit to the necessary control of energy consumption at substantially lower volume levels. An elevated price cannot be the only method of discouraging the consumption of transportation fuel unless radical changes in the distribution of purchasing power are anticipated. Political reality requires some balancing in the economic equation to provide for a minimally necessary transportation budget. The net effect of the increased cost of transportation will be deflationary. There will be less money in the family budget for other things. This clearly indicates the failure of the cost-of-living index as a measure of inflation in the world of tomorrow.

The subsidy of intercity mass transportation in the form of economical fares on subways, buses, and surface rail systems is the first and best solution to the problem. Under the financial incentive of substantially increased costs for private transportation, the required subsidy would be reduced as a consequence of the economics of scale. Bus service can be extended to the outlying, suburban areas. Factory bus shuttles can be required for employers located off economical public transportation corridors. For practical purposes, the necessity of a private automobile will have to be eliminated from the qualifications of a job seeker. A public transportation net must be established between mass employers and mass housing areas.

Negotiable gasoline ration coupons will probably be required to provide the fuel required for the worker-commuter, particularly during the transition period between the availability of mass transit and the reestablishment of housing patterns and working patterns that are compatible with a minimum transportation economy.

The individual's response to the transportation problem will require a choice of relocating his home, accepting the inconvenience of mass transportation dependence, or accepting substantially higher transportation costs. As long as a large proportion of the population continued to prefer the choice of high cost individual transportation, the cost of transportation fuel will have to continue to increase. In the absence of reliable information on the amount of price increase required to decrease gasoline consumption (economic elasticity), it cannot be reliably anticipated. The tax on gasoline purchases in excess of the rationed quantity might have to exceed $3 a gallon. For diesel fuels, which are interchangeable with home heating oil, this price structure would have to be coordinated. This might entail home heating rationing tickets for fuel oil users.

The central city will be the principal beneficiary of the energy economy in transportation. The affluent segments of the population will return. Life can become very satisfying in midtown residential areas populated by persons interested in maintaining their properties. These same areas will support high multiples of their original population in modern multiple family structures all within walking distance of cultural, recreational, and business interest. No innovation is required as these communities have been in various stages of development. The patterns have been established and only need to be implemented with modern, energy-conscious design improvements.

The individual will have an opportunity to reduce his transportation expense even though fuel costs quadruple. Electronic communications will take the place of transportation fuel consumption. Isolation in the sparsely populated suburban areas will be greater and will suit those individuals desiring isolation. The close knit suburban developments will organize their own bus services as transportation cost or the availability of ration coupons become a controlling factor. The reduced availability of transportation will increase the social dependence of communities. Home selection will relate to the transportation pattern and community tastes to a greater extent. The development of compatible communities will become more important in the success of real estate operations.

In the thirty years since World War II, we have lost our concern for transportation costs. The return of this dimension to social and economic planning should not be too difficult to accept.

FOOD

U. S. agriculture is dependent on petroleum for fertilizer, pesticides, and tractor fuel. Food processing and food transportation are heavy users of gas and oil. U. S. agriculture would have difficulty supplying the needs of its own small town agricultural communities if no petroleum were available. Even a small reduction in the quantity of gas and oil made available to the food industry would be felt in reduced food production.

The effect of increased costs for petroleum products will increase food prices before any inflation multiplier develops. U. S. agricultural commodity surpluses have been eliminated, removing the buffer between short term changes in the available food stocks, the insulation from world market price influence. The trading value of the U. S. agricultural commodity in the world market and the U. S. dependence on agricultural exports for petroleum imports creates a direct link between food prices and oil prices. This linkage will multiply the direct cost increase in agricultural products. This linkage will account for the real inflationary factor in the U. S. and world price systems.

For the individual, food costs can be expected to increase substantially. Home gardening, canning, and baking will be worth the effort.

RECREATION

Recreational opportunities will be radically altered by the reduced availability of petroleum and its substitutes. For many, the change will be welcome. For others, the frustration could create secondary social complications including increases in the divorce and suicide rate. The changes will be substantial.

The escape from the family will still be available without the private car and frustrations should dissipate more rapidly in walking and bicyling. The bus will offer a change in personal contact as well as a change in scenery.

Vacations on wheels will be purchasable but the wheels will not be private. The European travel card which allows unlimited use of all trains for a fixed period at a fixed cost could become attractive on the home lines.

There will be changes in the priority and the value of resort properties. Vacations will be longer and transportation will be confined to the coming and going. The arrived guest will expect to walk or bicycle on the land, and sail, paddle, or row on the water. He will not require wide horizons for his all-terrain vehicle, but he will require more area than the roadside entertainer can provide. Vacations will require more planning. There will be frustrations for the social groups accustomed to constantly moving about.

Science has prepared the way for reduced transportation in recreation. Television delivers entertainment to the home that was only imagined before World War II. Closed circuit television is already available and will be extended to permit personal hookups, first through communication centers and finally to individual homes. The telephone is taken for granted by most persons alive today, but it will remain the greatest transportation substitute both for business and pleasure. It will be used to greater advantage. Books, magazines, and newspapers are not in short supply. There will be time to read them at home, on the bus, and on the train.

Recreational patterns will follow housing patterns as communities develop more compatibility. Walking distance will be redefined and with reduced automotive travel, bicycling will be both a recreation and a means of transportation.

The advantages of reduced individually powered transportation exceed the disadvantages. Golf has greater health benefits without the cart. There will be no change in tennis, it has not been motorized. The argument between sailing and motorized fleets will be resolved with half the protagonists satisfied. The curtailment of snowmobiling will also come off with an equal number of victors and losers.

The infinite availability of the automobile will be missed and these machines will not disappear from the scene, but the tragedy for the individual who is not directly involved in the industry will not be great. The air pollution problems that created so much concern in the recent past will become difficult to imagine. The remains of the older generation will be called out to teach the young how to live and play. They may be quite busy.

POPULATION

The population grows slowly, but it increases geometrically and for a long time. Population growth has erased the benefits of technological advances in the developing world. In the future, material limits will be more obvious and the necessity for population control will have to be recognized.

The population problem impinges on all aspects of the future world. The control of population will require limitation on a freedom which has been considered to be primary and basic. It cannot be. Unlimited reproduction stands in opposition to every other freedom and every other hope for a manageable world.

Even in the United States, population increases will not be tolerable. We will have enough energy to support an increase in the population, but the reduced mobility, reduced opportunities for employment, and higher per capita living costs will make it more and more difficult to support unlimited population increases. The energy effect on population will be indirect but it will be pervasive. The energy problem in the world is the direct result of the excess world population and the United States is part of this world. Energy attrition equals population multiplied by affluence. Both affluence and population must be brought under control.

XV

A BEGINNING FOR CHANGE

We must find a beginning to the process of social change and we cannot wait for a generation to die. The beginning will not be dramatic. Drama would only intensify the resistance. The understanding for the necessity of change must be broadly based and false prophets must be allowed a quiet exit. Truth and education are the ingredients for the beginning. Then we can consider the explosive question of the definition of private property and its limitation.

TRUTH

Truth in reporting physical resource reserves is now missing. Truth is relative, but the relativities of truth in financial reporting are understood and responsibility for truth in the pecuniary processes is woven into the legal structure as well as the moral fabric of society. But it was not always that way and it may be necessary to look back on the development of social responsibility in financial reporting to gain perspective on the void that exists in physical resource counting.

The petroleum resource of the United States is a more critical inventory than the gold in Fort Knox. The gold is a psychological prop for the market economy and psychology cannot be ignored in this market, but a twenty-two times multiple in the reporting of the gold would not actually affect the market or the life of the nation. If the error were corrected after the bankers had been accustomed to the larger number reporting, a twenty-two times reduction of the nation's gold supply would have precipitated a Black Friday as actually occurred in the country's early financial history. But these events predate the Federal Reserve System, the Fort, and modern banking.

Conversely, physical economics is not a psychological phenomenon. The availability or unavailability of energy is real and controlling over the lives of the people of the world. A population that depends on energy which proves unavailable must die. In the natural world, no differential is drawn between the lemmings of the Arctic and the humans in the Asian subcontinent. The advanced civilizations are not immune.

Scientists are the keepers of truth in the material world. They have their own code of ethics which requires truth in reporting scientific fact. The experiment must be replicable. Another scientist free from any appointive process or selective qualification accepting only the employment of weights, measures, and established scientific law must be able to verify the conclusion accepted by the scientific world. It is the scientific process. It is the process without which there would be no scientific progress.

But the science community is not a world, it is only a part of the world society, subordinate to the political society and its legal, commercial, and religious agents. In speaking to the political society, the scientists are bound by no responsibility for truth except only the truth which can be discovered in the legal process of confrontation, unrestricted advocacy of opposing positions. Scientific truth is subtle. It begins with principles and process. The conclusion cannot be tested in the courtroom independent of the selection of materials to be presented and herein lies the problem of truth in material economics.

The critical resource for the American economy is crude oil. The critical information selection and publication is U. S. Geological Survey Circular 650. The critical statement in this release appears in the abstract "We estimate the total resource base for petroleum liquids to be about 2,900 billion barrels,---." This estimate is qualified in the following terms:

Identified reserves	52 billion barrels
Undiscovered recoverable	450 billion barrels
Submarginal identified	290 billion barrels
Submarginal undiscovered	2,100 billion barrels
Total	2,892 billion barrels

In actual practice, Circular 650 under various interpretations has been employed by all economic analyses projecting the future of the United States energy resource. The Circular 650 resource estimate multiplies by twenty-two the high probability minimum resource identified in the 1975 Circular 725 inventory.

The scientific basis for these estimates is not presented, violating the scientific principle of confirmation by independent research or review of the research process. The estimate is thrown to the non-scientific world of economists and politicians with a minimum of definition and with no advisory restraint. The identified and proved reserves are known to represent only a portion of the total resource. The economic interpreter is totally free to reach his own conclusion as to the numbers which he wishes to employ and the authentification of approximately 2,900 billion barrels carries the stamp of the office of the specifically identified authority in the United States Government.

The United States has no laws or commission for moral restraints on the use of erroneous or misleading information as to the petroleum resource. The chief executive officers of the country's leading corporations have employed these specific figures in their proofs of the adequacy of future fuel for their products. In 1976 the same executives are presenting the same arguments to the public and the politicians are seeking election on the basis of this same outdated but not outlawed information.

Coincident with the development of factual information as to the extent of the fossil fuel resource, a new problem is developing with truth in energy. The debate as to national policy in support of atomic energy in all its forms is producing a truth-damaging argument in both the scientific world and the public arena. The protagonists of atomic solutions to the United States and world energy problem and the environmentalists, who have singled out atomic energy as the ultimate evil, are locked in a battle that is destroying the means of objective analysis. Totally irresponsible information is being thrown out by both sides confusing the interpretation of factual data and destroying confidence in any information released in the public press. The origin must be known and discounted. The previously sacrosanct scientific community has all but lost its credentials with the public.

The restoration of responsibility in the scientific community is more important than any other consideration both for the resolution of the social and economic problems brought on by the energy short-fall and for the continued progress of the society which has become dependent on technological advances. It is difficult to overstate the importance of this problem or the need for its resolution. Truth in energy fact reporting is the first step and the most critical step in the resolution of our current problems.

When basic scientific data is alloyed with irresponsible economic theories and time sequences, a narcotic is produced that deadens the decision capacity of the nation. This combination becomes more lethal when it is voiced by otherwise responsible authorities. The most common combination is the overstatement of future U. S. oil and gas production in terms of years of supply and the understatement of the lead time required for alternative energy resources. Then we find an overstatement of the quantity of atomic energy which can be made available from year to year, the overstatement of the ultimate and year to year contribution of solar energy, and the understatement of the necessary reduction in per capita materials which equate to per capita Gross National Product. The objective of these errors and omissions is to pretend that the energy problem can be resolved without any sacrifice. The Gross National Product must continue to increase to support the free economy under the old rules. The big lies that would draw attention are easily disguised in projecting summary conclusions identified as "scenarios" with unauditable parameters.

Computer technology contributes substantially to the camouflage as it is usually impossible to approximate the computer produced conclusion. Thus, truth has come to require the avoidance of the computer technology. There are virtually no responsible sources of information or methods of authenticating unauditable general conclusions as to the future balance of energy supply and demand and the required sacrifice by individuals to maintain our free society. There is too much at stake to accept conclusion pronouncements that cannot be demonstrated. The opportunity and the temtation to ignore evidence and manufacture a formula that indicates that no changes are required has become the established pattern. This is a devastating conclusion. Neither authoritative persons nor the computer can be relied upon. The solution to the energy problem must be based on basic factual data and understandable employment of these data in reaching conclusions. There can be no gaps, no assumptions based on "obvious" relationships that everyone has come to accept. Two hundred years is not long enough to prove an unsound theory.

These are the problems that the academic community must resolve. The easy answers cannot be accepted. The comfortable occupants of authoritative chairs must lose their comfort. We must find a way to introduce anxiety or there will be no progress. Then, the resolution of the problem in public education will become primary.

EDUCATION

Public understanding of the energy problem is a prerequisite of the political conclusion. At the same time, no politician has been able to handle the energy question. It could not be an issue in the 1976 presidential election and it is doubtful that any politician will want to become involved soon. The absence of reliable facts is a principal contri-

butor, but more is involved. Confidence must be developed in organizations responsible for public information. The product must be reliable
and the new organization will be granted little tolerance.

Both the nation and the individual politicians must have a place to
go for information and the information source must be constantly updated.
Of equal importance, an audit function must be developed that identifies
false interpretations. Energy information must have the same status as
financial information. Counterfeit currency is not tolerable in a society
dependent on that currency.

The process of public education must begin slowly and have time to
develop. The dominoes of positive thinking must fall one at a time. The
Munich decisions since the Arab boycott must be accepted without rancor
but corrected. Truth as to the limited reserve must develop acceptance
and a national conscience must grow, supported by responsible leaders.
Then the politicians will be able to handle the energy problem and panic
can be avoided. It is a task for the time between elections and it will
take all of that time. It must begin with the recognition that the nation
and the world do not have another four years. There are not even another
two years of time to safely avoid the decisions that Congress must make.

X V I

A POTENTIAL ENERGY POLICY

Two ingredients are required for the development of a constructive energy policy in the United States. First, there must be comprehension of the nation's physical resource, the tremendous quantities of materials that are presently available. We know more about the wealth of the nation today than was known when our country was founded. The added knowledge of the limits of these resources is a secondary fact which cannot be ignored, but these limits are not a barrier to a constructive policy.

Second, the development of an energy policy requires recognition that change is possible in the relationship between men and the organizations they have created.

The material world, the world of nature is not infinitely malleable to the desires of men. There are things that cannot be changed in the material world. The habit of thinking that man's institutions can prevail over all material obstacles is at the bottom of the energy problem, the problem that has been developing since the beginning of the industrial revolution

The development of an energy policy begins with understanding the resistances in the social structure to changes which can now be demonstrated as absolutely essential. The source of the resistance must be understood before it can be overcome.

THE RESISTANCE

The utter necessity for recognition of the real nature of our energy dilemma is balanced by the universal resistance to recognition. The business community, which includes organized labor, is too committed to economic growth to accept the obvious total readjustment in the value of goods and services that would result from a socio-economic structure that places energy conservation ahead of labor, and this is the critically obvious conclusion that cannot be avoided. Energy will be dear because there will not be enough of it. Labor is already a commodity in excess supply, and it cannot be put to work by the traditional means of an expanding economy.

The reduction in available energy necessitates substitution of labor for energy, a reversal of the trend established at the beginning of the industrial revolution. This alteration in orientation must be recognized as equivalent to a second industrial revolution and more than ideologies will be altered. This conclusion may be too stark. It is certainly too simplistic, but the statement is necessary to place the problem in proper perspective. We can then consider the complexities of the actual situation wherein a reoriented economy can continue to be free and many of the parts of that economy will have to expand substantially, but the energy intensive part of that economy cannot continue to expand.

In terms of previous conflicts in ideology, the readjustment of the economy to accommodate a retreating energy supply has little to do with theories of equity or justice or the ideas which engendered resistance to the "isms" of the past. The reorganization of society is only secondarily economic and political. It is primarily a materially motivated alteration of the affairs of men, problems caused by the hard facts of physical limits, the inevitable conflict between the irresistible force and the immovable object with priorities altered.

The system as it has been known cannot continue and alteration of the system will deeply affect existing organizations and individuals whose skills and positions are based on the former expansion economics and the measure of success dictated by these economics. Every business organization — every trade union, every professional representative, every institution — functions to look after the economic interest of its members, whether they be individual or corporate. Every group and sub-group in the body politic wants to retreat to safe ground, the old ways. Emphasis shifts to the immediate future and concentrations turn to narrow member interests. The expansive, open, concern for the future of the nation is lost. The organization structure that has developed in the two hundred year history of our country and goes back to the society and culture from which we came is threatened and loses its constructive flexibility. Social organization can very well become the enemy of progress.

This is the general nature of the resistance that is developing. These are the dimensions of the obstacles that must be overcome, but they are not the measure. The resistance need not develop beyond manageable proportions controllable by a free society desiring to maintain its freedom. However, there is another difficulty, the difficulty of identifying any major segment of the society that is naturally oriented to assist in finding solutions, the bases for compromise and the source of leadership.

INVENTORY OF ATTITUDES IN THE SOCIAL STRUCTURE

Business is organized for profit and naturally inclines to a minimum of restriction, gravitationally attracted to the principles of laissez-faire, caveat emptor, and unlimited exploitation of the earth's resources. Labor is the greatest of these resources and business is responsible for its organization. Business has the greatest commitment in the expansionist economy and business owns the priests and the managers who administer their empire. Like Churchill, business is unlikely to undertake the liquidation of its empire, but the actual practice or the development of the controlled economy has witnessed the cooperation of business with minimum planning functions and this minimum can be extended. Business possesses the strength and the foresight to lead the nation if a goal and a beginning can be established.

The religious institutions have a very different problem but their capacity to represent the future and lead society out of its dilemma is limited by its history. The representatives of man's conscience have thus far failed to resolve the practical problem of the preservation of life in our society. Their focus has remained on the individual. Physical knowledge has been their enemy. Death has been their sacred trust but they have not resolved the dichotomy of its treatment in war and peace and have reversed nature's selectivity. The future of man depends on maintaining a balance between human life and the material world but only a small segment of the organized religions recognize this necessity today and teach a balanced world for tomorrow.

The cultural society of western civilization has not always been distinguishable from its origin, the combination of religious and economic development. The partners have produced the conquest of the physical world and the expansionist ideology. Peace, artistic development, and the necessity for a retreat, a place to hide, have been secondary. Primitive ritualistic murder was a religious ceremony. Modern war is a vast extension of ritualistic murder, substituting allegiance to the nation state. These primary social drives of conscious man will be most difficult to harness. It is against this background that the many social organizations of our society must be viewed in their potential contribution to a world of spiritual expansion that is restrained from physical conquest. Still, it is in this social area that leadership must be found to meet the challenges necessary for future development.

Grass roots political organizations are a questionable source of leadership. At the precinct level, the time spectrum cannot exceed the next election and the needs of the constituency until that election. Today's sacrifice for tomorrow's future is the last consideration that these tenuous organizations can tolerate.

Special interest lobbies may very well represent the balance of power in our political structure, leveraging the economic powers they represent. They have no identifiable independence, adding nothing to the time horizon so necessary to a constructive solution to our energy problems. Salesmen for economic interests are consciousless representatives required to play their role but denied the power of moral decision. Only when a political advantage can be identified or the collapse of the system is immediate and obvious can these conduits be expected to transmit information and contribute to the kind of adjustments in the economy that are required. They are the defenders of the developers, the primary advocates of expansion economics and they consider it irresponsible to promote alterations to the system that they nourish and are nourished by.

The bureaucracy has been identified as the independent and principal practitioner of government, and certainly the bureaucracy is an influential element in all governmental processes; but the bureaucracy is not equally influential in all situations. Its power and its independence relates to the multiplicity and volume of individual decisions which combine to produce government policy and administration. But the bureaucracy is subordinate to the political structure of the government, and the political and economic influences are very well able to exert their control over the bureaucracy when it is worth the effort.

Energy decisions have never been allowed to escape to the bureaucratic level of government. The decisions have always affected the seat of power and both the decision process and the bureaucratic organization have been controlled. The proof is in the history of energy law and administration. The government energy organization has been fragmented for reason. Little independence exists and only a small independent contribution can be expected.

The press in all its aspects has been the principal source of our information and its performance has been critically observed. Where we have been able to observe the fact and its reporting, there have been disappointments. Publishers cannot afford to print that which the public does not wish to read. Publishers have a stake in the established order and interpret their interest in its protection. Our press is free and the facts will be published, but the press cannot carry the burden of convincing the public that critical sacrifices must be made. As at the time of Munich, the press follows. Only a captive press employs its resources to mold and control public opinion.

The academic institutions have the longest gestation period. They react not at all to the present. Leadership can develop and can be the critical element in finding solutions to the energy problem, but the process has barely started. The academic institutions are organized to protect the thinking process of its individual members, not to focus attention on the solution to identified problems. There is no limit to the delay in this process. It may be decades before an energy discipline develops and becomes broadly recognized. In the meantime, the subject of energy is nowhere represented in the organization of the university. The supply of energy is material, treated in the college of physical sciences: the departments of biology, geology, physics, and chemistry. The demand for energy is treated in the college of humanities as economics with a little help from other social studies. The subject of energy falls between disciplinary lines in the academic no-man's land of general studies. The problem of finding energy resources, disposing of waste, and forecasting the availability of energy and the capacity of the biosphere to absorb waste should be a major consideration in economic studies. But the subject matter is unknown to the economists and the proper evaluation would destroy the presently accepted economic theories. It may be necessary to create a new economics. In the meantime, the resistance approaches infinity.

Privately endowed foundations are a potential source of leadership and intellectual power. The foundations are many and their resources are substantial, but compared to their size and number, they have shown very little interest in the energy problem. Most all foundations recognize the necessity of focusing their resources in areas where their contribution can be identified and their progress measured. The great majority are small and their target must be local. The Ford Foundation has staked out a primary energy concern and created a research organization with a long track record, but they have been almost alone in the field. Neither the foundations nor the independent research organizations have had any noticeable effect on the educational and political structure or the thought processes of the country. My survey of the 250 foundations represented by The Council on Foundations disclosed no interest in my energy research or any significant ongoing programs. The field was left to the Ford Foundation.

Professional organizations can have the greatest influence on national policy and its interpretation. Law and medicine, the most powerful professions are not directly involved, but the eighteen earth science organizations which make up the American Geological Institute and the more numerous organizations which represent the economists are very much involved. The influence of both of these professions is strongly oriented towards the maintenance of the status quo and there is substantial evidence of the strains on their professional objectivity in presenting and suppressing factual information which reflects the necessity for preparing for a future that is not dependent on the availability of increasing quantities of energy materials, traditional pecuniary measures of economic progress, and uninhibited exploitation of natural resources. The professional lives of the members of these organizations are committed to the accepted knowledge, the accepted practices, and the accepted measures of success and failure.

In summary, there is no identifiable segment of society, no organized group, no latent organizational structure with a charter to seek out solutions to the continued functioning of a free society in an energy poor world. There are few identifiable segments of the society that have accepted the significance of the fact of limited energy resources in their own future. No flag can be hoisted with assurance that individuals will recognize a place to gather and consider their future life together and the necessities for change. This is amazing against the history of the proliferation of organizations in the free society and the normally great number of individuals and corporate structures looking for a cause. "Isms" of past generations that struck fear in the conservative heart and set in motion their negative counterparts now demonstrate fear of association with a problem so universally endowed with negative attributes.

This is the background against which progress for the solution to the energy problem must be judged.

THE NATIONAL CONSTITUENCY NECESSITY

In the absence of any special interest group positively concerned with solutions to the energy problem, only one constituency remains, the nation as a whole. Only the representative of the nation can suggest the necessary adjustments that must be accepted by the special interests in their conflict with the nation's survival.

The President does not have a monopoly in representing the national constituency but he is their only elected representative and he is the only individual with the power, the responsibility, and the possibility of resisting pressures that will be directed at his administrators and at him directly or indirectly through the Congress. The elected President will have the power to resist these pressures. He will have the authority to directly affect the Administrative branch of government by appointment and by removal if he believes strongly in the necessity of specific courses of action. The dissemination of misinformation can be stopped at the source by him.

The President can avoid the delays that are the automatic consequences of the appointment of study commissions. The presently available information is adequate. The William S. Paley Commission appointed in 1951 provides sufficient information for primary decision and in the twenty-four years since the Commission's report was completed in June of 1952, the responsible updates by federal, state, and private organizations are easily identifiable. Since the middle of 1975, there is no need for doubt as to the extent of the oil and gas reserves within the United States as presented by the U. S. Geological Survey and the National Academy of Sciences conclusions.

The President has numerous inherited powers to streamline administrative organization, control material imports, and eliminate barriers to interstate commerce. The President can recommend legislation which offers solutions to the energy problem, legislation which can be judged palatable to a Congress that has been prepared with reliable information as to the facts of the nation's energy problem and the alternatives that are available for its solution. The national constituency cannot be ignored by the Congress.

THE ELEMENTS OF AN ENERGY POLICY

The specifics of a national energy policy develop directly from our physical economic analysis unalloyed by compromise. They can best be stated in outline form with a minimum of discussion, summarized under ten elements.

(1) Realistic energy supply forecasting

This elementary task requires very little additional information but a great deal of information censoring. Almost every department of the federal government has been releasing optimistic interpretations of the U. S. energy reserve. The Arabs are not fooled

and the country's interests are not served by this confusion. The
free economy cannot function in this atmosphere. Realistic year
to year production potential for each source of energy must be
available. The forecast must extend long enough to accommodate
the lead times required to put in place alternative sources of
energy, at least thirty years.

(2) Oil and gas conservation stimulation

In the free economy the consumption of oil and gas cannot
be reduced without substantial increases in their costs. The
price mechanism must be employed without compromise. Use taxes
are an obvious and efficient means. Natural gas prices must be
high enough to balance the cost of home insulation and encourage
the reduction of living space. Motor fuel costs must be high
enough to restrict by one-half the present use of liquid petroleum for this purpose, stimulating mass personnel transportation
and the most economical material transport systems.

(3) Physical energy resource supply planning

It is no longer possible to avoid recognizing the necessity for
identifying the nation's energy resources in physical terms. We must
know the energy conversion methods and the cost of each conversion.
All energy resources must be included. The lead times for the production of energy and the construction of conversion plants must be known.
The current mix between the government and private sectors of the economy
must be recognized as a necessity. The corollary is the recognition of
the failure of the free price structure to independently handle this
problem and the necessity of planning to preserve the free economy in
its broader aspects.

(4) Restricted use of oil and positive control of reserves

The price structure is inadequate to protect the single most versa-
tile source of fuel to the U. S. economy from extinction. Petroleum
reserves represent the most necessary energy assets of future generations and their dissipation cannot be permitted. The absence of alternatives to liquid petroleum and the cost of synthetic oil produced from
coal, shale, and other hydrocarbon resources is already in evidence.
The lead time constrictions and the costs implicit in these replacements
prohibit a smooth transition through the price mechanism alone. Unrestricted petroleum imports threaten the balance of trade, international
credit, and the value of the currency. The loss of petroleum reserves
threatens the security of the nation.

Solutions to the petroleum problem reverse economic theories and conventional wisdom. Unrestricted price increases will produce very little more oil from the domestic resource and that encouragement is not desired. The nation's oil reserves should be maintained in the ground to the maximum degree possible and these combined objectives can be realized only by direct physical controls.

(5) *Release of restrictions on the private financing of the electric power industry*

Electric power costs must increase to encourage necessary conservation. This increase may need to be substantial. The encouragement of power consumption by graduated rates is already being discouraged. Competition between the states based on publicly supported cheap power is not in the national interest. The return to financial health of the private sector power utility is desirable. All of these objectives can be realized with a minimum of federal legislation restricting the discouragement of necessary increases in electric power rates with a minimum of federal assistance in equalizing costs and responsible federal advice on alternative sources of energy to produce electric power.

(6) *Federal financing of substitute natural gas and the supply and processing of nuclear fuel*

The nuclear fuel processing function has been unable to successfully escape the public sector and it appears improbable that further attempts are in the national interest. There is no significant synthetic gas industry in the free economy, and the industry can be developed only under the protection of federal price control and federal financing. This industry includes synthetic gas from coal (SNG) and the development of a liquefied natural gas industry (LNG) based on foreign imports.

*(7) Coordination of the environmental protection and the energy
production responsibilities*

The conflict between environmental protection and energy production cannot continue. The agencies were created during different
periods of time representing different national priorities. The
separation of interests has provided the opportunity for the coali-
tion of opposing forces within the body politic, virtually stalemat-
ing the production of energy from coal, the source of energy which
will become most important in the immediate future.

(8) Direct federal subsidy of efficient transportation resources

The defacto federal subsidy of inefficient transportation
systems must be terminated. The fossil fuels are not free to the
economy and their taxation to benefit users in proporation to
their consumption is not equitable, desirable, or defensible.
The tax revenues which can be generated from the fossil fuel must
be employed to place the railroads on a competitive basis and
encourage their much more efficient operation as compared with
inter-city trucking. The same fossil fuel tax resources will
best serve the nation's interest in subsidizing both inter-and
intra-city bus transportation systems which can utilize the past
subsidy of the highway right of way.

(9) Zero energy subsidy by all governments

All costs relating to governmental assistance or actual operation of the energy system of the country should be balanced with
taxation of the fossil fuels and the processed nuclear fuels as
they are used. The tax base is adequate and the balance can be
maintained. The solution to the energy problem can and should be
non-inflationary. This objective requires the balancing of all
sources of energy revenue and all energy-related expenditures. It
also requires some redefinition of economic terms.

(10) Development and promotion of the conservation ethic

The conservation ethic directly or indirectly conflicts with economic theory and political expediency. The energy conservation ethic introduces problems in the general economy and the balance of power within and between political constituencies. These problems must be anticipated and recognized if the energy objectives are to be realized.

THE DESIRABLE BUT IMPROBABLE ENERGY AUTHORITY

The elements of energy policy identify the scope of the problem, the need for policy coordination, and the threat to the existing governmental structure. The forces involved in this balance are tremendous and their consequence for the future can hardly be overstated, but it is improbable that Congress will release the necessary authority soon.

The arguments in favor of an energy authority with very broad powers are persuasive. The authority can be circumscribed to limit the extent of powers, but the authority must coordinate policy in all aspects of energy administration and the authority must have sufficient lattitude to effectively restrain excess resource consumption, stimulate conservation, and provide for the financing of the conversion industry. The authority should not encourage governmental activities where the private economy can function, but the nation's future cannot be sacrificed for ideological free enterprise which is totally dependent on public sector financing and totally subservient to public sector economic decisions. The two most important functions of an energy authority are long range planning and the insulation of critical economic decisions from the Legislative and Administrative branches of the government.

Too little is known about the actual elasticity in the energy price structure to establish either subsidies or tax levels whose economic consequences can be anticipated for even a short period of time. Energy administration through the legislative process must be compared with control of the money supply and the maintenance of a balanced economy without the power and authority of the Federal Reserve Board. Less is known about energy economics. It will be impossible to legislate limits or state objectives in meaningful terms. The problem is compounded by the reluctance of economists to recognize their own limitations. There is little evidence of support for the release of the required broad prerogatives.

Thus, a total energy authority must be recognized as improbable. The objective can be set forth, coordination can be realized, and the beginnings of the necessary authority can be delegated. The need for this kind of authority was recognized by the 1952 Paley Commission and the evidence of need has been building since then, but there has been actual growth in the fragmentation of governmental power and authority, and the political and economic basis for these motivations has not diminished.

POSSIBLE LEGISLATION

While it is improbable that a total energy program will evolve early in the elected presidency, much can be done within the administrative structure of the government, without legislation, to coordinate policy and prepare the way for the national debate. This debate will be concerned with a step by step legislative process. The sequence in this process will be governed by necessity, the developing crisis in physical energy resource availability.

Natural gas price control

The relaxation of natural gas price control can be deferred only if the courts allow the Federal Power Commission ruling*to stand and if the interpretation of this decision is sufficiently relaxed to encourage the release of gas supplies to interstate commerce needed to meet the minimum requirements of the interstate pipeline companies. Controls will be *removed* only in an emergency situation which precludes proper study and debate. A substantial tax on gas use balancing the release from the price ceiling with a permanent relationship between price and tax is more probable. The natural gas price control debate should precipitate legislation coordinating a program for federal financing and control of natural gas substitutes.

Natural gas substitutes financing and control (LNG and SNG)

The home heating segment of the national economy has become dependent on the availability of pipeline grade natural gas. Significant portions of the commercial segment of the economy share this dependence and a number of industries are unable to convert to alternative fuels except at a cost which is so high that synthetic natural gas provides the more economical solution.

---

* See footnote Page 51

Very little resistance can be anticipated to recognizing the necessity of federal financing of a liquefied natural gas industry and a synthetic natural gas industry. The immense costs cannot be financed in the private sector and the private sector has little experience in the market. The industry will be totally dependent on the federally controlled prices which can be anticipated to remain politically necessary. Synthetic natural gas from coal and imported liquefied natural gas can be financed by taxation of the use of the remaining natural gas resource. This natural solution to the economic problem can be expected to be politically palatable.

Federally directed release of electric power utility rates

The uneconomical control of utility rates which jeopardize the viability of this industry, the development of publicly supported regional power authorities, and the tax free bond assistance to this industry precipitated by regional competition is clearly not in the national interest. General public education as to the necessity for the elimination of subsidized electric power should find support among conservatives and liberals. This is a natural development once the necessity for reduced consumption of electric power is recognized. The higher power costs as well as the higher fuel costs are required to stimulate the housing industry in free economic responses. Support for this legislation should be available.

Federal support of the nuclear fuels supply and processing industry

The inevitability of the public sector control of this industry has been amply demonstrated during the last few years. The stalemate in legislation should be broken. Legislation will probably include financing and authorization for commercial size experimental atomic plants, taking over the functions which have been abandoned by private industry. The electric power industry cannot be saddled with the cost of experimental plants and the separation of this economic responsibility will facilitate the return of the electric power utilities to a sound financial basis.

Removal of petroleum products price and product rationing controls

Controls over petroleum use and pricing must be revamped. This will become the critical area for political decision and the decision process may fail. Petroleum prices must increase. The revenues from petroleum use taxes are necessary to balance the federal government's energy budget. Failure to accept a program for increased prices, increased taxes, and the removal of the inequitable refinery rationing system will substantially increase inflationary pressures and can lead to more critical physical energy supply problems.

The taxation of petroleum products will test the legislative process. More accurately, it will be a test of the educational and communications function of the free society. The inflationary spiral cannot be controlled unless the consumption of unavailable materials is reduced. There is a critical difference between an inflationary spiral and an increase in costs resulting from the substitution of high cost, labor intensive materials for a low cost material that has been exhausted. The proposed tax on petroleum usage would become a tax on the remaining natural resource and if the tax were employed to finance the replacement industry, and if the tax was paid by the final user of the product, there would be no inflationary spiral. But, the cost-of-living index would go up, and labor costs geared to the cost of living would increase. The inflation would be a result of the indices and their operation, not the fundamental economic change. As previously discussed, fundamentals of the running out of cheap oil and gas will result in the creation of jobs and deflation of the economy. The secondary effects will be the consequence of a failure of the pecuniary economic measures, and their interpretation. The underlying fact is a reduction in the standard of living of the nation and the reluctance of either politicians or economists to recognize this fact and begin the educational process.

The current failure in the economic indices and the current failure in the economic comprehension of the energy problem almost guarantees a political failure. This is the basic problem. This is the problem that can be avoided by properly constituted energy authority. There does not appear to be time to develop the economic discipline and broad public comprehension needed for legislative control.

Combined environmental protection and coal industry production responsibility

The primary conflict between the environmental interests and the energy interests center in the coal industry. Solution to the future availability of energy produced from coal requires coordination of the activities of the organizations which impinge on this problem. Subordination of all organizations relating to the production of energy from coal and the protection of the environment represent a minimum step in the direction of necessary energy administration efficiency.

Coal will become the primary source of energy in the United States after the turn of the century. The coordination of the run-out of the natural gas and oil industries including imported oil could be best administered by an energy authority, but the production of coal is an established industry with a long history of control in the free economy. Coal has always been priced in relationship to the labor cost component of its removal. The production of coal should remain in the free economy with a minimum of governmental interference. New methods of controlling gaseous influence from burning coal appear to be on the horizon. Integrated controls of coal production and environmental protection with taxing authority should be able to control coal production and finance environmental protection.

Transportation

Control of the transportation industry faces the same problem as the control of the petroleum products. They are interdependent industries with the greatest political influence. The protection of their short term interests can bring down the free economy and the free society.

The economy cannot function without transportation and transportation cannot function without liquid petroleum. The remaining U. S. petroleum reserve will be required to finance the industry to provide the minimum liquid petroleum required for a reconstituted transportation industry requiring very substantially less petroleum to accomplish the nation's transportation purpose. The time to realize this transition must be bought from the world supply of petroleum and paid for with the U. S. agricultural surpluses. The balancing of this equation will require careful planning.

The details are somewhat incidental, but they include the necessity for balancing the governmental subsidy to automotive and truck transportation with a government subsidized railroad right of way. This subsidy too, can be paid for from the tax on the petroleum reserve as it is used.

XVII

THE ECONOMIC FICTIONS AND REALITY

Energy is one of the realities in a world that has become dominated by fiction. The real world of economics concerns man's relationship with his life support. It is the business of living, man's labor applied to the materials and living organisms of the earth that are the source of food and shelter. The reality of economics is physical.

The practice of economics is very different. The economists are concerned with measuring activity without regard for the purpose of that activity. They are the nation's accountants, charged with the responsibility of keeping the balance of the nation's wealth and spending. Their decisions determine the quantity of money that will be circulated and the rate of return on the investment in the nation's wealth. Their tools are principally statistical procedures and they are dependent on monetary denomination of all of the things of the world and the activities of men.

There are no limits in the economists' equations. The activities which they measure do not end with a lifetime. A resource that is depleted is replaced by another resource and the monetary valuation is assigned by the market, an automatic, continuous process free from any planning function. Economists are totally concerned with man's activity in producing goods and services and it is considered desirable, although not necessary, to maintain stability in the value of things. To accomplish this stability, the quantity of money must not be allowed to grow faster than the production of things.

Economists are not the custodians of the earth's resources. These resources have value only when they are extracted or traded and the value that is attached to the earth's resources relates to the value of the labor involved in the resource removal and the competition for that resource with other resources which perform the same service to man. The basic resource has no significant value until it becomes scarce within the economists' time horizons.

The time horizons of economists are very close and they are controlled by the monetary system and the measure of the value of money which is the rate of return, the annual interest paid to the owner of the monetarily denominated property. Money is both a property itself and a measure of the value of all properties. All things are valued by the rate of the return to the owner. If there is no return in the foreseeable future, there is no value. Even a sure return many years in the future has current value only in relationship to the expected year to year return which must begin with the present and which is based on the current expectancy, the rate of return or interest paid in the current market.

The complexities of the economic process must be reduced to monetary terms for the economists. They are concerned with the employment of these measures of economic activity as they affect the national and free world political decision process. In contrast with this perspective, I am concerned with the reality of the input figures. I am concerned with the availability of material and the consequence of this availability in the national and world economy. These materials are specific and cannot be dealt with in monetary terms only. Further, I am concerned with the validity of the economists' theory of growth which ignores the fact of limits.

THE REALITY OF THE EARTH

The biosphere is identified as the thin layer on the skin of the earth which supports life. It includes the depth of the seas, the land as far down as we can dig, and the atmosphere above the earth. The biosphere produced man, supports man, and represents the only livable area in the universe so far identified. The English economist, Kenneth Boulding, named the biosphere our space ship and introduced the concepts of our dependence on this earth to the economic discipline. However, he has had few followers.

The earth is finite and the identifiable quantities of many minerals as well as the fossil fuels are small in comparison with the quantity of these minerals required to maintain the world economy and the continuation of its growth. The finite nature of these resources conflicts with the economic theory of infinite expansion. In the scientific sense, this fact destroys the economic theory, but economics is not a science and economists have not accepted this fact nor attempted to adjust their concepts to it.

The living organisms of the biosphere relate to each other in a natural process identified by ecologists as bilaterally coupled and self-correcting. No species dominates the natural world or is indispensable to it. The higher species of animals feed on the lower species and the plants and bogs process the waste and regenerate the atmospheric elements in the air and sea. Excess populations are reduced when their numbers exceed the capacity of their biological supports.

Man is a part of the natural world and is dependent on the natural world, but his social structure and his political-economic system has set him in opposition to the natural world and he has assumed an independence. His independence is based on his scientific knowledge which has enabled him to control his environment and avoid the restraints on the increase in his population.

Man's escape from nature has been an evolutionary process beginning with the earliest development of civilization, but the acceleration of this process did not begin until the modern era. The scientific and industrial revolution of the 18th Century marked the start of the current acceleration, identifiable by the rate of growth of the population.

The economic theory of free enterprise and unrestricted exploitation accelerated man's conflict with the natural world. The economic theory replaced the bilateral feedback system of nature with a rational equivalent in the economists' market price control. Under this theory, the materials of the natural world can be freely taken until they approach extinction at which time the cost of their exploitation will increase, their unavailability will decrease the quantity in the market, and market demand will increase their price. At the higher price, alternative resources will become economical to produce and the cycle will be repeated, maintaining the supply of materials to man without limit and without the interference of unpredictable political motives.

In practice, the economic theory functions only for non-essential materials. The bilateral coupling of the system is subject to political interference necessitated by the humanity of the society man has created. Death in the natural world is automatic. Death in the human world is unacceptable unless planned in the ritual ceremonies which include war.

The time cycle in the feedback system of the natural world is very short. Winter eliminates the population which cannot be supported. In those parts of the world where the winters are inadequate to perform this function, the evolutionary process has been retarded. The year is a natural cycle.

Man's economic control system has pretended to reach into the future, applying man's capacity to understand his origins and foresee his direction. In actual practice, the present is dominant and the economic mechanisms have reinforced this dominance. It is virtually impossible to hold off from the market resources which have value today even though they may be almost infinitely more valuable in the future. The market strikes a balance in the weighting of the present as opposed to conservation for the future. The weighting of the present is increased with the activity of the market and equalitarian distribution of market power. The economic feedback system which in theory has infinite time horizons becomes in fact very little different from the annual cycle in nature except for one major difference.

Man's economic control of his relationship with the environment permits deferred decision and delayed reaction. The acceleration of man's capacity to exploit his environment is no different than the geometric multiplication of natural species that outrun their natural supports, but man's scientific capacity has permitted him to alter and hold back the restraining influences of the natural world. His pesticides and germicides have eliminated plagues that threatened to restrict his growth. Genetic manipulation has increased agricultural yield. He has employed the power taken from the natural world to dig deeper into the biosphere for his required supports. But all of his planning has been for a small multiple of years and most of his economic system operates on a single annual cycle. He has created political institutions geared to the short time response in his fear of even one day's delay in the achievement of his individual objectives. Democracy has created no long term planning capacity, no function, no structure.

Man has created a society that borrows from nature and is totally dependent on nature but which opposes nature. Man has created and fostered the illusion that his system can go on in perpetuity. His system depends on growth. His system has already grown too large. The option of reducing the dependence on growth and reducing his incursion on the natural world is running out.

THE SPECIAL NATURE OF ENERGY AND WASTE

Man's economic system will not function without energy and the disposal of waste. Both have a special relationship with the economic system as this system has operated in the past. Both have been almost totally neglected as an economic cost. They have been considered intangibles or by-products of the economic process which could be ignored except for the labor component of their service.

No greater error could have been introduced into the understanding of the economic process. Energy is the source of economic power in almost every industrial and commercial segment of the economy. In the modern world, energy is the single most important ingredient in the life support systems. Only energy from the sun and from the secondary effects of solar energy are renewable and independent of the functioning of the economic system. Primitive man can live with sun power, water power, and wind power but he can live only in reduced numbers. The population of the world today cannot be supported by these means.

Energy in the western world is fossil fuel energy. The use of energy is governed by the first and second laws of thermodynamics, physical laws which have not been altered in the two hundred year development of the modern society. The use of the fossil fuels for heat is governed by the first law, the energy process is non-reversible. Their use for power is governed by the second law, almost two-thirds of the input must be discarded as waste. The use of a fuel resource to produce energy is forever. It can not be recycled or regenerated.

Nature's capacity to process waste is also limited and this capacity has been even more neglected than energy resources by the economic system. The renewal capacities of streams, lakes, and the ocean are only now being determined and the waste absorbtion limits for many of these bodies have already been exceeded. Atmospheric absorption capacity is even more critical when the limits are approached. The earth's capacity to absorb solid waste is more obvious but less critical. So far, our economic system has been able to respond only to the solid waste problem which lends itself to the costing of labor and material required to handle the problem. The business sector which represents the practical functioning of the economic system has resisted responding to air and water pollution. The restraints have been political, not economic, and the resistance to the restraints has not abated.

THE FICTION OF MONEY AND CAPITAL

Capital represents deferred expenditure. Capital is man's labor and the employment of materials to build the engines that will serve man in the future. Capital is shelter and roadways and machines and the removal of overburden that makes possible the production of goods and services for daily consumption.

Capital is not money, bank accounts, or figures in the residual summation of the corporate balance sheet. Money is a symbol, a reflection of capital, a medium of exchange and a basis for recording the value of the real capital that it is employed to represent. Money is the only common measure of the economic world, but this common measure is a necessity only in reducing the complexity and manageability of the economy.

The primitive society can function without money. The political system dominated by a single individual can function without money. It is doubtful that a free society with its free economy dependence can function without money.

The confusion of money and capital and the assumption of money's primary importance contributes to economic fictions which are a barrier to comprehension.

THE REALITY OF INFLATION AND ITS MEASURE

Inflation is a relationship between the sum of the monetary supplies of the country with the sum of the capital and the inventories of the country. Inflation occurs when the money supply increases more rapidly than the capital accumulation. Inflation can be controlled by controlling the money supply. All values can be shrunk if the relative supply of money is less than the true value of the nation's capital. The converse is also true.

The definition of inflation is simple but its measure is difficult. Only the money supply can be counted. The value of the nation's capital can be assumed to be growing in response to time and the rate of industrial and commercial activity, but the proof of the actual amount of capital that has been put in place in a short time span is not possible. Only the money supply can be counted statistically.

In the true accounting of inflation, changes in the nation's primary reserves of resource materials cannot be counted as these reserves do not actually enter the economic equation. The reserves are represented only as a reflection of their existence or nonexistence in the exchange of property. The reserve itself, its latent contribution is not recognized. Thus, a sudden and dramatic change in its value introduces the necessity for eliminating the effect in the inflation balance.

The discovery of large reserves of valuable minerals will have an initial inflationary effect on the economy as a consequence of the day to day conversion of these minerals into exchange media. Value will be created at the location of the mineral finding, and the material balance will be thrown out with the movement of people and the slower movement of materials. The inflationary waves will move through the economy relative to the value of the total economy. The lasting effect is neither inflationary nor deflationary, if the money supply is kept in balance.

Conversely, the running out of a resource must introduce a deflationary cycle. The year to year production of that resource is reduced, there is less economic activity, fewer people are involved, fewer materials are moved, and less money is required to circulate. But the money supply also must be reduced and this reduction is much more difficult in the deflationary cycle. Modern economics advises against this deflation introducing theories of employment maintenance and economic stimulation of growth, turning the fundamental deflation into a fundamental inflation.

THE INFLATION FICTIONS

The existence or nonexistence of inflation cannot be measured in terms of the level of prosperity. Inflation is a process, a developing condition which endangers relative values and the smooth operation of the economy. Inflation enriches the debtor and the owner of marketable property. Inflation impoverishes the fixed income dependent, the retiree. Money loses its value.

Money does not lose its value and inflation does not develop as a consequence of the running out of a primary natural resource; but the replacement of that resource with a more expensive material may substantially increase the proportion of every man's income that must be reserved for that replacement resource. With no change in the individual's income, he will have less available money to bid for other materials in the economy. There will in fact be a deflation comparable to this shift in purchasing power. But these circumstances will also result in an increase in the cost-of-living index as computed.

The secondary effect of a cost-of-living index increase can and will trigger labor cost increases in broad segments of the economy. These increases are definitely inflationary. They will begin to balance the deflationary effect of the primary resource substitution, but then the increases will set in motion an inflationary spiral. Thus, the cost-of-living index is not a measure of inflation. It can become the principal cause of inflation.

Keynesian political-economic theory suggests deliberate fiscal and monetary stimulation of the economy, advancing the probability of an actual inflationary spiral. In the instance of a primary change in resource availability, monetary supply increase is the wrong medicine.

The precise circumstances of the running out of the world's gas and oil resource compounds problems of economic prediction. The material standard of living of the nation will be substantially reduced. This is a physical fact which cannot be overcome. Monetary stimulation under these circumstances will be totally inflationary. Money pumped into the economy to pay for petroleum products that are not available at any price can only bid up the value of all other commodities. Theoretically, the cost-of-living index could approach infinity as no amount of money will purchase the amount of petroleum product established by the index as necessary for the average family.

The temptation will be to tinker with the cost-of-living index in the anticipation that this tinkering will return the validity of the measure. In fact, the cost-of-living index is only accidentally a measure of inflation. Specifically, the cost-of-living index can be considered a measure of inflation only in a relatively stable material economy, one in which the primary materials required for the support of the economy are in stable supply. These conditions will not be available in the immediate future and the cost-of-living index cannot be employed in its traditional manner.

Very similar circumstances will affect the validity of the wholesale price index and virtually all of the indices employed by economists to measure the stability of the economy. It has taken a generation to put together the statistical procedures for establishing these indices, and it will be most difficult for economists to establish new measures of equilibrium and predict their fulfillment.

THE VOID IN THE NATION'S BALANCE SHEET AND THE FICTION OF THE GROSS NATIONAL PRODUCT

Accountants measure the balance sheet of a corporation in terms of total assets, total liabilities, and capital. These balance sheets are heavily weighted for consideration of historic costs or historic market values. The balance sheet is a fossil record which only nominally considers the value of the primary resources which the corporation may own. Extraction industries almost totally discount or ignore the latent value of their raw material reserves.

In the national accounting, economists do not consider the balance sheet. Economics has not yet advanced to that state. There is no accounting for the nation's reserves and no recognition of their depletion. The understatement by the corporate accountant becomes infinite in the national economic balance. It is zero each year.

The Gross National Product measures the activity of the nation in terms of all economic inputs. It includes both the flow of value into capital investment and the flow to consumption. It is the value that the market puts on that which is *taken out of the nation's resources*. It is labor and compensation for capital and compensation to the owners of the right to remove materials from the earth, but it includes no consideration for those values over and above these compensations. Net national product is very similar except that the capital accounts are subtracted.

Gross National Product is not a measure of the nation's wealth. It comes close to measuring the subtraction from the nation's wealth, a subtraction which includes both the renewable and non-renewable resources of the nation.

There is no measure of the wealth of the nation as it changes from year to year. For most of the nations of the world, that measure would be negative and for the United States the negative quantity has been growing exponentially during the last two hundred years.

To the extent that the Gross National Product measures the nation's wealth and the change in its wealth, the GNP is a negative or reciprocal measure. This is unsettling and it is significant, but it is not directly useful. The primary significance is the evidence of the limited extent of our economic knowledge and the danger of plunging ahead with solutions to the problems of the immediate future based on the economic measures which have been developed and which have assumed importance but which cannot be supported.

LABOR, CAPITAL, AND THE INFLATION SYNDROME

The reality and the fiction of inflation become mixed in the political-economic syndrome of the oil and gas depletion. Inflation can be controlled or avoided if the capital for the replacement of natural gas and petroleum is generated by taxing the remaining resource and building the plants that manufacture oil and gas from coal and transporting the foreign natural gas that is now wasted. Inflation can be avoided if the price

structure is used to decrease the demand for gas and oil and encourage
energy efficient transportation and energy efficient space heating.
Inflation will be avoided if the price structure is employed to reduce
the consumption of all materials and encourage the design of all machines
and utilities to lengthen their life and reduce waste in replacement and
unnecessary recycling. Inflation will be avoided if unemployed labor is
put to work in the recycling industries and in the maintenance of the
nation's capital goods, including the railway right of way.

The inflation spiral will be turned loose if the fundamental fact
of the end of the oil and gas age is not recognized and accepted. Energy
is involved in every material that goes into the cost of living. A
reduced supply of energy requires a reduction in the supply of the materials
which the nation consumes and the per capita consumption must come down.
To maintain the balance, the price of all goods must go up, the cost of
living will increase and the wage dollar will buy less of the world's
goods.

The only possible, constructive response to the energy attrition is
a reduction in those activities which are most energy intensive. Labor
and time must begin to replace cheap energy: labor in the form of walking
and bicycling, time waiting for materials to arrive by rail, labor to insu-
late existing homes and factories, labor to repair machines that were discarded under the old economy of labor cost priority. In monetary terms,
the standard of living will go down. The net national product and the
national product per capita will go down. Growth in the industries supplying consumption products will go down. Most of the economic indicators
will signal a depression, but there need not be a depression. The depression can be totally avoided by a combination of properly stimulated free
economy response and a minimum of responsible long range planning.

The constructive, non-inflationary response to the retreating supply
of cheap energy is not automatic. Quite to the contrary, the laws and
the habits of the free economy of the United States directly oppose a responsive and constructive reaction to the problems created by the energy
decline. Collective bargaining privileges guarantee a demand by labor
for increased wages to offset the higher cost of home heating, transportation fuel, and every material the household consumes. The inflationary
spiral will be initiated by these demands and there is no limit in this
process. The value system of the free economy can be totally destroyed
in the inflation spiral.

A second contributor to the destruction of the free economy is the attrition of planning time. If the transition from energy consumption encouragement to energy conservation is not begun soon enough, there will not be enough energy available to realize the transition: the construction of the more energy economical transportation system, the insulation to avoid energy losses in home heating, the design of longer life machines serving the necessary functions of the economy, and the curtailment of the population spiral that reduces available materials and living space to every individual. The time horizon of the individual and the time horizon of the free economy institution is too short to avoid the consequences of this disaster syndrome. Planning must intervene. Political-economic leadership must be awakened.

The third contributor to the potential disaster is capital and the money illusion. Money is not capital and capital is not created in the money markets. The money markets do serve the formation of capital and the money markets have functioned and the money markets can function again, but they cannot be relied upon to solve the problem of the transition from a labor-efficient to an energy-efficient economy.

The rewards for capital accumulation in the free economy are profits and interest. As the sum of all profits over all cycles of the free economy tend to equal zero, interest is the principal factor in the reward system. The capital accumulation task in the transition to an energy-efficient economy will overload the capital accumulation machinery of the free economy. The rate of interest cannot be high enough to encourage the accumulation. The base for the accumulation is not large enough. An attempt to employ this machinery would increase income distribution inequality in addition to wasting time to prove in practice that which can be foreseen without going through the process.

The capital accumulation can be realized only by extending the base for the capital input. The base must include the total population, not just those individuals in the population able and willing to save. Taxation is the method of capital accumulation in the public sector. The effectiveness of public sector financing is assisted by the fact of the large proportion of the population presently compensated as unemployed. The unemployed can be put to work at a small cost, if wages are not artificially established above their market value.

XVIII

THE SOCIAL CONTRACT AND THE

LEADERSHIP DECISION

There are no real barriers to a solution to the energy problem of this country and the free world. But there are many ideological problems, legal problems, and social problems. The problems can be resolved. A free society can be maintained. The essential characteristics of the free economy can be protected and can be constructively employed in the solution.

The problem with the problems is their extensiveness. They go to the root of every concept, every established privilege, every assumed necessity in the free society. Limitations must be accepted where freedom from any limitation has been preached, claimed, and defended for more than two hundred years.

The nation and the free world face only one decision. The choice lies between accepting the reality of the world that produced man and limits man, or rejecting that reality for the impossible dream. There is poetry and romance in the dream. The dream has sustained generations. To a very considerable extent, we have built our civilization on the dream and we have credited the dream with our success.

The reality behind the dream is the natural resource of the world. Oil and gas represent a single commodity in this world but they are the commodity upon which we have become most dependent and the running out of this commodity brings the moment of truth. Our dream has been supported by many commodities and many have already run out. Their running out was not critical. The theory of replacement under the price structure handled the energy predecessors to gas and oil smoothly and efficiently, but this past experience cannot be projected.

There is a great temptation to assume that science will perform the miracle in replacing oil and gas with unlimited energy from a controlled nuclear fusion reaction, the same process that energizes the solar system and produced all life, all cultures, everything that is anything. The fusion solution would regenerate the dream if energy were the only problem. But energy is not the only problem. Other critical materials are in short supply and the protection of the environment from waste disposal is only a little way over the time horizon. It would soon take over the job of establishing limits to man's growth if the energy problem were resolved.

The dream of infinite expansion and infinite domination of the world by man is an impossible dream. A delay in recognizing its impossibility will spell the end of the western world civilization. After that, there may be a regeneration reflecting the thoughts of Aldous Huxley, a new world built with man's inventions and a new respect for accommodation to nature, a world of totally controlled humanity.

The immediate question concerns the sanctity of contracts, the privileges of private property, the prerogatives of political authority, the definition of civil liberty and the rights of the individual. These questions can be answered only in terms of the single decision. Are we a part of the world we live in or are we its controllers? Either way or both, we must accept the necessity for the rational employment of our power and find ways to protect the fragile nature of the rational process. Unfortunately, there is no natural law of economic control. The natural law for man is his extinction.

THE DECISION

Survival is not a decision. Survival is an instinct and even man, who is born with few natural instincts, shares the instinct for survival with the animal world. The extinction of the human race will not follow as the natural consequence of the worship of false prophets. Before extinction, false doctrine will be recognized. Decision will follow recognition and will determine the doctrine and choice of leadership. The consequence of this decision will determine the extent of the chaos or its avoidance. The process begins with understanding man's origin.

Man is a creature of the biosphere. This is how it began and this recognition can start the process of finding solutions for the problems of the future. The recognition can provide the weighting in the selection between ideas in conflict, the selection between the doctrines of alternative disciplines and the conclusions they have developed.

Scientific truth has been based on the natural world. Science is natural science. Disciplines that claim to represent the scientific process but ignore the facts of the natural world are not science.

Mathematics has been considered a pure science. This claim can mislead and confuse. Mathematics is a science only within its own sphere, the development of numerical relationships. Mathematics in its application is not a science. Mathematics is only useful to investigation and it can be misused producing totally unscientific conclusions.

The social disciplines have been led by philosophy and religion in the development of ideas. When these ideas could be grounded in the observable facts of the natural world, natural sciences were formed. Where ideas could not be grounded, social disciplines developed, partly in search of their grounding, partly oblivious to the necessity of developing common bases in their hoped for contribution to society. The meeting place of the social disciplines is the moral code of the society they represent. It is the common point of departure and the place to where they must return.

There is only one test of a moral code. That test is the survival of the society. All religions, all social disciplines are subject to the test. The greatest sin for man is the activities and beliefs that endanger his survival, and he cannot survive alone. His society must be protected.

TIME AND THE TWO ECONOMIC DISCIPLINES

Time is both the ultimate resource and also the ultimate measure of the energy problem and its solution. As individuals, we can lay claim to only a limited amount of time. As a society, we can look back on thousands of generations and millions of years in the development. There have been many breaks, many beginnings and endings for the parts, but the whole has continued to develop.

The critical problem is the neglect of time in the pecuniary economists' methodology. The neglect is not recognized. The neglect of time has been both the creed and privilege of the pecuniary economists. They do not believe in the significance of time or the necessity for its consideration. Their market will adjust in the time that it takes and the measure of that time is not important because it has never been important. Time is too difficult a concept to be understood by the voting public. The political leaders cannot deal with the concept of the engineering parameters and their consequences. Physical economics is a branch of engineering and time is a primary consideration.

The economics of today is pecuniary economics. The importance of physical economics and its time concept is not recognized.

Time enters the economic equation in its relationship with the availability of materials and the availability of material processes to produce materials when they are required. Time is critical in the formation of capital. Capital is material and labor reserved from current consumption to produce the resources that are needed to manufacture or make available products that will be required in the future.

The quantification of time and materials is critical to physical economics. Time is limited. Time cannot be manufactured. Once expended, time cannot be recaptured or recycled. Materials expended today will not be available tomorrow. Materials required tomorrow that are not available in their natural state or cannot be produced by processes that are available today can only be produced tomorrow when the time and materials have been saved and applied in the construction of the required processes. The future flow of materials is controlled by projectable time sequences and is limited by these same time sequences.*

---

* All of the analysis procedures in Part Two and the preview of these conclusions in Part One represent time denominated material economics. This begins with Exhibit 2 on Page 16 and continues through Figure 27 on Page 123. The time denominated material economic conclusions are contrasted with the time ignoring econometric projections of the Federal Energy Administration on Figure 15 (Page 95), Figure 16 (Page 97) and Figure 25 (Page 115). The contrast is also drawn in comparison with the Interior Department's forecast in Figure 17 (Page 99).

By definition, time controls the rate of material production. The feasibility of the rate conclusion is indicated in plotting production against time. Rate changes that are physically impossible become obvious in these plottings. Visual extrapolation of possible changes in rate (the slope of the line) and possible production (the level reached in the charting) obviate repeated numerical projections.

Pecuniary economics is the economics of the main line economists of the United States today. They are the protectors of the free market and the free society. They are the principal advisers to the political powers at all levels of government and business. In their market concepts, energy is a material which may represent a slightly larger proportion of the Gross National Product than had been recognized in the past.

In physical economics, energy is the partner of time. Energy and time must be applied to materials to produce capital facilities, and more energy and time are required in combination with capital facilities to produce goods and services for consumption.

Physical economics is not new. Physical economics is a branch of engineering, but it has not been identified by the engineering discipline in its broader aspects. The mathematics of physical economics involve probability and time sequence projections. These mathematics are not untested. They are firmly grounded in natural science.

M. King Hubbert's* projection of the full petroleum production cycle is an exercise in physical economics. This 1956 projection identified the 1970 peaking of oil production in the United States within a very narrow tolerance. He also projected the world petroleum cycle. Both are now controlling on the whole economics of the free world.

The methodologies in our analysis of the supply and demand of energy to the U. S. economy is physical economics. This Chapter VI discussion which develops the critical 1979 failure of supply to satisfy demand is physical economics. This procedure and this conclusion will be rejected by pecuniary economists. It will be rejected because it is not understood.

Physical economics is concerned with the supply and demand equation only secondarily. Physical economics recognizes that demand cannot always dominate the equation. The history of the demand dominance has nothing to do with the facts which must be recognized in the future.

The failure of the supply/demand balance in or about 1979 is not a total material supply failure. Physical economists are no more concerned with absolutes than are pecuniary economists. The Chapter VI projection identifies the time when demand will no longer dominate the energy supply equation. An adjustment must be made in demand as well

_____
* Figure 4, Page 70 and Figure 5, Page 73. All of Dr. Hubbert's projections are secondarily or primarily time denominated.

as in supply. The Chapter VI projection assumes a demand which cannot be realized. This time sequence projection, employing physical economic methodology, is necessary to probe the future. This projection is important because time is important.*

There will not be time to put in place the energy conversion industry required by our economy as it operates today. With or without growth in the economy, we will not be able to supply the economy with the energy in the past quantities when the flow of energy from the natural resources runs out. This is the significant fact today which develops the critical decision for the United States economy. This is the fact which was indicated by Dr. Hubbert's 1956 projection of the complete petroleum cycle. This is the fact that is denied in *economic* theory. This is the information which the leaders of our business and political institutions must use to allow the survival of our society. The problem is the conflict between the material economists' advice and the pecuniary economists' denial of the existence of a problem. Finally, the problem is the preponderance in the influence of pecuniary economic theory in the academic community, the business community, and the political community.

---

* The economic literature includes myriad references to economic indices related to historic periods. The extrapolation of these economic measures is the most visible activity of professional economists. However, this employment of time in identifying economic events should not be confused with its employment as a substantive factor in the definition of a process.

Economists also employ time in establishing the relative value of benefits available now and in the future. This employment of time determines the rate of interest earned on invested capital and the present and future value of the income stream which is expected. These employments of time relate to the banking and investment banking function which is only peripheral to basic economics.

Time does not enter into the economic determination of the quantity of goods and services that can be expected from the economic system as this system is presented in economic theory. In economic theory, the quantity of supply is controlled by price and market demand. The relationship of supply, demand, and price are independent of time in this theory, which is the heart of economics. Economic predictions of supply ignore the time factor in capital accumulation, in the social process, and in the physical process.

(Footnote continued on next page)

THE CONFLICT BETWEEN THE FREE ECONOMY AND THE FREE SOCIETY

The free economy is represented today by the pecuniary economists,
their principles and their beliefs. Their principles are amoral, and
they conflict with the necessities of a free society.

The market governs distribution. It is a primitive market borrowed
from primitive societies and in this sense it is a part of the natural
development of man and his society. There has always been a market and
there will always be a market.

Price is determined in the market by the balance of supply and
demand. There are no upper or lower limits to price in the free market.
The free market economy tends to produce more than can be consumed,
shifting the weight of control of the market process to demand and the
influence of the supply of money. This historic evidence has been considered an economic law. It is based on the ingenuity of man and his
capacity to find substitute materials to maintain supply. Reliance on
this market principle has introduced conflict with the reality of the
political processes.

The free society has interceded and overruled the free economy in
two vital areas. First, the free distribution of income has been curtailed by the tax structure and by social welfare distribution. Second
and more important, the free society has interfered with the market price
mechanism. Commodities which are vital to the free society — food, shelter, and energy — have not been allowed to be curtailed in their distribution by the rise in price. The price has been controlled and the
encouragement to produce the quantities required and the encouragement
to substitute materials to meet demand has been taken out of the system.

Physical processes not only occur in time, they require time. Time
is an integral part of the process and the time ingredient defines the
product that can be expected from the process.

Physical economics employs time in projecting probable expectancies
in both micro- and macro-economic references. Neither economics can
function without physical process. Ignorance of these processes and
their time dependence is excusable in the micro-economics so long as the
time related tasks are represented by other disciplines. Ignorance of
time in macro-economics attacks the validity of economic theory.

Economists are agents of the free economy. Their system has been damaged and they believe it should be repaired and allowed to function; the free price structure should be allowed to clear the market, returning the incentive to produce and supply all materials in that market for the benefit of the free society. The market is not concerned with the welfare of the individual no matter how great his numbers or how great his need. The market ignores the political process, the needs of people in a specific time frame. When necessary, people must die.

THE PROBABILITY FOR SURVIVAL AND THE SIGNIFICANCE OF THE NATIONAL CONSTITUENCY IMPERATIVE

Survival must be defined in terms of the continuity of the free society institutions which include the political, the business, the religious, the cultural, and the educational. These institutions have survived the Revolutionary War, Civil War, World War, and the world depression in the two hundred year history of the United States. Western civilization is rooted in the five thousand year recorded history. Whole civilizations have developed and disappeared during this time span. Man will survive. Some of his institutions will survive. The question is which institutions and how much of his society.

The probability of the survival of our society as it exists today is not good. The twenty year delay in the recognition of physical economics and our dependence on a depleting energy resource may be damning.

Pecuniary economic concepts dominate the society. They control almost every political and business institution. These dominant segments of the society control the religious, educational, and cultural institutions. As a consequence of the control of ideas and concepts, the critical information — the physical economics, the significance of time in the survival equation — is not available for consideration.

Economic theory does not require a time denominated projection of the supply and demand balance. Society must wait for the market to determine the price and for the price to stimulate men to produce that which is needed for the free economy. The market will take care of the future. The tools of the engineer are not appropriate.

The *economic* prescription spells failure for both the free society and the free economy. Actually, neither the free society nor the free economy is dependent on the *established economics*. Physical economics

in combination with pecuniary economics is available to the free society
and the majority of our institutions can be salvaged through the development of an economics for the free society that is not rooted in conflict
and outmoded assumptions.

These considerations lead to the question of the source of leadership and the development of political and economic principles. The
absence of a broadly based compatible political and economic discipline
becomes a serious problem. The national constituency imperative which I
discussed in Chapter XVI necessitates a highly centralized leadership and
a very substantial reduction in the prerogatives of individuals and their
independent institutions.

My greatest hope for a solution to this problem has been based on
the universities. They are vital to a free society. They are broadly
distributed geographically. They have already corraled a substantial
segment of the thinking population. They are organized to preserve freedom. But the universities are also organized to avoid decision, and the
required development of broad interdisciplinary relationships is almost
impossible. The university protects the individual scholar who is established in the university. The university protects the discipline that
has been accepted. The university discourages innovation both within
and between disciplines. Knowledge can be extended but the new must not
encroach on the established, and conflicts between the disciplines are
resolved by isolation. There is no interdisciplinary authority except
the administration, and within the university, the administration has
become the enemy.

The frustrations of the university are a reflection of the frustrations of the society. The university could lead the society out of its
frustrations. But what are the probabilities? They are not good. Mighty
Gulliver cannot escape his bonds.

In the Middle Ages the monasteries maintained the cultural inheritance of civilization and developed the forms of our modern society. It
may be necessary to think in these terms. Democracy in the political
process will be curtailed, and the political process will accelerate its
encroachment on the free economy. The availability of energy will determine the speed of this process and the ultimate survival of the works of
man.

Only the energy that remains in the biosphere or enters from the sun is available in resolving the problem of the future. Only future time can be employed. And only net energy which can be processed in the sequential time frames of capital accumulation can be counted. The laws of physics cannot be violated. Will man alter his relationships to accomodate necessity? It remains a question. There is no current evidence that he will in time to avoid more economic chaos than the world has seen.

APPENDIX

SUMMATION OF HISTORIC U. S. PETROLEUM PRODUCTION
AND TEN YEAR <u>KNOWN OIL FORECAST</u>

Based on F.E.A. Sample of Fields Accounting for 52% of U. S. Proved Reserves
and U. S. Department of Interior Monthly Petroleum Statement

Billions of Barrels Per Year

	55 Selected Lower 48 State Fields	Remaining Lower 48 State Fields	Subtotal Lower 48 Sts.(CO+LC) Production	Alaska Including Prudhoe Bay	Natural Gas Liquids, Incl. Alaska After 1981	Total Domestic Production
1973	1.008	2.281	3.289	.072	.634	3.995
1974	.989	2.143	3.132	.071	.616	3.819
1975	.949	2.033	2.982	.070	.596	3.648
1976	.888	1.912	2.800	.070	.546	3.416
1977	.812	1.808	2.620	.146	.498	3.264
1978	.743	1.697	2.440	.515	.451	3.406
1979	.680	1.580	2.260	.548	.407	3.215
1980	.616	1.464	2.080	.548	.364	2.992
1981	.563	1.337	1.900	.548	.323	2.771
1982	.514	1.211	1.725	.548	.340	2.613
1983	.469	1.071	1.540	.547	.301	2.388
1984	.421	.939	1.360	.547	.266	2.173
1985	.375	.803	1.178	.547	.232	1.957

DOMESTIC DEMAND FOR REFINED PRODUCTS
(Billions of Barrels/Year)

Source: US Bureau of Mines, Department of Interior

Projected Demand at Zero Per Capita Consumption
Increase & 1½% Annual Adult Population Increase

Historic		Projected	
1947	2.003	1976	6.080
1948	2.122	1977	6.173
1949	2.120	1978	6.266
1950	2.393	1979	6.360
1951	2.579	1980	6.455
1952	2.668	1981	6.552
1953	2.777	1982	6.651
1954	2.834	1983	6.750
1955	3.089	1984	6.852
1956	3.215	1985	6.954
1957	3.222	1986	7.059
1958	3.328	1987	7.165
1959	3.477	1988	7.272
1960	3.586	1989	7.381
1961	3.641	1990	7.492
1962	3.796	1991	7.604
1963	3.922	1992	7.718
1964	4.034	1993	7.834
1965	4.202	1994	7.952
1966	4.411	1995	8.071
1967	4.584	1996	8.192
1968	4.902	1997	8.315
1969	5.160	1998	8.440
1970	5.364	1999	8.566
1971	5.553	2000	8.695
1972	5.990		
1973	6.317	2005	9.367
1974	6.078		
1975	5.946	2010	10.091

EEEe Revised Study May 1976

THE DECLINING SUPPLY OF DOMESTIC CRUDE OIL
(Billions of Barrels)
Source: American Petroleum Institute

Year	Proved Reserve Additions	Proved Reserves At Year End	Reserve/ Demand Ratio	Year	Proved Reserve Additions	Proved Reserves At Year End	Reserve/ Demand Ratio
1900	-	1.000	-	1970	3.089*	29.401*	5.5*
1905	-	1.800	-	1971	2.318	28.463*	5.1*
1910	-	2.800	-	1972	1.558	26.739*	4.5*
1915	-	3.800	-	1973	2.146	25.700*	4.1*
1920	-	5.500	-	1974	1.994	24.700*	4.1*
1925	-	9.000	-	1975	1.300	23.100*	3.9*
1930	-	13.200	-				
1935	-	13.000	-	* Excludes 9.6 Billion Bbl.			
1940	-	19.000	-	Prudhoe Bay Discovery			
1945	-	20.500	-				
1946	2.658	20.874	-				
1947	2.465	21.488	10.7				
1948	3.795	23.280	11.0				
1949	3.188	24.649	11.6				
1950	2.563	25.268	10.6				
1951	4.414	27.468	10.7	1970	12.689**	39.001**	7.3**
1952	2.749	27.961	10.5	1971	2.318	38.063**	6.9**
1953	3.296	28.945	10.4	1972	1.558	36.339**	6.1**
1954	2.873	29.561	10.4	1973	2.146	35.300**	5.6**
1955	2.871	30.012	9.7	1974	1.994	34.300**	5.6**
1956	2.974	30.435	9.5	1975	1.300	32.700**	5.5**
1957	2.425	30.300	9.4				
1958	2.608	30.536	9.2	** Includes 9.6 Billion Bbl.			
1959	3.667	31.719	9.1	Prudhoe Bay Discovery			
1960	2.365	31.613	8.8				
1961	2.658	31.759	8.7				
1962	2.181	31.389	8.3				
1963	2.174	30.970	7.9				
1964	2.665	30.991	7.7				
1965	3.048	31.352	7.5				
1966	2.964	31.452	7.1				
1967	2.962	31.377	6.8				
1968	2.455	30.707	6.3				
1969	2.120	29.632	5.7				

EEEe Revised Study May 1976

HISTORIC DOMESTIC PRODUCTION OF LIQUID HYDROCARBONS

Source: US Bureau of Mines, Department of Interior
(Billion Barrels/Year)

| | CONTERMINOUS U.S. | | | ALASKA | | Total Domestic Production |
Year	Crude Oil	Lease Condensate	Natural Gas Liquids	Crude Oil + Lease Condensate	Natural Gas Liquids	Crude Oil + Lease Condensate + Natural Gas Liquids + Alaksa
1975	2.850	.132	.596	.070	Neg.	3.648
1974	2.986	.146	.616	.071	Neg.	3.819
1973	3.134	.155	.634	.072	Neg.	3.995
1972	3.220	.162	.638	.073	Neg.	4.093
1971	3.219	.157	.618	.078	Neg.	4.072
1970	3.268	.167	.606	.083	Neg.	4.124
1969	3.130	.168	.580	.074	Neg.	3.952
1968	3.104	.159	.550	.066	Neg.	3.879
1967		3.187	.514	.029	Neg.	3.730
1966		3.014	.469	.014	Neg.	3.497
1965		2.837	.442	.011	Neg.	3.290
1964		2.776	.423	.011	Neg.	3.210
1963		2.742	.401	.011	Neg.	3.154
1962		2.666	.373	.010	Neg.	3.049
1961		2.616	.362	.006	Neg.	2.984
1960		2.574	.340	.001	Neg.	2.915
1959		2.574	.321	Neg.	Neg.	2.895
1958		2.449	.295	Neg.	Neg.	2.744
1957		2.617	.295	Neg.	Neg.	2.912
1956		2.617	.293	Neg.	Neg.	2.910
1955		2.484	.281	Neg.	Neg.	2.765
1954		2.315	.252	Neg.	Neg.	2.567
1953		2.357	.239	Neg.	Neg.	2.596
1952		2.290	.224	Neg.	Neg.	2.514
1951		2.248	.205	Neg.	Neg.	2.453
1950		1.974	.182	Neg.	Neg.	2.156
1949		1.842	.157	Neg.	Neg.	1.999
1948		2.020	.147	Neg.	Neg.	2.167
1947		1.857	.132	Neg.	Neg.	1.989
1946		1.734	.111	Neg.	Neg.	1.845
1945		1.714	.098	Neg.	Neg.	1.812
1944		1.678	.084	Neg.	Neg.	1.762
1943		1.506	.065	Neg.	Neg.	1.571
1942		1.387	.050	Neg.	Neg.	1.437
1941		1.402	.042	Neg.	Neg.	1.444
1940		1.353	.027	Neg.	Neg.	1.380

EEEe Revised Study May 1976

Measured Reserve   = 24.156
Indicated Reserve   =   4.623
Inferred Reserve   = 16.900
Undiscovered Rec Res = 81.000
Remaining Reserve: 126.679

CONTERMINOUS US CRUDE OIL PRODUCTION
(Excludes LC, NGL's, & Alaska)
Maximum Approach (232.205 ORO)*

Year	% WR	Multiplier	Starting Reserve	Remaining Reserve	Crude Oil Production	Cumulative Production	% ORO	% ORO Remaining
1940	.62%	.9938	(208.567)=	207.279	1.288	24.926	10.7%	89.3%
1941	.64%	.9936	(207.279)=	205.944	1.335	26.261	11.3%	88.7%
1942	.64%	.9936	(205.944)=	204.623	1.321	27.582	11.9%	88.1%
1943	.70%	.9930	(204.623)=	203.189	1.424	29.016	12.5%	87.5%
1944	.79%	.9921	(203.189)=	201.591	1.598	30.614	13.2%	86.8%
1945	.81%	.9919	(201.591)=	199.959	1.632	32.246	13.9%	86.1%
1946	.83%	.9917	(199.959)=	198.308	1.651	33.897	14.6%	85.4%
1947	.89%	.9911	(198.308)=	196.540	1.768	35.665	15.4%	84.6%
1948	.98%	.9902	(196.540)=	194.617	1.923	37.588	16.2%	83.8%
1949	.90%	.9910	(194.617)=	192.863	1.754	39.342	16.9%	83.1%
1950	.97%	.9903	(192.863)=	190.983	1.880	41.222	17.8%	82.2%
1951	1.12%	.9888	(190.983)=	188.842	2.141	43.363	18.7%	81.3%
1952	1.15%	.9885	(188.842)=	186.661	2.181	45.544	19.6%	80.4%
1953	1.20%	.9880	(186.661)=	184.417	2.244	47.788	20.6%	79.4%
1954	1.20%	.9880	(184.417)=	182.213	2.204	49.992	21.5%	78.5%
1955	1.30%	.9870	(182.213)=	179.848	2.365	52.357	22.6%	77.4%
1956	1.39%	.9861	(179.848)=	177.356	2.492	54.849	23.6%	76.4%
1957	1.41%	.9859	(177.356)=	174.864	2.492	57.341	24.7%	75.3%
1958	1.33%	.9867	(174.864)=	172.532	2.332	59.673	25.7%	74.3%
1959	1.42%	.9858	(172.532)=	170.081	2.451	62.124	26.8%	73.2%
1960	1.44%	.9856	(170.081)=	167.630	2.451	64.575	27.8%	72.2%
1961	1.49%	.9851	(167.630)=	165.139	2.491	67.066	28.9%	71.1%
1962	1.54%	.9846	(165.139)=	162.600	2.539	69.605	30.0%	70.0%
1963	1.61%	.9839	(162.600)=	159.989	2.611	72.216	31.1%	68.9%
1964	1.65%	.9835	(159.989)=	157.346	2.643	74.859	32.2%	67.8%
1965	1.72%	.9828	(157.346)=	154.645	2.701	77.560	33.4%	66.6%
1966	1.86%	.9814	(154.645)=	151.775	2.870	80.430	34.6%	65.4%
1967	2.00%	.9800	(151.775)=	148.740	3.035	83.465	35.9%	64.1%
1968	2.09%	.9791	(148.740)=	145.636	3.104	86.569	37.3%	62.7%
1969	2.15%	.9785	(145.636)=	142.506	3.130	89.699	38.6%	61.4%
1970	2.29%	.9771	(142.506)=	139.238	3.268	92.967	40.0%	60.0%
1971	2.31%	.9769	(139.238)=	136.019	3.219	96.186	41.4%	58.6%
1972	2.37%	.9763	(136.019)=	132.799	3.220	99.406	42.8%	57.2%
1973	2.36%	.9764	(132.799)=	129.665	3.134	102.540	44.2%	55.8%
1974	2.30%	.9770	(129.665)=	126.679	2.986	105.526	45.5%	54.5%
1975	2.25%	.9775	(126.679)=	123.829	2.850	108.376	46.7%	53.3%

*Original recoverable oil Ref. Exhibit I

EEEe Revised Study May 1976

Measured Reserve   = 24.156
Indicated Reserve   = 4.623
Inferred Reserve   = 16.900
Undiscovered Rec Res = 36.000
Remaining Reserve: 81.679

CONTERMINOUS US CRUDE OIL PRODUCTION
(Excludes LC, NGL's, & Alaska)
Minimum Approach (187.205 ORO)*

Year	% WR	Multiplier	Starting Reserve	Remaining Reserve	Crude Oil Production	Cumulative Production	% ORO	% ORO Remaining
1940	.79%	.9921	(163.567)=	162.279	1.288	24.926	13.3%	86.7%
1941	.82%	.9918	(162.279)=	160.944	1.335	26.261	14.0%	86.0%
1942	.82%	.9918	(160.944)=	159.623	1.321	27.582	14.7%	85.3%
1943	.90%	.9910	(159.623)=	158.189	1.434	29.016	15.5%	84.5%
1944	1.01%	.9899	(158.189)=	156.591	1.598	30.614	16.4%	83.6%
1945	1.04%	.9896	(156.591)=	154.959	1.632	32.246	17.2%	82.8%
1946	1.07%	.9893	(154.959)=	153.308	1.651	33.897	18.1%	81.9%
1947	1.15%	.9885	(153.308)=	151.540	1.768	35.665	19.1%	80.9%
1948	1.27%	.9873	(151.540)=	149.617	1.923	37.588	20.1%	79.9%
1949	1.17%	.9883	(149.863)=	147.863	1.754	39.342	21.0%	79.0%
1950	1.27%	.9873	(147.863)=	145.983	1.880	41.222	22.0%	78.0%
1951	1.47%	.9853	(145.983)=	143.842	2.141	43.363	23.2%	76.8%
1952	1.52%	.9848	(143.842)=	141.661	2.181	45.544	24.3%	75.7%
1953	1.58%	.9842	(141.661)=	139.417	2.244	47.788	25.5%	74.5%
1954	1.58%	.9842	(139.417)=	137.213	2.204	49.992	26.7%	73.3%
1955	1.72%	.9828	(137.213)=	134.848	2.365	52.357	28.0%	72.0%
1956	1.85%	.9815	(134.848)=	132.356	2.492	54.849	29.3%	70.7%
1957	1.88%	.9812	(132.356)=	129.864	2.492	57.341	30.6%	69.4%
1958	1.80%	.9820	(129.864)=	127.532	2.332	59.673	31.9%	68.1%
1959	1.92%	.9808	(127.532)=	125.081	2.451	62.124	33.2%	66.8%
1960	1.96%	.9804	(125.081)=	122.630	2.451	64.575	34.5%	65.5%
1961	2.03%	.9797	(122.630)=	120.139	2.491	67.066	35.8%	64.2%
1962	2.11%	.9789	(120.139)=	117.600	2.539	69.605	37.2%	62.8%
1963	2.22%	.9778	(117.600)=	114.989	2.611	72.216	38.6%	61.4%
1964	2.30%	.9770	(114.989)=	112.346	2.643	74.859	40.0%	60.0%
1965	2.40%	.9760	(112.346)=	109.645	2.701	77.560	41.4%	58.6%
1966	2.62%	.9738	(109.645)=	106.775	2.870	80.430	43.0%	57.0%
1967	2.84%	.9716	(106.775)=	103.740	3.035	83.465	44.6%	55.4%
1968	2.99%	.9701	(103.740)=	100.636	3.104	86.569	46.2%	53.8%
1969	3.11%	.9689	(100.636)=	97.506	3.130	89.699	47.9%	52.1%
1970	3.35%	.9665	(97.506)=	94.238	3.268	92.967	49.7%	50.3%
1971	3.42%	.9658	(94.238)=	91.019	3.219	96.186	51.4%	48.6%
1972	3.54%	.9646	(91.019)=	87.799	3.220	99.406	53.1%	46.9%
1973	3.57%	.9643	(87.799)=	84.665	3.134	102.540	54.8%	45.2%
1974	3.53%	.9647	(84.665)=	<u>81.679</u>	2.986	105.526	56.4%	43.6%
1975	3.49%	.9651	(<u>81.679</u>)=	78.829	2.850	108.376	57.9%	42.1%

*Original recoverable oil, Ref. Exh. I   -195-

EEEe Revised Study May 1976

SUMMARY OF DOMESTIC LIQUID HYDROCARBON PRODUCTION

Maximum Approach

(Billion Bbls/Year)

Year	Conterminous U.S. Crude Oil	Conterminous U.S. Lease Condensate	Conterminous U.S. NGL's	Alaska Crude Oil	Alaska Lease Condensate	Alaska NGL's	Total Liquid Hydrocarbon Production
1975	2.850	.132	.596	.070	–	–	3.648
1976	2.691	.121	.538	.070	–	–	3.420
1977	2.552	.112	.510	.146	–	–	3.320
1978	2.410	.103	.482	.515	–	–	3.510
1979	2.348	.097	.458	.547	–	–	3.450
1980	2.284	.092	.434	.585	–	–	3.395
1981	2.231	.087	.413	.657	–	–	3.388
1982	2.186	.083	.394	.767	–	.077	3.507
1983	2.143	.079	.375	.875	–	.087	3.559
1984	2.099	.075	.357	.875	–	.087	3.493
1985	2.058	.071	.340	.875	.004	.087	3.435
1986	2.017	.067	.323	.875	.009	.087	3.378
1987	1.976	.063	.306	.875	.013	.087	3.320
1988	1.937	.060	.291	.875	.018	.087	3.268
1989	1.897	.056	.275	.875	.022	.087	3.212
1990	1.860	.053	.260	.875	.026	.088	3.162
1991	1.823	.049	.246	.875	.031	.088	3.112
1992	1.787	.046	.232	.875	.035	.088	3.063
1993	1.750	.043	.219	.875	.035	.088	3.010
1994	1.716	.040	.206	.875	.035	.088	2.960
1995	1.681	.038	.193	.875	.031	.088	2.906
1996	1.648	.035	.181	.875	.026	.088	2.853
1997	1.614	.032	.170	.875	.022	.088	2.801
1998	1.583	.030	.158	.875	.018	.087	2.751
1999	1.551	.027	.147	.857	.013	.086	2.681
2000	1.519	.025	.137	.841	.008	.084	2.614
2005	1.373	.014	.089	.770	–	.077	2.323
2010	1.242	.005	.050	.705	–	.071	2.073

Measured Reserve = 24.156
Indicated Reserve = 4.623
Inferred Reserve = 16.900
Undiscovered Rec Res = 81.000
Remaining Reserve: 126.679

CONTERMINOUS U.S. CRUDE OIL PROJECTED PRODUCTION
(Excludes LC & NGL's)   (On & Offshore)
Maximum Approach (232.205 ORO)*

Year	% WR	Multiplier	Starting Reserve	Remaining Reserve	Crude Oil Production	Cumulative Production	% ORO	% ORO Remaining
1975	2.25%	.9775	(126.679)=	123.829	2.850	108.376	46.7%	53.3%
1976	2.17%	.9783	(123.829)=	121.138	2.691	111.067	47.8%	52.2%
1977	2.11%	.9789	(121.138)=	118.586	2.552	113.619	48.9%	51.1%
1978	2.03%	.9797	(118.586)=	116.176	2.410	116.029	50.0%	50.0%
1979	2.02%	.9798	(116.176)=	113.828	2.348	118.377	51.0%	49.0%
1980	2.01%	.9799	(113.828)=	111.544	2.284	120.661	52.0%	48.0%
1981	2.00%	.9800	(111.544)=	109.313	2.231	122.892	52.9%	47.1%
1982	2.00%	.9800	(109.313)=	107.127	2.186	125.078	53.9%	46.1%
1983	2.00%	.9800	(107.127)=	104.984	2.143	127.221	54.8%	45.2%
1984	2.00%	.9800	(104.984)=	102.885	2.099	129.320	55.7%	44.3%
1985	2.00%	.9800	(102.885)=	100.827	2.058	131.378	56.6%	43.4%
1986	2.00%	.9800	(100.827)	98.810	2.017	133.395	57.5%	42.5%
1987	2.00%	.9800	(98.810)=	96.834	1.976	135.371	58.3%	41.7%
1988	2.00%	.9800	(96.834)=	94.897	1.937	137.308	59.1%	40.9%
1989	2.00%	.9800	(94.897)=	93.000	1.897	139.205	60.0%	40.0%
1990	2.00%	.9800	(93.000)=	91.140	1.860	141.065	60.8%	39.2%
1991	2.00%	.9800	(91.140)=	89.317	1.823	142.888	61.5%	38.5%
1992	2.00%	.9800	(89.317)=	87.530	1.787	144.675	62.3%	37.7%
1993	2.00%	.9800	(87.530)=	85.780	1.750	146.425	63.1%	36.9%
1994	2.00%	.9800	(85.780)=	84.064	1.716	148.141	63.8%	36.2%
1995	2.00%	.9800	(84.064)=	82.383	1.681	149.822	64.5%	35.5%
1996	2.00%	.9800	(82.383)=	80.735	1.648	151.470	65.2%	34.8%
1997	2.00%	.9800	(80.735)=	79.121	1.614	153.084	65.9%	34.1%
1998	2.00%	.9800	(79.121)=	77.538	1.583	154.667	66.6%	33.4%
1999	2.00%	.9800	(77.538)=	75.987	1.551	156.218	67.3%	32.7%
2000	2.00%	.9800	(75.987)=	74.468	1.519	157.737	67.9%	32.1%
2005	2.00%	.9800	(68.686)=	67.313	1.373	164.892	71.0%	29.0%
2010	2.00%	.9800	(62.087)=	60.845	1.242	171.360	73.8%	26.2%

*Original recoverable oil, Ref. Exh. 1

EEEe Revised Study May 1976

Measured Reserve   = 10.094
Indicated Reserve   =   .013
Inferred Reserve   = 6.200
Undiscovered Rec Res = 50.000
Remaining Reserve: 66.307

ALASKA CRUDE OIL PROJECTED PRODUCTION
(Excludes LC & NGL's)
Maximum Approach (66.917 ORO)*

Year	% WR	Multiplier	Starting Reserve	Remaining Reserve	Crude Oil Production	Cumulative Production	% ORO	% ORO Remaining
1975	.11%	.9989	(66.307)=	66.237	.070	.680	1.0%	99.0%
1976	.11%	.9989	(66.237)=	66.167	.070	.750	1.1%	98.9%
1977	.22%	.9978	(66.167)=	66.021	.146	.896	1.3%	98.7%
1978	.78%	.9922	(66.021)=	65.506	.515	1.411	2.1%	97.9%
1979	.84%	.9916	(65.506)=	64.959	.547	1.958	2.9%	97.1%
1980	.90%	.9910	(64.959)=	64.374	.585	2.543	3.8%	96.2%
1981	1.02%	.9898	(64.374)=	63.717	.657	3.200	4.8%	95.2%
1982	1.20%	.9880	(63.717)=	62.950	.767	3.967	5.9%	94.1%
1983	1.39%	.9861	(62.950)=	62.075	.875	4.842	7.2%	92.8%
1984	1.41%	.9859	(62.075)=	61.200	.875	5.717	8.5%	91.5%
1985	1.43%	.9857	(61.200)=	60.325	.875	6.592	9.9%	90.1%
1986	1.45%	.9855	(60.325)=	59.450	.875	7.467	11.2%	88.8%
1987	1.47%	.9853	(59.450)=	58.575	.875	8.342	12.5%	87.5%
1988	1.49%	.9851	(58.575)=	57.700	.875	9.217	13.8%	86.2%
1989	1.52%	.9848	(57.700)=	56.825	.875	10.092	15.1%	84.9%
1990	1.54%	.9846	(56.825)=	55.950	.875	10.967	16.4%	83.6%
1991	1.56%	.9844	(55.950)=	55.075	.875	11.842	17.7%	82.3%
1992	1.59%	.9841	(55.075)=	54.200	.875	12.717	19.0%	81.0%
1993	1.61%	.9839	(54.200)=	53.325	.875	13.592	20.3%	79.7%
1994	1.64%	.9836	(53.325)=	52.450	.875	14.467	21.6%	78.4%
1995	1.67%	.9833	(52.450)=	51.575	.875	15.342	22.9%	77.1%
1996	1.70%	.9830	(51.575)=	50.700	.875	16.217	24.2%	75.8%
1997	1.73%	.9827	(50.700)=	49.825	.875	17.092	25.5%	74.5%
1998	1.76%	.9824	(49.825)=	48.950	.875	17.967	26.9%	73.1%
1999	1.75%	.9825	(48.950)=	48.093	.857	18.824	28.1%	71.9%
2000	1.75%	.9825	(48.093)=	47.252	.841	19.665	29.4%	70.6%
2005	1.75%	.9825	(44.030)=	43.260	.770	23.657	35.4%	64.6%
2010	1.75%	.9825	(40.310)=	39.605	.705	27.312	40.8%	59.2%

*Original recoverable oil, Ref. Exh. I

EEEe Revised Study May 1976

SUMMARY OF DOMESTIC LIQUID HYDROCARBON PRODUCTION

Minimum Approach

(Billion Bbls/Year)

Year	Conterminous U.S. Crude Oil	Conterminous U.S. Lease Condensate	Conterminous U.S. NGL's	Alaska Crude Oil	Alaska Lease Condensate	Alaska NGL's	Total Liquid Hydrocarbon Production
1975	2.850	.132	.596	.070	-	-	3.648
1976	2.691	.121	.538	.070	-	-	3.420
1977	2.552	.112	.510	.146	-	-	3.320
1978	2.410	.103	.482	.515	-	-	3.510
1979	2.348	.097	.458	.547	-	-	3.450
1980	2.284	.092	.434	.585	-	-	3.395
1981	2.216	.087	.410	.657	-	-	3.370
1982	2.142	.081	.386	.694	-	.069	3.372
1983	2.071	.076	.362	.693	-	.069	3.271
1984	2.002	.071	.340	.694	-	.069	3.176
1985	1.935	.066	.319	.693	.004	.069	3.086
1986	1.871	.062	.299	.694	.007	.069	3.002
1987	1.808	.058	.280	.674	.010	.067	2.897
1988	1.748	.054	.262	.650	.013	.065	2.792
1989	1.690	.050	.245	.627	.016	.063	2.691
1990	1.634	.046	.229	.606	.018	.061	2.594
1991	1.579	.043	.213	.584	.020	.058	2.497
1992	1.527	.040	.199	.564	.023	.056	2.409
1993	1.476	.037	.185	.544	.022	.054	2.318
1994	1.426	.034	.171	.525	.021	.053	2.230
1995	1.380	.031	.159	.506	.018	.051	2.145
1996	1.333	.028	.147	.489	.015	.049	2.061
1997	1.289	.026	.135	.472	.012	.047	1.981
1998	1.246	.023	.125	.455	.009	.046	1.904
1999	1.204	.021	.114	.440	.007	.044	1.830
2000	1.165	.019	.105	.424	.004	.042	1.759
2005	.983	.010	.064	.355	-	.036	1.448
2010	.830	.004	.033	.297	-	.030	1.194

Measured Reserve   = 24.156
Indicated Reserve   = 4.623
Inferred Reserve   = 16.900
Undiscovered Rec Res = 36.000
Remaining Reserve: 81.679

CONTERMINOUS U.S. CRUDE OIL PROJECTED PRODUCTION
(Excludes LC & NGL's)   (On & Offshore)
Minimum Approach (187.205 ORO) *

Year	% WR	Multiplier	Starting Reserve	Remaining Reserve	Crude Oil Production	Cumulative Production	% ORO	% ORO Remaining
1975	3.49%	.9651	(81.679)=	78.829	2.850	108.376	57.9%	42.1%
1976	3.41%	.9659	(78.829)=	76.138	2.691	111.067	59.3%	40.7%
1977	3.35%	.9665	(76.138)=	73.586	2.552	113.619	60.7%	39.3%
1978	3.28%	.9672	(73.586)=	71.176	2.410	116.029	62.0%	38.0%
1979	3.30%	.9670	(71.176)=	68.828	2.348	118.377	63.2%	36.8%
1980	3.32%	.9668	(68.828)=	66.544	2.284	120.661	64.5%	35.5%
1981	3.33%	.9667	(66.544)=	64.328	2.216	122.877	65.6%	34.4%
1982	3.33%	.9667	(64.328)=	62.186	2.142	125.019	66.8%	33.2%
1983	3.33%	.9667	(62.186)=	60.115	2.071	127.090	67.9%	32.1%
1984	3.33%	.9667	(60.115)=	58.113	2.002	129.092	69.0%	31.0%
1985	3.33%	.9667	(58.113)=	56.178	1.935	131.027	70.0%	30.0%
1986	3.33%	.9667	(56.178)=	54.307	1.871	132.898	71.0%	29.0%
1987	3.33%	.9667	(54.307)=	52.499	1.808	134.706	72.0%	28.0%
1988	3.33%	.9667	(52.499)=	50.751	1.748	136.454	72.9%	27.1%
1989	3.33%	.9667	(50.751)=	49.061	1.690	138.144	73.8%	26.2%
1990	3.33%	.9667	(49.061)=	47.427	1.634	139.778	74.7%	25.3%
1991	3.33%	.9667	(47.427)=	45.848	1.579	141.357	75.5%	24.5%
1992	3.33%	.9667	(45.858)=	44.321	1.527	142.884	76.3%	23.7%
1993	3.33%	.9667	(44.321)=	42.845	1.476	144.360	77.1%	22.9%
1994	3.33%	.9667	(42.845)=	41.419	1.426	145.786	77.9%	22.1%
1995	3.33%	.9667	(41.419)=	40.039	1.380	147.166	78.6%	21.4%
1996	3.33%	.9667	(40.039)=	38.706	1.333	148.499	79.3%	20.7%
1997	3.33%	.9667	(38.706)=	37.417	1.289	149.788	80.0%	20.0%
1998	3.33%	.9667	(37.417)=	36.171	1.246	151.034	80.7%	19.3%
1999	3.33%	.9667	(36.171)=	34.967	1.204	152.238	81.3%	18.7%
2000	3.33%	.9667	(34.967)=	33.802	1.165	153.403	81.9%	18.1%
2005	3.33%	.9667	(29.520)=	28.537	.983	158.668	84.8%	15.2%
2010	3.33%	.9667	(24.921)=	24.091	.830	163.114	87.1%	12.9%

*Original recoverable oil, Ref. Exh. 1

EEEe Revised Study May 1976   -200-

Measured Reserve	= 10.094
Indicated Reserve	= .013
Inferred Reserve	= 6.200
Undiscovered Rec Res	= 9.000
Remaining Reserve:	25.307

ALASKA CRUDE OIL PROJECTED PRODUCTION
(Excludes LC & NGL's)
Minimum Approach (25.917 ORO)*

Year	% WR	Multiplier	Starting Reserve	Remaining Reserve	Crude Oil Production	Cumulative Production	% ORO	% ORO Remaining
1975	.28%	.9972	(25.307)=	25.237	.070	.680	2.6%	97.4%
1976	.28%	.9972	(25.237)=	25.167	.070	.750	2.9%	97.1%
1977	.58%	.9942	(25.167)=	25.021	.146	.896	3.5%	96.5%
1978	2.06%	.9794	(25.021)=	24.506	.515	1.411	5.4%	94.6%
1979	2.23%	.9777	(24.506)=	23.959	.547	1.958	7.6%	92.4%
1980	2.44%	.9756	(23.959)=	23.374	.585	2.543	9.8%	90.2%
1981	2.81%	.9719	(23.374)=	22.717	.657	3.200	12.4%	87.6%
1982	3.05%	.9695	(22.717)=	22.023	.694	3.894	15.0%	85.0%
1983	3.15%	.9685	(22.023)=	21.330	.693	4.587	17.7%	82.3%
1984	3.25%	.9675	(21.330)=	20.636	.694	5.281	20.4%	79.6%
1985	3.36%	.9664	(20.636)=	19.943	.693	5.974	23.1%	76.9%
1986	3.48%	.9652	(19.943)=	19.249	.694	6.668	25.7%	74.3%
1987	3.50%	.9650	(19.249)=	18.575	.674	7.342	28.3%	71.7%
1988	3.50%	.9650	(18.575)=	17.925	.650	7.992	30.8%	69.2%
1989	3.50%	.9650	(17.925)=	17.298	.627	8.619	33.3%	66.7%
1990	3.50%	.9650	(17.298)=	16.692	.606	9.225	35.6%	64.4%
1991	3.50%	.9650	(16.692)=	16.108	.584	9.809	37.9%	62.1%
1992	3.50%	.9650	(16.108)=	15.544	.564	10.373	40.0%	60.0%
1993	3.50%	.9650	(15.544)=	15.000	.544	10.917	42.1%	57.9%
1994	3.50%	.9650	(15.000)=	14.475	.525	11.442	44.2%	55.8%
1995	3.50%	.9650	(14.475)=	13.969	.506	11.948	46.1%	53.9%
1996	3.50%	.9650	(13.969)=	13.480	.489	12.437	48.0%	52.0%
1997	3.50%	.9650	(13.480)=	13.008	.472	12.909	49.8%	50.2%
1998	3.50%	.9650	(13.008)=	12.553	.455	13.364	51.6%	48.4%
1999	3.50%	.9650	(12.553)=	12.113	.440	13.804	53.3%	46.7%
2000	3.50%	.9650	(12.113)=	11.689	.424	14.228	54.9%	45.1%
2005	3.50%	.9650	(10.137)=	9.782	.355	16.135	62.3%	37.7%
2010	3.50%	.9650	(8.483)=	8.186	.297	17.731	68.4%	31.6%

*Original recoverable oil, Ref. Exh. I

Federal Energy Administration

"1976 NATIONAL ENERGY OUTLOOK"

Revised Domestic Production Projections

Billion Bbls Liquid Hydrocarbons

Reference — Pages G-2 thru G-24

	$8.00/Bbl.	$13.00/Bbl.	$16.00/Bbl.
1985 Reference Case	4.15	5.06	5.46
1985 Conservation Case	4.05	5.11	5.51
1985 Accelerated Case	4.69	5.84	6.29
1985 Accelerated Supply, BAU Demand W/O Load Mgmt.	4.71	6.42	6.79
1985 $7.50 Regulation Case	-	3.61	3.61
1985 $9.00 Regulation Case	-	4.18	4.18
1985 Electrification Case	4.12	5.04	5.45
1985 Regional Limitation Case #1, With Conservation Demand	4.02	4.98	5.18
1985 Regional Limitation Case #2	4.02	4.99	5.19
1985 Supply Pessimism Case	-	3.50	3.50
1980 Reference Case	4.36	4.66	4.77
1990 Reference Case	3.22	5.05	5.57

EEEe Revised Study May 1976

SUMMARY OF MAXIMUM APPROACH,
HISTORIC & PROJECTED NATURAL GAS REGIONAL PRODUCTION - TCF/Yr
Revised 5/5/76

Maximum Approach

Year	Region 1 On & Off	Region 2 On & Off	Region 3	Region 4	Region 5	Region 6 On Only	Region 7	Regions 8,9,10,11 + Misc. On Only	Region 11A Off Only	Region 6A Off Only	Maximum Domestic Production
1965	.008	.628	.598	.448	1.903	8.029	3.192	.458	-	.989	16.253
1966	.013	.686	.627	.435	2.003	8.421	3.416	.461	-	1.347	17.409
1967	.023	.660	.657	.428	2.084	8.533	3.663	.487	-	1.827	18.362
1968	.042	.685	.716	.458	2.312	8.942	3.737	.496	-	2.288	19.676
1969	.081	.659	.664	.482	2.532	9.341	3.984	.475	-	2.733	20.951
1970	.145	.636	.635	.490	3.015	9.429	4.218	.505	-	3.200	22.273
1971	.154	.572	.675	.501	3.122	9.278	3.804	.485	-	3.423	22.014
1972	.147	.499	.704	.531	3.349	9.215	3.967	.475	-	3.873	22.760
1973	.136	.478	.682	.549	3.350	8.565	3.882	.480	-	4.169	22.291
1974	.144	.357	.677	.490	3.377	7.820	3.850	.506	-	4.095	21.316
1975	.155	.332	.662	.465	2.950	6.829	3.687	.521	-	4.119	19.720
1976	.154	.307	.665	.457	2.657	6.101	3.543	.530	-	4.106	18.520
1977	.172	.283	.663	.442	2.379	5.438	3.401	.536	-	4.092	17.406
1978	.197	.260	.665	.433	2.114	4.773	3.265	.544	-	4.073	16.324
1979	.197	.258	.652	.429	2.082	4.702	3.192	.535	-	3.981	16.028
1980	.202	.256	.640	.426	2.052	4.632	3.120	.527	-	3.892	15.747
1981	.303	.254	.628	.423	2.020	4.562	3.050	.519	-	3.805	15.564
1982	.584	.252	.616	.420	1.990	4.493	2.981	.512	-	3.719	15.567
1983	.875	.250	.604	.489	1.960	4.426	2.914	.504	-	3.635	15.657
1984	.981	.249	.592	.551	1.931	4.360	2.848	.496	-	3.553	15.561
1985	1.073	.247	.582	.616	1.902	4.294	2.785	.489	.003	3.474	15.465
1986	1.066	.245	.570	.674	1.873	4.230	2.722	.481	.018	3.395	15.274
1987	1.060	.243	.559	.735	1.846	4.167	2.660	.475	.031	3.319	15.095
1988	1.054	.241	.549	.787	1.817	4.104	2.601	.467	.043	3.244	14.907
1989	1.047	.240	.539	.776	1.791	4.042	2.542	.460	.058	3.171	14.666
1990	1.042	.237	.528	.764	1.763	3.982	2.485	.453	.072	3.100	14.426
1991	1.035	.236	.518	.752	1.737	3.922	2.429	.447	.088	3.030	14.194
1992	1.029	.234	.508	.742	1.711	3.863	2.374	.440	.103	2.962	13.966
1993	1.023	.232	.499	.730	1.685	3.806	2.321	.433	.114	2.896	13.739
1994	1.017	.231	.489	.719	1.660	3.748	2.269	.426	.127	2.830	13.516
1995	1.010	.229	.480	.708	1.635	3.692	2.217	.421	.138	2.766	13.296
1996	1.004	.227	.471	.698	1.611	3.636	2.168	.414	.152	2.704	13.085
1997	.998	.225	.461	.687	1.586	3.583	2.119	.408	.166	2.644	12.877
1998	.993	.224	.453	.677	1.563	3.528	2.071	.401	.178	2.584	12.672
1999	.987	.222	.445	.667	1.539	3.475	2.025	.396	.191	2.526	12.473
2000	.981	.220	.436	.657	1.516	3.424	1.979	.389	.203	2.468	12.273
	81.2%	46.7%	46.5%	61.7%	48.0%	42.1%	32.6%	35.4%	88.0%	47.6%	

Original Recoverable Gas Remaining

Proved Rec Res (On) = 30.325
Inferred Rec Res (On) = 14.053
Undiscovered (On) = ‒

44.378 TCF

PROJECTED PRODUCTION OF PRUDHOE BAY AS PER FEA, 93-275, Sec 15(b), Oct. 1975

NONASSOCIATED & ASSOCIATED NATURAL GAS PRODUCTION - TCF/YR*

Year	% WR	Multiplier	Remaining Reserve		Production	Cumulative Production	(44.378) % ORG	% ORG Remain
1975	0%	100%	(44.378)	= 44.378	0	0	0	100%
1976	0%	100%	(44.378)	= 44.378	0	0	0	100%
1977	.04%	.9996	(44.378)	= 44.360	.0182	.0182	.04%	99.96%
1978	.08%	.9992	(44.360)	= 44.323	.0365	.0547	.12%	99.88%
1979	.08%	.9992	(44.323)	= 44.287	.0365	.0912	.21%	99.79%
1980	.08%	.9992	(44.287)	= 44.250	.0365	.1277	.29%	99.71%
1981	.08%	.9992	(44.250)	= 44.214	.0365	.1642	.37%	99.63%
1982	.50%	.9950	(44.214)	= 43.993	.2205	.3847	.87%	99.13%
1983	.94%	.9906	(43.993)	= 43.578	.4151	.7998	1.80%	98.20%
1984	.98%	.9902	(43.578)	= 43.153	.4257	1.2255	2.76%	97.24%
1985	.99%	.9901	(43.153)	= 42.727	.4257	1.6512	3.72%	96.28%
1986	1.00%	.9900	(42.727)	= 42.301	.4257	2.0769	4.68%	95.32%
1987	1.01%	.9899	(42.301)	= 41.876	.4257	2.5026	5.64%	94.36%
1988	1.02%	.9898	(41.876)	= 41.450	.4257	2.9283	6.60%	93.40%
1989	1.03%	.9897	(41.450)	= 41.024	.4257	3.3540	7.56%	92.44%
1990	1.04%	.9896	(41.024)	= 40.599	.4257	3.7797	8.52%	91.48%
1991	1.05%	.9895	(40.599)	= 40.173	.4257	4.2054	9.48%	90.52%
1992	1.06%	.9894	(40.173)	= 39.747	.4257	4.6311	10.44%	89.56%
1993	1.07%	.9893	(39.747)	= 39.321	.4257	5.0568	11.39%	88.61%
1994	1.08%	.9892	(39.321)	= 38.896	.4257	5.4825	12.35%	87.65%
1995	1.10%	.9890	(38.896)	= 38.470	.4257	5.9082	13.31%	86.69%
1996	1.11%	.9889	(38.470)	= 38.044	.4257	6.3339	14.27%	85.73%
1997	1.12%	.9888	(38.044)	= 37.619	.4257	6.7596	15.23%	84.77%
1998	1.13%	.9887	(37.619)	= 37.193	.4257	7.1853	16.19%	83.81%
1999	1.15%	.9885	(37.193)	= 36.767	.4257	7.6110	17.15%	82.85%
2000	1.16%	.9884	(36.767)	= 36.342	.4257	8.0367	18.11%	81.89%

*Thousand cubic feet/yr.

Measured Res (On)	= 1.397
Inferred Res (On)	= .647
Undiscovered Max (On)	= 57.000
Measured Res (Off)	= .145
Inferred Res (Off)	= .100
Undiscovered Min (Off)	= 8.000
	67.289 TCF

HISTORIC & PROJECTED PRODUCTION OF ALASKA (EXCLUDING PRUDHOE BAY)

NONASSOCIATED & ASSOCIATED NATURAL GAS PRODUCTION - TCF/YR*

REALISTIC MAXIMUM APPROACH

Year	% WR	Multiplier	Remaining Reserve	Production	Cumulative Production	(68.194) % ORG	% ORG Remain
1965	.01%	.9999	(68.182) = 68.174	.008	.020	.03%	99.97%
1966	.02%	.9998	(68.174) = 68.161	.013	.033	.05%	99.95%
1967	.03%	.9997	(68.161) = 68.138	.023	.056	.08%	99.92%
1968	.06%	.9994	(68.138) = 68.096	.042	.098	.14%	99.86%
1969	.12%	.9988	(68.096) = 68.015	.081	.179	.26%	99.74%
1970	.21%	.9979	(68.015) = 67.870	.145	.324	.48%	99.52%
1971	.23%	.9977	(67.870) = 67.716	.154	.478	.70%	99.30%
1972	.22%	.9978	(67.716) = 67.569	.147	.625	.92%	99.08%
1973	.20%	.9980	(67.569) = 67.433	.136	.761	1.12%	98.88%
1974	.21%	.9979	(67.433) = 67.289	.144	.905	1.33%	98.67%
1975	.23%	.9977	(67.289) = 67.134	.155	1.060	1.55%	98.45%
1976	.23%	.9977	(67.134) = 66.980	.154	1.214	1.78%	98.22%
1977	.23%	.9977	(66.980) = 66.826	.154	1.368	2.01%	97.99%
1978	.24%	.9976	(66.826) = 66.665	.161	1.529	2.24%	97.76%
1979	.24%	.9976	(66.665) = 66.505	.160	1.689	2.48%	97.52%
1980	.25%	.9975	(66.505) = 66.339	.166	1.855	2.72%	97.28%
1981	.40%	.9960	(66.339) = 66.073	.266	2.121	3.11%	96.89%
1982	.55%	.9945	(66.873) = 65.710	.363	2.484	3.64%	96.36%
1983	.70%	.9930	(65.710) = 65.250	.460	2.944	4.32%	95.68%
1984	.85%	.9915	(65.250) = 64.695	.555	3.499	5.13%	94.87%
1985	1.0%	.9900	(64.695) = 64.048	.647	4.146	6.08%	93.92%
1986	1.0%	.9900	(64.048) = 63.408	.640	4.786	7.02%	92.98%
1987	1.0%	.9900	(63.408) = 62.774	.634	5.420	7.95%	92.05%
1988	1.0%	.9900	(62.774) = 62.146	.628	6.048	8.87%	91.13%
1989	1.0%	.9900	(62.146) = 61.525	.621	6.669	9.78%	90.22%
1990	1.0%	.9900	(61.525) = 60.909	.616	7.285	10.68%	89.32%
1991	1.0%	.9900	(60.909) = 60.300	.609	7.894	11.58%	88.42%
1992	1.0%	.9900	(60.300) = 59.697	.603	8.497	12.46%	87.54%
1993	1.0%	.9900	(59.697) = 59.100	.597	9.094	13.34%	86.66%
1994	1.0%	.9900	(59.100) = 58.509	.591	9.685	14.20%	85.80%
1995	1.0%	.9900	(58.509) = 57.924	.585	10.270	15.06%	84.94%
1996	1.0%	.9900	(57.924) = 57.345	.579	10.849	15.91%	84.09%
1997	1.0%	.9900	(57.345) = 56.772	.573	11.422	16.75%	83.25%
1998	1.0%	.9900	(56.772) = 56.204	.568	11.990	17.58%	82.42%
1999	1.0%	.9900	(56.204) = 55.642	.562	12.552	18.41%	81.59%
2000	1.0%	.9900	(55.642) = 55.086	.556	13.108	19.22%	80.78%

*Thousand cubic feet/yr.

SUMMARY OF THE HISTORIC & PROJECTED PRODUCTION OF REGION #1

NA & ASSOC. NATURAL GAS PRODUCTION - TCF/YR*

Year	Prudhoe Bay Production	Maximum Remain Alaska	Minimum Remain Alaska	Maximum Total Alaska Production	Minimum Total Alaska Production
1965	-	.008	.008	.008	.008
1966	-	.013	.013	.013	.013
1967	-	.023	.023	.023	.023
1968	-	.042	.042	.042	.042
1969	-	.081	.081	.081	.081
1970	-	.145	.145	.145	.145
1971	-	.154	.154	.154	.154
1972	-	.147	.147	.147	.147
1973	-	.136	.136	.136	.136
1974	-	.144	.144	.144	.144
1975	-	.155	.155	.155	.155
1976	-	.154	.154	.154	.154
1977	.018	.154	.153	.172	.171
1978	.036	.161	.153	.197	.189
1979	.037	.160	.151	.197	.188
1980	.036	.166	.153	.202	.189
1981	.037	.266	.173	.303	.210
1982	.221	.363	.191	.584	.412
1983	.415	.460	.206	.875	.621
1984	.426	.555	.233	.981	.659
1985	.426	.647	.245	1.073	.671
1986	.426	.640	.243	1.066	.669
1987	.426	.634	.241	1.060	.667
1988	.426	.628	.239	1.054	.665
1989	.426	.621	.236	1.047	.662
1990	.426	.616	.233	1.042	.659
1991	.426	.609	.232	1.035	.658
1992	.426	.603	.229	1.029	.655
1993	.426	.597	.226	1.023	.652
1994	.426	.591	.225	1.017	.651
1995	.425	.585	.222	1.010	.647
1996	.425	.579	.220	1.004	.645
1997	.425	.573	.218	.998	.643
1998	.425	.568	.215	.993	.640
1999	.425	.562	.214	.987	.639
2000	.425	.556	.211	.981	.636

*Thousand cubic feet/yr.

Measured Res (On)	=	4.732	
Inferred Res (On)	=	4.000	
Undiscovered (On)	=	20.000	
Measured Res (Off)	=	.463	
Inferred Res (Off)	=	.400	
Undiscovered (Off)	=	6.000	

MAXIMUM APPROACH

35.595 TCF

HISTORIC & PROJECTED PRODUCTION OF REGION #2 (ON & OFF)

NONASSOCIATED & ASSOCIATED NATURAL GAS PRODUCTION - TCF/YR[*]
(TCF)

Year	Annual % Withdrawal	Multiplier	Remaining Reserve	(62.465) % ORG Remaining	Production
1965	1.51%	.9849	(41.455) = 40.827	65.4%	.628
1966	1.68%	.9832	(40.827) = 40.141	64.3%	.686
1967	1.64%	.9836	(40.141) = 39.481	63.2%	.660
1968	1.74%	.9826	(39.481) = 38.796	62.1%	.685
1969	1.70%	.9830	(38.796) = 38.137	61.0%	.659
1970	1.67%	.9833	(38.137) = 37.501	60.0%	.636
1971	1.53%	.9847	(37.501) = 36.929	59.1%	.572
1972	1.35%	.9865	(36.929) = 36.430	58.3%	.499
1973	1.31%	.9869	(36.430) = 35.952	57.6%	.478
1974	.99%	.9901	(35.952) = 35.595	57.0%	.357
1975	.93%	.9907	(35.595) = 35.263	56.5%	.332
1976	.87%	.9913	(35.263) = 34.956	56.0%	.307
1977	.81%	.9919	(34.956) = 34.673	55.5%	.283
1978	.75%	.9925	(34.673) = 34.413	55.1%	.260
1979	.75%	.9925	(34.413) = 34.155	54.7%	.258
1980	.75%	.9925	(34.155) = 33.899	54.3%	.256
1981	.75%	.9925	(33.899) = 33.645	53.9%	.254
1982	.75%	.9925	(33.645) = 33.393	53.5%	.252
1983	.75%	.9925	(33.393) = 33.143	53.1%	.250
1984	.75%	.9925	(33.143) = 32.894	52.7%	.249
1985	.75%	.9925	(32.894) = 32.647	52.3%	.247
1986	.75%	.9925	(32.647) = 32.402	51.9%	.245
1987	.75%	.9925	(32.402) = 32.159	51.5%	.243
1988	.75%	.9925	(32.159) = 31.918	51.1%	.241
1989	.75%	.9925	(31.918) = 31.678	50.7%	.240
1990	.75%	.9925	(31.678) = 31.441	50.3%	.237
1991	.75%	.9925	(31.441) = 31.205	50.0%	.236
1992	.75%	.9925	(31.205) = 30.971	49.6%	.234
1993	.75%	.9925	(30.971) = 30.739	49.2%	.232
1994	.75%	.9925	(30.739) = 30.508	48.8%	.231
1995	.75%	.9925	(30.508) = 30.279	48.5%	.229
1996	.75%	.9925	(30.279) = 30.052	48.1%	.227
1997	.75%	.9925	(30.052) = 29.827	47.7%	.225
1998	.75%	.9925	(29.827) = 29.603	47.4%	.224
1999	.75%	.9925	(29.603) = 29.381	47.0%	.222
2000	.75%	.9925	(29.381) = 29.161	46.7%	.220

*Thousand cubic feet/yr.

Measured Res (On)	=	9.081
Inferred Res (On)	=	2.900
Undiscovered (On)	=	25.000
Measured Res (Off)	=	-
Inferred Res (Off)	=	-
Undiscovered (Off)	=	-
		36.981 TCF

MAXIMUM APPROACH

HISTORIC & PROJECTED PRODUCTION OF REGION #3

NONASSOCIATED & ASSOCIATED NATURAL GAS PRODUCTION - TCF/YR
(TCF)

Year	Annual % Withdrawal	Multiplier	Remaining Reserve	(48.443) % ORG Remaining	Production
1965	1.37%	.9863	(43.616) = 43.018	88.8%	.598
1966	1.46%	.9854	(43.018) = 42.391	87.5%	.627
1967	1.55%	.9845	(42.391) = 41.734	86.2%	.657
1968	1.72%	.9828	(41.734) = 41.018	84.7%	.716
1969	1.62%	.9838	(41.018) = 40.354	83.3%	.664
1970	1.57%	.9843	(40.354) = 39.719	82.0%	.635
1971	1.70%	.9830	(39.719) = 39.044	80.6%	.675
1972	1.80%	.9820	(39.044) = 38.340	79.1%	.704
1973	1.78%	.9822	(38.340) = 37.658	77.7%	.682
1974	1.80%	.9820	(37.658) = 36.981	76.3%	.677
1975	1.79%	.9821	(36.981) = 36.319	75.0%	.662
1976	1.83%	.9817	(36.319) = 35.654	73.6%	.665
1977	1.86%	.9814	(35.654) = 34.991	72.2%	.663
1978	1.90%	.9810	(34.991) = 34.326	70.9%	.665
1979	1.90%	.9810	(34.326) = 33.674	69.5%	.652
1980	1.90%	.9810	(33.674) = 33.034	68.2%	.640
1981	1.90%	.9810	(33.034) = 32.406	66.9%	.628
1982	1.90%	.9810	(32.406) = 31.790	65.6%	.616
1983	1.90%	.9810	(31.790) = 31.186	64.4%	.604
1984	1.90%	.9810	(31.186) = 30.594	63.2%	.592
1985	1.90%	.9810	(30.594) = 30.012	62.0%	.582
1986	1.90%	.9810	(30.012) = 29.442	60.8%	.570
1987	1.90%	.9810	(29.442) = 28.883	59.6%	.559
1988	1.90%	.9810	(28.883) = 28.334	58.5%	.549
1989	1.90%	.9810	(28.334) = 27.795	57.4%	.539
1990	1.90%	.9810	(27.795) = 27.267	56.3%	.528
1991	1.90%	.9810	(27.267) = 26.749	55.2%	.518
1992	1.90%	.9810	(26.749) = 26.241	54.2%	.508
1993	1.90%	.9810	(26.241) = 25.742	53.1%	.499
1994	1.90%	.9810	(25.742) = 25.253	52.1%	.489
1995	1.90%	.9810	(25.253) = 24.773	51.1%	.480
1996	1.90%	.9810	(24.773) = 24.302	50.2%	.471
1997	1.90%	.9810	(24.302) = 23.841	49.2%	.461
1998	1.90%	.9810	(23.841) = 23.388	48.3%	.453
1999	1.90%	.9810	(23.388) = 22.943	47.4%	.445
2000	1.90%	.9810	(22.943) = 22.507	46.5%	.436

Measured Res (On)	=	6.754
Inferred Res (On)	=	5.300
Undiscovered (On)	=	47.000
Measured Res (Off)	=	-
Inferred Res (Off)	=	-
Undiscovered (Off)	=	-
		59.054 TCF

MAXIMUM APPROACH

HISTORIC & PROJECTED PRODUCTION OF REGION #4

NONASSOCIATED & ASSOCIATED NATURAL GAS PRODUCTION - TCF/YR

Year	Annual % Withdrawal	Multiplier	(TCF) Remaining Reserve	(69.874) % ORG Remaining	Production
1965	.70%	.9930	(63.866) = 63.418	90.8%	.448
1966	.69%	.9931	(63.418) = 62.983	90.1%	.435
1967	.68%	.9932	(62.983) = 62.555	89.5%	.428
1968	.73%	.9927	(62.555) = 62.097	88.9%	.458
1969	.78%	.9922	(62.097) = 61.615	88.2%	.482
1970	.80%	.9920	(61.615) = 61.125	87.5%	.490
1971	.82%	.9918	(61.125) = 60.624	86.8%	.501
1972	.88%	.9912	(60.624) = 60.093	86.0%	.531
1973	.91%	.9909	(60.093) = 59.544	85.2%	.549
1974	.82%	.9918	(59.544) = 59.054	84.5%	.490
1975	.79%	.9921	(59.054) = 58.589	83.9%	.465
1976	.78%	.9922	(58.589) = 58.132	83.2%	.457
1977	.76%	.9924	(58.132) = 57.690	82.6%	.442
1978	.75%	.9925	(57.690) = 57.257	81.9%	.433
1979	.75%	.9925	(57.257) = 56.828	81.3%	.429
1980	.75%	.9925	(56.828) = 56.402	80.7%	.426
1981	.75%	.9925	(56.402) = 55.979	80.1%	.423
1982	.75%	.9925	(55.979) = 55.559	79.5%	.420
1983	.88%	.9912	(55.559) = 55.070	78.8%	.489
1984	1.00%	.9900	(55.070) = 54.519	78.0%	.551
1985	1.13%	.9887	(54.519) = 53.903	77.1%	.616
1986	1.25%	.9875	(53.903) = 53.229	76.2%	.674
1987	1.38%	.9862	(53.229) = 52.494	75.1%	.735
1988	1.50%	.9850	(52.494) = 51.707	74.0%	.787
1989	1.50%	.9850	(51.707) = 50.931	72.9%	.776
1990	1.50%	.9850	(50.931) = 50.167	71.8%	.764
1991	1.50%	.9850	(50.167) = 49.415	70.7%	.752
1992	1.50%	.9850	(49.415) = 48.673	69.7%	.742
1993	1.50%	.9850	(48.673) = 47.943	68.6%	.730
1994	1.50%	.9850	(47.943) = 47.224	67.6%	.719
1995	1.50%	.9850	(47.224) = 46.516	66.6%	.708
1996	1.50%	.9850	(46.516) = 45.818	65.6%	.698
1997	1.50%	.9850	(45.818) = 45.131	64.6%	.687
1998	1.50%	.9850	(45.131) = 44.454	63.6%	.677
1999	1.50%	.9850	(44.454) = 43.787	62.7%	.667
2000	1.50%	.9850	(43.787) = 43.130	61.7%	.657

		Measured Res (On)	=	24.624
		Inferred Res (On)	=	23.300
		Undiscovered (On)	=	101.000
		Measured Res (Off)	=	-
		Inferred Res (Off)	=	-
		Undiscovered (Off)	=	-

MAXIMUM APPROACH

148.924 TCF

HISTORIC & PROJECTED PRODUCTION OF REGION #5

NONASSOCIATED & ASSOCIATED NATURAL GAS PRODUCTION - TCF/YR
(TCF)

Year	Annual % Withdrawal	Multiplier	Remaining Reserve	(207.592) % ORG Remaining	Production
1965	1.08%	.9892	(175.971) = 174.068	83.9%	1.903
1966	1.15%	.9885	(174.068) = 172.065	82.9%	2.003
1967	1.21%	.9879	(172.065) = 169.981	81.9%	2.084
1968	1.36%	.9864	(169.981) = 167.669	80.8%	2.312
1969	1.51%	.9849	(167.669) = 165.137	79.6%	2.532
1970	1.83%	.9817	(165.137) = 162.122	78.1%	3.015
1971	1.93%	.9807	(162.122) = 159.000	76.6%	3.122
1972	2.11%	.9789	(159.000) = 155.651	75.0%	3.349
1973	2.15%	.9785	(155.651) = 152.301	73.4%	3.350
1974	2.22%	.9778	(152.301) = 148.924	71.7%	3.377
1975	1.98%	.9802	(148.924) = 145.974	70.3%	2.950
1976	1.82%	.9818	(145.974) = 143.317	69.0%	2.657
1977	1.66%	.9834	(143.317) = 140.938	67.9%	2.379
1978	1.50%	.9850	(140.938) = 138.824	66.9%	2.114
1979	1.50%	.9850	(138.824) = 136.742	65.9%	2.082
1980	1.50%	.9850	(136.742) = 134.690	64.9%	2.052
1981	1.50%	.9850	(134.690) = 132.670	63.9%	2.020
1982	1.50%	.9850	(132.670) = 130.680	63.0%	1.990
1983	1.50%	.9850	(130.680) = 128.720	62.0%	1.960
1984	1.50%	.9850	(128.720) = 126.789	61.1%	1.931
1985	1.50%	.9850	(126.789) = 124.887	60.2%	1.902
1986	1.50%	.9850	(124.887) = 123.014	59.3%	1.873
1987	1.50%	.9850	(123.014) = 121.168	58.4%	1.846
1988	1.50%	.9850	(121.168) = 119.351	57.5%	1.817
1989	1.50%	.9850	(119.351) = 117.560	56.6%	1.791
1990	1.50%	.9850	(117.560) = 115.797	55.8%	1.763
1991	1.50%	.9850	(115.797) = 114.060	54.9%	1.737
1992	1.50%	.9850	(114.060) = 112.349	54.1%	1.711
1993	1.50%	.9850	(112.349) = 110.664	53.3%	1.685
1994	1.50%	.9850	(110.664) = 109.004	52.5%	1.660
1995	1.50%	.9850	(109.004) = 107.369	51.7%	1.635
1996	1.50%	.9850	(107.369) = 105.758	50.9%	1.611
1997	1.50%	.9850	(105.758) = 104.172	50.2%	1.586
1998	1.50%	.9850	(104.172) = 102.609	49.4%	1.563
1999	1.50%	.9850	(102.609) = 101.070	48.7%	1.539
2000	1.50%	.9850	(101.070) = 99.554	48.0%	1.516

Measured Res (On) = 81.903
Inferred Res (On) = 58.700
Undiscovered (On) = 196.000
Measured Res (Off) = -
Inferred Res (Off) = -
Undiscovered (Off) = -

MAXIMUM APPROACH

336.603 TCF

HISTORIC & PROJECTED PRODUCTION OF REGION #6

NONASSOCIATED & ASSOCIATED NATURAL GAS PRODUCTION - TCF/YR
(TCF)

Year	Annual % Withdrawal	Multiplier	Remaining Reserve	(533.626) % ORG Remaining	Production
1965	1.89%	.9811	(424.176) = 416.147	78.0%	8.029
1966	2.02%	.9798	(416.147) = 407.726	76.4%	8.421
1967	2.09%	.9791	(407.726) = 399.193	74.8%	8.533
1968	2.24%	.9776	(399.193) = 390.251	73.1%	8.942
1969	2.39%	.9761	(390.251) = 380.910	71.4%	9.341
1970	2.48%	.9752	(380.910) = 371.481	69.6%	9.429
1971	2.50%	.9750	(371.481) = 362.203	67.9%	9.278
1972	2.54%	.9746	(362.203) = 352.988	66.2%	9.215
1973	2.43%	.9757	(352.988) = 344.423	64.5%	8.565
1974	2.27%	.9773	(344.423) = 336.603	63.1%	7.820
1975	2.03%	.9797	(336.603) = 329.774	61.8%	6.829
1976	1.85%	.9815	(329.774) = 323.673	60.7%	6.101
1977	1.68%	.9832	(323.673) = 318.235	59.6%	5.438
1978	1.50%	.9850	(318.235) = 313.462	58.7%	4.773
1979	1.50%	.9850	(313.462) = 308.760	57.9%	4.702
1980	1.50%	.9850	(308.760) = 304.128	57.0%	4.632
1981	1.50%	.9850	(304.128) = 299.566	56.1%	4.562
1982	1.50%	.9850	(299.566) = 295.073	55.3%	4.493
1983	1.50%	.9850	(295.073) = 290.647	54.5%	4.426
1984	1.50%	.9850	(290.647) = 286.287	53.6%	4.360
1985	1.50%	.9850	(286.287) = 281.993	52.8%	4.294
1986	1.50%	.9850	(281.993) = 277.763	52.1%	4.230
1987	1.50%	.9850	(277.763) = 273.596	51.3%	4.167
1988	1.50%	.9850	(273.596) = 269.492	50.5%	4.104
1989	1.50%	.9850	(269.492) = 265.450	49.7%	4.042
1990	1.50%	.9850	(265.450) = 261.468	49.0%	3.982
1991	1.50%	.9850	(261.468) = 257.546	48.3%	3.922
1992	1.50%	.9850	(257.546) = 253.683	47.5%	3.863
1993	1.50%	.9850	(253.683) = 249.877	46.8%	3.806
1994	1.50%	.9850	(249.877) = 246.129	46.1%	3.748
1995	1.50%	.9850	(246.129) = 242.437	45.4%	3.692
1996	1.50%	.9850	(242.437) = 238.801	44.8%	3.636
1997	1.50%	.9850	(238.801) = 235.218	44.1%	3.583
1998	1.50%	.9850	(235.218) = 231.690	43.4%	3.528
1999	1.50%	.9850	(231.690) = 228.215	42.8%	3.475
2000	1.50%	.9850	(228.215) = 224.791	42.1%	3.424

Measured Res (Off) = 35.348
Inferred Res (Off) = 67.000
Undiscovered (Off) = 91.000
193.348 TCF

MAXIMUM APPROACH

HISTORIC & PROJECTED PRODUCTION OF REGION #6A (GULF OF MEXICO)

NONASSOCIATED & ASSOCIATED NATURAL GAS PRODUCTION - TCF/YR

Year	Annual % Withdrawal	Multiplier	(TCF) Remaining Reserve	(225.491) % ORG Remaining	Production
1965	.45%	.9955	(221.292) = 220.303	97.7%	.989
1966	.61%	.9939	(220.303) = 218.956	97.1%	1.347
1967	.83%	.9917	(218.956) = 217.129	96.3%	1.827
1968	1.05%	.9895	(217.129) = 214.841	95.3%	2.288
1969	1.27%	.9873	(214.841) = 212.108	94.1%	2.733
1970	1.51%	.9849	(212.108) = 208.908	92.7%	3.200
1971	1.64%	.9836	(208.908) = 205.485	91.1%	3.423
1972	1.88%	.9812	(205.485) = 201.612	89.4%	3.873
1973	2.07%	.9793	(201.612) = 197.443	87.6%	4.169
1974	2.07%	.9793	(197.443) = 193.348	85.8%	4.095
1975	2.13%	.9787	(193.348) = 189.229	83.9%	4.119
1976	2.17%	.9783	(189.229) = 185.123	82.1%	4.106
1977	2.21%	.9779	(185.123) = 181.031	80.3%	4.092
1978	2.25%	.9775	(181.031) = 176.958	78.5%	4.073
1979	2.25%	.9775	(176.958) = 172.977	76.7%	3.981
1980	2.25%	.9775	(172.977) = 169.085	75.0%	3.892
1981	2.25%	.9775	(169.085) = 165.280	73.3%	3.805
1982	2.25%	.9775	(165.280) = 161.561	71.6%	3.719
1983	2.25%	.9775	(161.561) = 157.926	70.0%	3.635
1984	2.25%	.9775	(157.926) = 154.373	68.5%	3.553
1985	2.25%	.9775	(154.373) = 150.899	66.9%	3.474
1986	2.25%	.9775	(150.899) = 147.504	65.4%	3.395
1987	2.25%	.9775	(147.504) = 144.185	63.9%	3.319
1988	2.25%	.9775	(144.185) = 140.941	62.5%	3.244
1989	2.25%	.9775	(140.941) = 137.770	61.1%	3.171
1990	2.25%	.9775	(137.770) = 134.670	59.7%	3.100
1991	2.25%	.9775	(134.670) = 131.640	58.4%	3.030
1992	2.25%	.9775	(131.640) = 128.678	57.1%	2.962
1993	2.25%	.9775	(128.678) = 125.782	55.8%	2.896
1994	2.25%	.9775	(125.782) = 122.952	54.5%	2.830
1995	2.25%	.9775	(122.952) = 120.186	53.3%	2.766
1996	2.25%	.9775	(120.186) = 117.482	52.1%	2.704
1997	2.25%	.9775	(117.482) = 114.838	50.9%	2.644
1998	2.25%	.9775	(114.838) = 112.254	49.8%	2.584
1999	2.25%	.9775	(112.254) = 109.728	48.7%	2.526
2000	2.25%	.9775	(109.728) = 107.260	47.6%	2.468

Measured Res (On) =   34.150
Inferred Res (On) =   20.600
Undiscovered (On) = 101.000
Measured Res (Off) =   -
Inferred Res (Off) =   -
Undiscovered (Off) = _____
                        155.750 TCF

MAXIMUM APPROACH

HISTORIC & PROJECTED PRODUCTION OF REGION #7

NONASSOCIATED & ASSOCIATED NATURAL GAS PRODUCTION - TCF/YR

Year	Annual % Withdrawal	Multiplier	(TCF) Remaining Reserve	(263.417) % ORG Remaining	Production
1965	1.65%	.9835	(193.463) = 190.271	72.2%	3.192
1966	1.80%	.9820	(190.271) = 186.855	70.9%	3.416
1967	1.96%	.9804	(186.855) = 183.192	69.5%	3.663
1968	2.04%	.9796	(183.192) = 179.455	68.1%	3.737
1969	2.22%	.9778	(179.455) = 175.471	66.6%	3.984
1970	2.40%	.9760	(175.471) = 171.253	65.0%	4.218
1971	2.22%	.9778	(171.253) = 167.449	63.6%	3.804
1972	2.37%	.9763	(167.449) = 163.482	62.1%	3.967
1973	2.37%	.9763	(163.482) = 159.600	60.6%	3.882
1974	2.41%	.9759	(159.600) = 155.750	59.1%	3.850
1975	2.37%	.9763	(155.750) = 152.063	57.7%	3.687
1976	2.33%	.9767	(152.063) = 148.520	56.4%	3.543
1977	2.29%	.9771	(148.520) = 145.119	55.1%	3.401
1978	2.25%	.9775	(145.119) = 141.854	53.9%	3.265
1979	2.25%	.9775	(141.854) = 138.662	52.6%	3.192
1980	2.25%	.9775	(138.662) = 135.542	51.5%	3.120
1981	2.25%	.9775	(135.542) = 132.492	50.3%	3.050
1982	2.25%	.9775	(132.492) = 129.511	49.2%	2.981
1983	2.25%	.9775	(129.511) = 126.597	48.1%	2.914
1984	2.25%	.9775	(126.597) = 123.749	47.0%	2.848
1985	2.25%	.9775	(123.749) = 120.964	45.9%	2.785
1986	2.25%	.9775	(120.964) = 118.242	44.9%	2.722
1987	2.25%	.9775	(118.242) = 115.582	43.9%	2.660
1988	2.25%	.9775	(115.582) = 112.981	42.9%	2.601
1989	2.25%	.9775	(112.981) = 110.439	41.9%	2.542
1990	2.25%	.9775	(110.439) = 107.954	41.0%	2.485
1991	2.25%	.9775	(107.954) = 105.525	40.1%	2.429
1992	2.25%	.9775	(105.525) = 103.151	39.2%	2.374
1993	2.25%	.9775	(103.151) = 100.830	38.3%	2.321
1994	2.25%	.9775	(100.830) = 98.561	37.4%	2.269
1995	2.25%	.9775	(98.561) = 96.344	36.6%	2.217
1996	2.25%	.9775	(96.344) = 94.176	35.8%	2.168
1997	2.25%	.9775	(94.176) = 92.057	34.9%	2.119
1998	2.25%	.9775	(92.057) = 89.986	34.2%	2.071
1999	2.25%	.9775	(89.986) = 87.961	33.4%	2.025
2000	2.25%	.9775	(87.961) = 85.982	32.6%	1.979

Measured Res (On)	=	8.210
Inferred Res (On)	=	4.600
Undiscovered (On)	=	25.000
Measured Res (Off)	=	-
Inferred Res (Off)	=	-
Undiscovered (Off)	=	-
		37.810 TCF

MAXIMUM APPROACH

HISTORIC & PROJECTED PRODUCTION OF REGIONS #8, 9, 10, 11 + MISCELLANEOUS

NONASSOCIATED & ASSOCIATED NATURAL GAS PRODUCTION - TCF/YR

Year	Annual % Withdrawal	Multiplier	(TCF) Remaining Reserve	(72.270) % ORG Remaining	Production
1965	1.07%	.9893	(42.638) = 42.180	58.4%	.458
1966	1.09%	.9891	(42.180) = 41.719	57.7%	.461
1967	1.17%	.9883	(41.719) = 41.232	57.1%	.487
1968	1.20%	.9880	(41.232) = 40.736	56.4%	.496
1969	1.17%	.9883	(40.736) = 40.261	55.7%	.475
1970	1.25%	.9875	(40.261) = 39.756	55.0%	.505
1971	1.22%	.9878	(39.756) = 39.271	54.3%	.485
1972	1.21%	.9879	(39.271) = 38.796	53.7%	.475
1973	1.24%	.9876	(38.796) = 38.316	53.0%	.480
1974	1.30%	.9870	(38.316) = 37.810	52.3%	.506
1975	1.38%	.9862	(37.810) = 37.289	51.6%	.521
1976	1.42%	.9858	(37.289) = 36.759	50.9%	.530
1977	1.46%	.9854	(36.759) = 36.223	50.1%	.536
1978	1.50%	.9850	(36.223) = 35.679	49.4%	.544
1979	1.50%	.9850	(35.679) = 35.144	48.6%	.535
1980	1.50%	.9850	(35.144) = 34.617	47.9%	.527
1981	1.50%	.9850	(34.617) = 34.098	47.2%	.519
1982	1.50%	.9850	(34.098) = 33.586	46.5%	.512
1983	1.50%	.9850	(33.586) = 33.082	45.8%	.504
1984	1.50%	.9850	(33.082) = 32.586	45.1%	.496
1985	1.50%	.9850	(32.586) = 32.097	44.4%	.489
1986	1.50%	.9850	(32.097) = 31.616	43.7%	.481
1987	1.50%	.9850	(31.616) = 31.141	43.1%	.475
1988	1.50%	.9850	(31.141) = 30.674	42.4%	.467
1989	1.50%	.9850	(30.674) = 30.214	41.8%	.460
1990	1.50%	.9850	(30.214) = 29.761	41.2%	.453
1991	1.50%	.9850	(29.761) = 29.314	40.6%	.447
1992	1.50%	.9850	(29.314) = 28.874	40.0%	.440
1993	1.50%	.9850	(28.874) = 28.441	39.4%	.433
1994	1.50%	.9850	(28.441) = 28.015	38.8%	.426
1995	1.50%	.9850	(28.015) = 27.594	38.2%	.421
1996	1.50%	.9850	(27.594) = 27.180	37.6%	.414
1997	1.50%	.9850	(27.180) = 26.772	37.0%	.408
1998	1.50%	.9850	(26.772) = 26.371	36.5%	.401
1999	1.50%	.9850	(26.371) = 25.975	35.9%	.396
2000	1.50%	.9850	(25.975) = 25.586	35.4%	.389

Measured Res (Off) =   -

Inferred Res (Off) =   -

Undiscovered (Off) = <u>14.000</u>

14.000 TCF

MAXIMUM APPROACH

HISTORIC & PROJECTED PRODUCTION OF REGION #11A (ATLANTIC COAST OFFSHORE)

NONASSOCIATED & ASSOCIATED NATURAL GAS PRODUCTION - TCF/YR

Year	Annual % Withdrawal	Multiplier	(TCF) Remaining Reserve	(14.000) % ORG Remaining	Production
1965	0%		14.000	100%	0
1966					
1967					
1968					
1969					
1970					
1971					
1972					
1973					
1974					
1975					
1976					
1977					
1978					
1979					
1980					
1981					
1982					
1983					
1984					
1985	.025%	.99975	(14.000) = 13.997	100%	.003
1986	.125%	.99875	(13.997) = 13.979	99.9%	.018
1987	.225%	.99775	(13.979) = 13.948	99.6%	.031
1988	.305%	.99695	(13.948) = 13.905	99.3%	.043
1989	.415%	.99585	(13.905) = 13.847	98.9%	.058
1990	.525%	.99475	(13.847) = 13.775	98.4%	.072
1991	.635%	.99365	(13.775) = 13.687	97.8%	.088
1992	.755%	.99245	(13.687) = 13.584	97.0%	.103
1993	.84%	.9916	(13.584) = 13.470	96.2%	.114
1994	.94%	.9906	(13.470) = 13.343	95.3%	.127
1995	1.035%	.98965	(13.343) = 13.205	94.3%	.138
1996	1.15%	.9885	(13.205) = 13.053	93.2%	.152
1997	1.27%	.9873	(13.053) = 12.887	92.1%	.166
1998	1.385%	.98615	(12.887) = 12.709	90.8%	.178
1999	1.50%	.9850	(12.709) = 12.518	89.4%	.191
2000	1.625%	.98375	(12.518) = 12.315	88.0%	.203

SUMMARY OF MINIMUM APPROACH,
HISTORIC & PROJECTED NATURAL GAS REGIONAL PRODUCTION - TCF/Yr
Revised 5/5/76

Minimum Approach

Year	Region 1 On & Off	Region 2 On & Off	Region 3	Region 4	Region 5	Region 6 On Only	Region 7	Regions 8,9,10,11 + Misc. On Only	Region 11A Off Only	Region 6A Off Only	Minimum Domestic Production
1965	.008	.628	.598	.448	1.903	8.029	3.192	.458	-	.989	16.253
1966	.013	.686	.627	.435	2.003	8.421	3.416	.461	-	1.347	17.409
1967	.023	.660	.657	.428	2.084	8.533	3.663	.487	-	1.827	18.362
1968	.042	.685	.716	.458	2.312	8.942	3.737	.496	-	2.288	19.676
1969	.081	.659	.664	.482	2.532	9.341	3.984	.475	-	2.733	20.951
1970	.145	.636	.635	.490	3.015	9.429	4.218	.505	-	3.200	22.273
1971	.154	.572	.675	.501	3.122	9.278	3.804	.485	-	3.423	22.014
1972	.147	.499	.704	.531	3.349	9.215	3.967	.475	-	3.873	22.760
1973	.136	.478	.682	.549	3.350	8.565	3.882	.480	-	4.169	22.291
1974	.144	.357	.677	.490	3.377	7.820	3.850	.506	-	4.095	21.316
1975	.155	.332	.662	.465	2.950	6.829	3.687	.521	-	4.119	19.720
1976	.154	.314	.641	.453	2.695	6.235	3.517	.524	-	4.010	18.543
1977	.171	.296	.622	.443	2.465	5.696	3.356	.524	-	3.894	17.467
1978	.189	.279	.602	.430	2.245	5.171	3.202	.526	-	3.791	16.435
1979	.188	.276	.580	.424	2.177	5.042	3.094	.511	-	3.659	15.951
1980	.189	.272	.557	.418	2.112	4.916	2.988	.496	-	3.531	15.479
1981	.210	.267	.537	.411	2.048	4.793	2.887	.482	-	3.407	15.042
1982	.412	.263	.517	.405	1.987	4.673	2.789	.468	-	3.288	14.802
1983	.621	.260	.498	.399	1.928	4.556	2.694	.454	-	3.172	14.582
1984	.659	.256	.478	.393	1.869	4.442	2.602	.441	-	3.062	14.202
1985	.671	.251	.461	.388	1.814	4.332	2.514	.428	.001	2.955	13.815
1986	.669	.248	.444	.381	1.759	4.223	2.428	.416	.006	2.851	13.425
1987	.667	.245	.427	.376	1.706	4.117	2.346	.404	.012	2.751	13.051
1988	.665	.241	.410	.370	1.655	4.015	2.266	.392	.015	2.655	12.684
1989	.662	.237	.396	.364	1.606	3.914	2.189	.380	.021	2.563	12.332
1990	.659	.233	.381	.359	1.557	3.816	2.114	.370	.025	2.472	11.986
1991	.658	.230	.366	.354	1.511	3.721	2.043	.359	.032	2.386	11.660
1992	.655	.226	.353	.349	1.465	3.628	1.973	.348	.037	2.302	11.336
1993	.652	.223	.339	.343	1.421	3.537	1.906	.339	.040	2.222	11.022
1994	.651	.220	.327	.338	1.379	3.449	1.842	.328	.046	2.144	10.724
1995	.647	.217	.314	.333	1.337	3.362	1.778	.319	.049	2.069	10.425
1996	.645	.213	.303	.327	1.297	3.279	1.719	.310	.054	1.997	10.144
1997	.643	.210	.291	.323	1.259	3.196	1.659	.301	.059	1.927	9.868
1998	.640	.207	.280	.319	1.220	3.117	1.604	.292	.064	1.859	9.602
1999	.639	.203	.270	.313	1.184	3.038	1.529	.283	.068	1.794	9.321
2000	.636	.201	.260	.309	1.149	2.963	1.496	.276	.073	1.731	9.094
	80.0%	28.4%	22.6%	49.6%	26.2%	27.3%	20.0%	17.0%	88.0%	31.3%	

Original Recoverable Gas Remaining

Proved Rec Res (On)   = 30.325
Inferred Rec Res (On) = 14.053
Undiscovered (On)   = ___-___
                                   44.378 TCF

PROJECTED PRODUCTION OF PRUDHOE BAY AS PER FEA, 93-275, Sec 15(b), Oct. 1975

NONASSOCIATED & ASSOCIATED NATURAL GAS PRODUCTION - TCF/YR

Year	% WR	Multiplier	Remaining Reserve	Production	Cumulative Production	(44.378) % ORG	% ORG Remain
1975	0%	100%	(44.378) = 44.378	0	0	0	100%
1976	0%	100%	(44.378) = 44.378	0	0	0	100%
1977	.04%	.9996	(44.378) = 44.360	.0182	.0182	.04%	99.96%
1978	.08%	.9992	(44.360) = 44.323	.0365	.0547	.12%	99.88%
1979	.08%	.9992	(44.323) = 44.287	.0365	.0912	.21%	99.79%
1980	.08%	.9992	(44.287) = 44.250	.0365	.1277	.29%	99.71%
1981	.08%	.9992	(44.250) = 44.214	.0365	.1642	.37%	99.63%
1982	.50%	.9950	(44.214) = 43.993	.2205	.3847	.87%	99.13%
1983	.94%	.9906	(43.993) = 43.578	.4151	.7998	1.80%	98.20%
1984	.98%	.9902	(43.578) = 43.153	.4257	1.2255	2.76%	97.24%
1985	.99%	.9901	(43.153) = 42.727	.4257	1.6512	3.72%	96.28%
1986	1.00%	.9900	(42.727) = 42.301	.4257	2.0769	4.68%	95.32%
1987	1.01%	.9899	(42.301) = 41.876	.4257	2.5026	5.64%	94.36%
1988	1.02%	.9898	(41.876) = 41.450	.4257	2.9283	6.60%	93.40%
1989	1.03%	.9897	(41.450) = 41.024	.4257	3.3540	7.56%	92.44%
1990	1.04%	.9896	(41.024) = 40.599	.4257	3.7797	8.52%	91.48%
1991	1.05%	.9895	(40.599) = 40.173	.4257	4.2054	9.48%	90.52%
1992	1.06%	.9894	(40.173) = 39.747	.4257	4.6311	10.44%	89.56%
1993	1.07%	.9893	(39.747) = 39.321	.4257	5.0568	11.39%	88.61%
1994	1.08%	.9892	(39.321) = 38.896	.4257	5.4825	12.35%	87.65%
1995	1.10%	.9890	(38.896) = 38.470	.4257	5.9082	13.31%	86.69%
1996	1.11%	.9889	(38.470) = 38.044	.4257	6.3339	14.27%	85.73%
1997	1.12%	.9888	(38.044) = 37.619	.4257	6.7596	15.23%	84.77%
1998	1.13%	.9887	(37.619) = 37.193	.4257	7.1853	16.19%	83.81%
1999	1.15%	.9885	(37.193) = 36.767	.4257	7.6110	17.15%	82.85%
2000	1.16%	.9884	(36.767) = 36.342	.4257	8.0367	18.11%	81.89%

Measured Res (On)   = 1.397
Inferred Res (On)   =   .647
Undiscovered Min (On) = 16.000
Measured Res (Off)   =   .145
Inferred Res (Off)   =   .100
Undiscovered Min (Off) = 8.000
                         26.289 TCF

HISTORIC & PROJECTED PRODUCTION OF ALASKA (EXCLUDING PRUDHOE BAY)

NONASSOCIATED & ASSOCIATED NATURAL GAS PRODUCTION - TCF/YR

MINIMUM APPROACH

Year	% WR	Multiplier	Remaining Reserve	Production	Cumulative Production	(27.194) % ORG	% ORG Remain
1965	.03%	.9997	(27.182) = 27.174	.008	.020	.07%	99.93%
1966	.05%	.9995	(27.174) = 27.161	.013	.033	.12%	99.88%
1967	.08%	.9992	(27.161) = 27.138	.023	.056	.21%	99.79%
1968	.15%	.9985	(27.138) = 27.096	.042	.098	.36%	99.64%
1969	.30%	.9970	(27.096) = 27.015	.081	.179	.66%	99.34%
1970	.54%	.9946	(27.015) = 26.870	.145	.324	1.19%	98.81%
1971	.57%	.9943	(26.870) = 26.716	.154	.478	1.76%	98.24%
1972	.55%	.9945	(26.716) = 26.569	.147	.625	2.30%	97.70%
1973	.51%	.9949	(26.569) = 26.433	.136	.761	2.80%	97.20%
1974	.54%	.9946	(26.433) = 26.289	.144	.905	3.33%	96.67%
1975	.59%	.9941	(26.289) = 26.134	.155	1.060	3.90%	96.10%
1976	.59%	.9941	(26.134) = 25.980	.154	1.214	4.46%	95.54%
1977	.59%	.9941	(25.980) = 25.827	.153	1.367	5.03%	94.97%
1978	.59%	.9941	(25.827) = 25.674	.153	1.520	5.59%	94.41%
1979	.59%	.9941	(25.674) = 25.523	.151	1.671	6.14%	93.86%
1980	.60%	.9940	(25.523) = 25.370	.153	1.824	6.71%	93.29%
1981	.68%	.9932	(25.370) = 25.197	.173	1.997	7.34%	92.66%
1982	.76%	.9924	(25.197) = 25.006	.191	2.188	8.05%	91.95%
1983	.84%	.9916	(25.006) = 24.800	.206	2.394	8.80%	91.20%
1984	.92%	.9908	(24.800) = 24.567	.233	2.627	9.66%	90.34%
1985	1.0%	.9900	(24.567) = 24.322	.245	2.872	10.56%	89.44%
1986	1.0%	.9900	(24.322) = 24.079	.243	3.115	11.45%	88.55%
1987	1.0%	.9900	(24.079) = 23.838	.241	3.356	12.34%	87.66%
1988	1.0%	.9900	(23.838) = 23.599	.239	3.595	13.22%	86.78%
1989	1.0%	.9900	(23.599) = 23.363	.236	3.831	14.09%	85.91%
1990	1.0%	.9900	(23.363) = 23.130	.233	4.064	14.94%	85.06%
1991	1.0%	.9900	(23.130) = 22.898	.232	4.296	15.80%	84.20%
1992	1.0%	.9900	(22.898) = 22.669	.229	4.525	16.64%	83.36%
1993	1.0%	.9900	(22.669) = 22.443	.226	4.751	17.47%	82.53%
1994	1.0%	.9900	(22.443) = 22.218	.225	4.976	18.30%	81.70%
1995	1.0%	.9900	(22.218) = 21.996	.222	5.198	19.11%	80.89%
1996	1.0%	.9900	(21.996) = 21.776	.220	5.418	19.92%	80.08%
1997	1.0%	.9900	(21.776) = 21.558	.218	5.636	20.73%	79.27%
1998	1.0%	.9900	(21.558) = 21.343	.215	5.851	21.52%	78.48%
1999	1.0%	.9900	(21.343) = 21.129	.214	6.065	22.30%	77.70%
2000	1.0%	.9900	(21.129) = 20.918	.211	6.276	23.08%	76.92%

SUMMARY OF THE HISTORIC & PROJECTED PRODUCTION OF REGION #1

NA & ASSOC. NATURAL GAS PRODUCTION - TCF/YR

Year	Prudhoe Bay Production	Maximum Remain Alaska	Minimum Remain Alaska	Maximum Total Alaska Production	Minimum Total Alaska Production
1965	-	.008	.008	.008	.008
1966	-	.013	.013	.013	.013
1967	-	.023	.023	.023	.023
1968	-	.042	.042	.042	.042
1969	-	.081	.081	.081	.081
1970	-	.145	.145	.145	.145
1971	-	.154	.154	.154	.154
1972	-	.147	.147	.147	.147
1973	-	.136	.136	.136	.136
1974	-	.144	.144	.144	.144
1975	-	.155	.155	.155	.155
1976	-	.154	.154	.154	.154
1977	.018	.154	.153	.172	.171
1978	.036	.161	.153	.197	.189
1979	.037	.160	.151	.197	.188
1980	.036	.166	.153	.202	.189
1981	.037	.266	.173	.303	.210
1982	.221	.363	.191	.584	.412
1983	.415	.460	.206	.875	.621
1984	.426	.555	.233	.981	.659
1985	.426	.647	.245	1.073	.671
1986	.426	.640	.243	1.066	.669
1987	.426	.634	.241	1.060	.667
1988	.426	.628	.239	1.054	.665
1989	.426	.621	.236	1.047	.662
1990	.426	.616	.233	1.042	.659
1991	.426	.609	.232	1.035	.658
1992	.426	.603	.229	1.029	.655
1993	.426	.597	.226	1.023	.652
1994	.426	.591	.225	1.017	.651
1995	.425	.585	.222	1.010	.647
1996	.425	.579	.220	1.004	.645
1997	.425	.573	.218	.998	.643
1998	.425	.568	.215	.993	.640
1999	.425	.562	.214	.987	.639
2000	.425	.556	.211	.981	.636

Measured Res (On)	4.732
Inferred Res (On)	4.000
Undiscovered (On)	8.000
Measured Res (Off)	.463
Inferred Res (Off)	.400
Undiscovered (Off) =	2.000
	19.595 TCF

MINIMUM APPROACH

HISTORIC & PROJECTED PRODUCTION OF REGION #2 (ON & OFF)

NONASSOCIATED & ASSOCIATED NATURAL GAS PRODUCTION - TCF/YR

Year	Annual % Withdrawal	Multiplier	(TCF) Remaining Reserve	(46.465) % ORG Remaining	Production
1965	2.47%	.9753	(25.455) = 24.827	53.4%	.628
1966	2.76%	.9724	(24.827) = 24.141	52.0%	.686
1967	2.73%	.9727	(24.141) = 23.481	50.5%	.660
1968	2.92%	.9708	(23.481) = 22.796	49.1%	.685
1969	2.89%	.9711	(22.796) = 22.137	47.6%	.659
1970	2.87%	.9713	(22.137) = 21.501	46.3%	.636
1971	2.66%	.9734	(21.501) = 20.929	45.0%	.572
1972	2.38%	.9762	(20.929) = 20.430	44.0%	.499
1973	2.36%	.9766	(20.430) = 19.952	42.9%	.478
1974	1.79%	.9821	(19.952) = 19.595	42.2%	.357
1975	1.69%	.9831	(19.595) = 19.263	41.5%	.332
1976	1.63%	.9837	(19.263) = 18.949	40.8%	.314
1977	1.56%	.9844	(18.949) = 18.653	40.1%	.296
1978	1.50%	.9850	(18.653) = 18.374	39.5%	.279
1979	1.50%	.9850	(18.374) = 18.098	38.9%	.276
1980	1.50%	.9850	(18.098) = 17.826	38.4%	.272
1981	1.50%	.9850	(17.826) = 17.559	37.8%	.267
1982	1.50%	.9850	(17.559) = 17.296	37.2%	.263
1983	1.50%	.9850	(17.296) = 17.036	36.7%	.260
1984	1.50%	.9850	(17.036) = 16.780	36.1%	.256
1985	1.50%	.9850	(16.780) = 16.529	35.6%	.251
1986	1.50%	.9850	(16.529) = 16.281	35.0%	.248
1987	1.50%	.9850	(16.281) = 16.036	34.5%	.245
1988	1.50%	.9850	(16.036) = 15.795	34.0%	.241
1989	1.50%	.9850	(15.795) = 15.558	33.5%	.237
1990	1.50%	.9850	(15.558) = 15.325	33.0%	.233
1991	1.50%	.9850	(15.325) = 15.095	32.5%	.230
1992	1.50%	.9850	(15.095) = 14.869	32.0%	.226
1993	1.50%	.9850	(14.869) = 14.646	31.5%	.223
1994	1.50%	.9850	(14.646) = 14.426	31.0%	.220
1995	1.50%	.9850	(14.426) = 14.209	30.6%	.217
1996	1.50%	.9850	(14.209) = 13.996	30.1%	.213
1997	1.50%	.9850	(13.996) = 13.786	29.7%	.210
1998	1.50%	.9850	(13.786) = 13.579	29.2%	.207
1999	1.50%	.9850	(13.579) = 13.376	28.8%	.203
2000	1.50%	.9850	(13.376) = 13.175	28.4%	.201

Measured Res (On) = 9.081
Inferred Res (On) = 2.900
Undiscovered (On) = 6.000
Measured Res (Off) = -
Inferred Res (Off) = -
Undiscovered (Off) = -
_____
17.981 TCF

MINIMUM APPROACH

HISTORIC & PROJECTED PRODUCTION OF REGION #3

NONASSOCIATED & ASSOCIATED NATURAL GAS PRODUCTION - TCF/YR

(TCF)

Year	Annual % Withdrawal	Multiplier	Remaining Reserve	(29.443) % ORG Remaining	Production
1965	2.43%	.9757	(24.616) = 24.018	81.6%	.598
1966	2.61%	.9739	(24.018) = 23.391	79.5%	.627
1967	2.81%	.9719	(23.391) = 22.734	77.2%	.657
1968	3.15%	.9685	(22.734) = 22.018	74.8%	.716
1969	3.02%	.9698	(22.018) = 21.354	72.5%	.664
1970	2.97%	.9703	(21.354) = 20.719	70.4%	.635
1971	3.26%	.9674	(20.719) = 20.044	68.1%	.675
1972	3.51%	.9649	(20.044) = 19.340	65.7%	.704
1973	3.53%	.9647	(19.340) = 18.658	63.4%	.682
1974	3.63%	.9637	(18.658) = 17.981	61.1%	.677
1975	3.68%	.9632	(17.981) = 17.319	58.8%	.662
1976	3.70%	.9630	(17.319) = 16.678	56.6%	.641
1977	3.73%	.9627	(16.678) = 16.056	54.5%	.622
1978	3.75%	.9625	(16.056) = 15.454	52.5%	.602
1979	3.75%	.9625	(15.454) = 14.874	50.5%	.580
1980	3.75%	.9625	(14.874) = 14.317	48.6%	.557
1981	3.75%	.9625	(14.317) = 13.780	46.8%	.537
1982	3.75%	.9625	(13.780) = 13.263	45.0%	.517
1983	3.75%	.9625	(13.263) = 12.765	43.4%	.498
1984	3.75%	.9625	(12.765) = 12.287	41.7%	.478
1985	3.75%	.9625	(12.287) = 11.826	40.2%	.461
1986	3.75%	.9625	(11.826) = 11.382	38.7%	.444
1987	3.75%	.9625	(11.382) = 10.955	37.2%	.427
1988	3.75%	.9625	(10.955) = 10.545	35.8%	.410
1989	3.75%	.9625	(10.545) = 10.149	34.5%	.396
1990	3.75%	.9625	(10.149) = 9.768	33.2%	.381
1991	3.75%	.9625	(9.768) = 9.402	31.9%	.366
1992	3.75%	.9625	(9.402) = 9.049	30.7%	.353
1993	3.75%	.9625	(9.049) = 8.710	29.6%	.339
1994	3.75%	.9625	(8.710) = 8.383	28.5%	.327
1995	3.75%	.9625	(8.383) = 8.069	27.4%	.314
1996	3.75%	.9625	(8.069) = 7.766	26.4%	.303
1997	3.75%	.9625	(7.766) = 7.475	25.4%	.291
1998	3.75%	.9625	(7.475) = 7.195	24.4%	.280
1999	3.75%	.9625	(7.195) = 6.925	23.5%	.270
2000	3.75%	.9625	(6.925) = 6.665	22.6%	.260

Measured Res (On)	=	6.754
Inferred Res (On)	=	5.300
Undiscovered (On)	=	18.000
Measured Res (Off)	=	-
Inferred Res (Off)	=	-
Undiscovered (Off)	=	-
		30.054 TCF

MINIMUM APPROACH

HISTORIC & PROJECTED PRODUCTION OF REGION #4

NONASSOCIATED & ASSOCIATED NATURAL GAS PRODUCTION - TCF/YR
(TCF)

Year	Annual % Withdrawal	Multiplier	Remaining Reserve	(40.874) % ORG Remaining	Production
1965	1.28%	.9872	(34.866) = 34.418	84.2%	.448
1966	1.26%	.9874	(34.418) = 33.983	83.1%	.435
1967	1.26%	.9874	(33.983) = 33.555	82.1%	.428
1968	1.36%	.9864	(33.555) = 33.097	81.0%	.458
1969	1.46%	.9854	(33.097) = 32.615	79.8%	.482
1970	1.50%	.9850	(32.615) = 32.125	78.6%	.490
1971	1.56%	.9844	(32.125) = 31.624	77.4%	.501
1972	1.68%	.9832	(31.624) = 31.093	76.1%	.531
1973	1.77%	.9823	(31.093) = 30.544	74.7%	.549
1974	1.60%	.9840	(30.544) = 30.054	73.5%	.490
1975	1.55%	.9845	(30.054) = 29.589	72.4%	.465
1976	1.53%	.9847	(29.589) = 29.136	71.3%	.453
1977	1.52%	.9848	(29.136) = 28.693	70.2%	.443
1978	1.50%	.9850	(28.693) = 28.263	69.1%	.430
1979	1.50%	.9850	(28.263) = 27.839	68.1%	.424
1980	1.50%	.9850	(27.839) = 27.421	67.1%	.418
1981	1.50%	.9850	(27.421) = 27.010	66.1%	.411
1982	1.50%	.9850	(27.010) = 26.605	65.1%	.405
1983	1.50%	.9850	(26.605) = 26.206	64.1%	.399
1984	1.50%	.9850	(26.206) = 25.813	63.2%	.393
1985	1.50%	.9850	(25.813) = 25.425	62.2%	.388
1986	1.50%	.9850	(25.425) = 25.044	61.3%	.381
1987	1.50%	.9850	(25.044) = 24.668	60.4%	.376
1988	1.50%	.9850	(24.668) = 24.298	59.4%	.370
1989	1.50%	.9850	(24.298) = 23.934	58.6%	.364
1990	1.50%	.9850	(23.934) = 23.575	57.7%	.359
1991	1.50%	.9850	(23.575) = 23.221	56.8%	.354
1992	1.50%	.9850	(23.221) = 22.872	56.0%	.349
1993	1.50%	.9850	(22.872) = 22.529	55.1%	.343
1994	1.50%	.9850	(22.529) = 22.191	54.3%	.338
1995	1.50%	.9850	(22.191) = 21.858	53.5%	.333
1996	1.50%	.9850	(21.858) = 21.531	52.7%	.327
1997	1.50%	.9850	(21.531) = 21.208	51.9%	.323
1998	1.50%	.9850	(21.208) = 20.889	51.1%	.319
1999	1.50%	.9850	(20.889) = 20.576	50.3%	.313
2000	1.50%	.9850	(20.576) = 20.267	49.6%	.309

Measured Res (On) = 24.624
Inferred Res (On) = 23.300
Undiscovered (On) = 35.000
Measured Res (Off) = -
Inferred Res (Off) = -
Undiscovered (Off) = -

82.924 TCF

MINIMUM APPROACH

HISTORIC & PROJECTED PRODUCTION OF REGION #5

NONASSOCIATED & ASSOCIATED NATURAL GAS PRODUCTION - TCF/YR

				(TCF)	(141.592)	
Year	Annual % Withdrawal	Multiplier		Remaining Reserve	% ORG Remaining	Production
1965	1.73%	.9827	(109.971) =	108.068	76.3%	1.903
1966	1.85%	.9815	(108.068) =	106.065	74.9%	2.003
1967	1.96%	.9804	(106.065) =	103.981	73.4%	2.084
1968	2.22%	.9778	(103.981) =	101.669	71.8%	2.312
1969	2.49%	.9751	(101.669) =	99.137	70.0%	2.532
1970	3.04%	.9696	(99.137) =	96.122	67.9%	3.015
1971	3.25%	.9675	(96.122) =	93.000	65.7%	3.122
1972	3.60%	.9640	(93.000) =	89.651	63.3%	3.349
1973	3.74%	.9626	(89.651) =	86.301	61.0%	3.350
1974	3.91%	.9609	(86.301) =	82.924	58.6%	3.377
1975	3.56%	.9644	(82.924) =	79.974	56.5%	2.950
1976	3.37%	.9663	(79.974) =	77.279	54.6%	2.695
1977	3.19%	.9681	(77.279) =	74.814	52.8%	2.465
1978	3.00%	.9700	(74.814) =	72.569	51.3%	2.245
1979	3.00%	.9700	(72.569) =	70.392	49.7%	2.177
1980	3.00%	.9700	(70.392) =	68.280	48.2%	2.112
1981	3.00%	.9700	(68.280) =	66.232	46.8%	2.048
1982	3.00%	.9700	(66.232) =	64.245	45.4%	1.987
1983	3.00%	.9700	(64.245) =	62.317	44.0%	1.928
1984	3.00%	.9700	(62.317) =	60.448	42.7%	1.869
1985	3.00%	.9700	(60.448) =	58.634	41.4%	1.814
1986	3.00%	.9700	(58.634) =	56.875	40.2%	1.759
1987	3.00%	.9700	(56.875) =	55.169	39.0%	1.706
1988	3.00%	.9700	(55.169) =	53.514	37.8%	1.655
1989	3.00%	.9700	(53.514) =	51.908	36.7%	1.606
1990	3.00%	.9700	(51.908) =	50.351	35.6%	1.557
1991	3.00%	.9700	(50.351) =	48.840	34.5%	1.511
1992	3.00%	.9700	(48.840) =	47.375	33.5%	1.465
1993	3.00%	.9700	(47.375) =	45.954	32.5%	1.421
1994	3.00%	.9700	(45.954) =	44.575	31.5%	1.379
1995	3.00%	.9700	(44.575) =	43.238	30.5%	1.337
1996	3.00%	.9700	(43.238) =	41.941	29.6%	1.297
1997	3.00%	.9700	(41.941) =	40.682	28.7%	1.259
1998	3.00%	.9700	(40.682) =	39.462	27.9%	1.220
1999	3.00%	.9700	(39.462) =	38.278	27.0%	1.184
2000	3.00%	.9700	(38.278) =	37.129	26.2%	1.149

Measured Res (On)	= 81.903
Inferred Res (On)	= 58.700
Undiscovered (On)	= 85.000
Measured Res (Off)	= -
Inferred Res (Off)	= -
Undiscovered (Off)	= -

MINIMUM APPROACH   225.603 TCF

HISTORIC & PROJECTED PRODUCTION OF REGION #6

NONASSOCIATED & ASSOCIATED NATURAL GAS PRODUCTION - TCF/YR
(TCF)

Year	Annual % Withdrawal	Multiplier		Remaining Reserve	(422.626) % ORG Remaining	Production
1965	2.56%	.9744	(313.176) =	305.147	72.2%	8.029
1966	2.76%	.9724	(305.147) =	296.726	70.2%	8.421
1967	2.88%	.9712	(296.726) =	288.193	68.2%	8.533
1968	3.10%	.9690	(288.193) =	279.251	66.1%	8.942
1969	3.35%	.9665	(279.251) =	269.910	63.9%	9.341
1970	3.49%	.9651	(269.910) =	260.481	61.6%	9.429
1971	3.56%	.9644	(260.481) =	251.203	59.4%	9.278
1972	3.67%	.9633	(251.203) =	241.988	57.3%	9.215
1973	3.54%	.9646	(241.988) =	233.423	55.2%	8.565
1974	3.35%	.9665	(233.423) =	225.603	53.4%	7.820
1975	3.03%	.9697	(225.603) =	218.774	51.8%	6.829
1976	2.85%	.9715	(218.774) =	212.539	50.3%	6.235
1977	2.68%	.9732	(212.539) =	206.843	48.9%	5.696
1978	2.50%	.9750	(206.843) =	201.672	47.7%	5.171
1979	2.50%	.9750	(201.672) =	196.630	46.5%	5.042
1980	2.50%	.9750	(196.630) =	191.714	45.4%	4.916
1981	2.50%	.9750	(191.714) =	186.921	44.2%	4.793
1982	2.50%	.9750	(186.921) =	182.248	43.1%	4.673
1983	2.50%	.9750	(182.248) =	177.692	42.0%	4.556
1984	2.50%	.9750	(177.692) =	173.250	41.0%	4.442
1985	2.50%	.9750	(173.250) =	168.918	40.0%	4.332
1986	2.50%	.9750	(168.918) =	164.695	39.0%	4.223
1987	2.50%	.9750	(164.695) =	160.578	38.0%	4.117
1988	2.50%	.9750	(160.578) =	156.563	37.0%	4.015
1989	2.50%	.9750	(156.563) =	152.649	36.1%	3.914
1990	2.50%	.9750	(152.649) =	148.833	35.2%	3.816
1991	2.50%	.9750	(148.833) =	145.112	34.3%	3.721
1992	2.50%	.9750	(145.112) =	141.484	33.5%	3.628
1993	2.50%	.9750	(141.484) =	137.947	32.6%	3.537
1994	2.50%	.9750	(137.947) =	134.498	31.8%	3.449
1995	2.50%	.9750	(134.498) =	131.136	31.0%	3.362
1996	2.50%	.9750	(131.136) =	127.857	30.3%	3.279
1997	2.50%	.9750	(127.857) =	124.661	29.5%	3.196
1998	2.50%	.9750	(124.661) =	121.544	28.8%	3.117
1999	2.50%	.9750	(121.544) =	118.506	28.0%	3.038
2000	2.50%	.9750	(118.506) =	115.543	27.3%	2.963

Measured Res (Off) = 35.348
Inferred Res (Off) = 67.000
Undiscovered (Off) = 18.000
—————
120.348 TCF

MINIMUM APPROACH

HISTORIC & PROJECTED PRODUCTION OF REGION #6A (GULF OF MEXICO)

NONASSOCIATED & ASSOCIATED NATURAL GAS PRODUCTION - TCF/YR

Year	Annual % Withdrawal	Multiplier	(TCF) Remaining Reserve	(152.401) % ORG Remaining	Production
1965	.67%	.9933	(148.292) = 147.303	96.6%	.989
1966	.91%	.9909	(147.303) = 145.956	95.7%	1.347
1967	1.25%	.9875	(145.956) = 144.129	94.5%	1.827
1968	1.59%	.9841	(144.129) = 141.841	93.0%	2.288
1969	1.93%	.9807	(141.841) = 139.108	91.2%	2.733
1970	2.30%	.9770	(139.108) = 135.908	89.1%	3.200
1971	2.52%	.9748	(135.908) = 132.485	86.9%	3.423
1972	2.92%	.9708	(132.485) = 128.612	84.3%	3.873
1973	3.24%	.9676	(128.612) = 124.443	81.6%	4.169
1974	3.29%	.9671	(124.443) = 120.348	78.9%	4.095
1975	3.42%	.9658	(120.348) = 116.229	76.2%	4.119
1976	3.45%	.9655	(116.229) = 112.219	73.6%	4.010
1977	3.47%	.9653	(112.219) = 108.325	71.0%	3.894
1978	3.5%	.9650	(108.325) = 104.534	68.6%	3.791
1979	3.5%	.9650	(104.534) = 100.875	66.2%	3.659
1980	3.5%	.9650	(100.875) = 97.344	63.8%	3.531
1981	3.5%	.9650	(97.344) = 93.937	61.6%	3.407
1982	3.5%	.9650	(93.937) = 90.649	59.4%	3.288
1983	3.5%	.9650	(90.649) = 87.477	57.4%	3.172
1984	3.5%	.9650	(87.477) = 84.415	55.4%	3.062
1985	3.5%	.9650	(84.415) = 81.460	53.4%	2.955
1986	3.5%	.9650	(81.460) = 78.609	51.5%	2.851
1987	3.5%	.9650	(78.609) = 75.858	49.7%	2.751
1988	3.5%	.9650	(75.858) = 73.203	48.0%	2.655
1989	3.5%	.9650	(73.203) = 70.640	46.3%	2.563
1990	3.5%	.9650	(70.640) = 68.168	44.7%	2.472
1991	3.5%	.9650	(68.168) = 65.782	43.1%	2.386
1992	3.5%	.9650	(65.782) = 63.480	41.6%	2.302
1993	3.5%	.9650	(63.480) = 61.258	40.2%	2.222
1994	3.5%	.9650	(61.258) = 59.114	38.8%	2.144
1995	3.5%	.9650	(59.114) = 57.045	37.4%	2.069
1996	3.5%	.9650	(57.045) = 55.048	36.1%	1.997
1997	3.5%	.9650	(55.048) = 53.121	34.8%	1.927
1998	3.5%	.9650	(53.121) = 51.262	33.6%	1.859
1999	3.5%	.9650	(51.262) = 49.468	32.4%	1.794
2000	3.5%	.9650	(49.468) = 47.737	31.3%	1.731

Measured Res (On)	=	34.150
Inferred Res (On)	=	20.600
Undiscovered (On)	=	50.000
Measured Res (Off)	=	-
Inferred Res (Off)	=	-
Undiscovered (Off)	=	-
		104.750 TCF

MINIMUM APPROACH

HISTORIC & PROJECTED PRODUCTION OF REGION #7

NONASSOCIATED & ASSOCIATED NATURAL GAS PRODUCTION - TCF/YR

Year	Annual % Withdrawal	Multiplier	(TCF) Remaining Reserve	(212.417) % ORG Remaining	Production
1965	2.24%	.9776	(142.463) = 139.271	65.6%	3.192
1966	2.45%	.9755	(139.271) = 135.855	64.0%	3.416
1967	2.70%	.9730	(135.855) = 132.192	62.2%	3.663
1968	2.83%	.9717	(132.192) = 128.455	60.5%	3.737
1969	3.10%	.9690	(128.455) = 124.471	58.6%	3.984
1970	3.39%	.9661	(124.471) = 120.253	56.6%	4.218
1971	3.16%	.9684	(120.253) = 116.449	54.8%	3.804
1972	3.41%	.9659	(116.449) = 112.482	53.0%	3.967
1973	3.45%	.9655	(112.482) = 108.600	51.1%	3.882
1974	3.55%	.9645	(108.600) = 104.750	49.3%	3.850
1975	3.52%	.9648	(104.750) = 101.063	47.6%	3.687
1976	3.48%	.9652	(101.063) = 97.546	45.9	3.517
1977	3.44%	.9656	(97.546) = 94.190	44.3%	3.356
1978	3.40%	.9660	(94.190) = 90.988	42.8%	3.202
1979	3.40%	.9660	(90.988) = 87.894	41.4%	3.094
1980	3.40%	.9660	(87.894) = 84.906	40.0%	2.988
1981	3.40%	.9660	(84.906) = 82.019	38.6%	2.887
1982	3.40%	.9660	(82.019) = 79.230	37.3%	2.789
1983	3.40%	.9660	(79.230) = 76.536	36.0%	2.694
1984	3.40%	.9660	(76.536) = 73.934	34.8%	2.602
1985	3.40%	.9660	(73.934) = 71.420	33.6%	2.514
1986	3.40%	.9660	(71.420) = 68.992	32.5%	2.428
1987	3.40%	.9660	(68.992) = 66.646	31.4%	2.346
1988	3.40%	.9660	(66.646) = 64.380	30.3%	2.266
1989	3.40%	.9660	(64.380) = 62.191	29.3%	2.189
1990	3.40%	.9660	(62.191) = 60.077	28.3%	2.114
1991	3.40%	.9660	(60.077) = 58.034	27.3%	2.043
1992	3.40%	.9660	(58.034) = 56.061	26.4%	1.973
1993	3.40%	.9660	(56.061) = 54.155	25.5%	1.906
1994	3.40%	.9660	(54.155) = 52.313	24.6%	1.842
1995	3.40%	.9660	(52.313) = 50.535	23.8%	1.778
1996	3.40%	.9660	(50.535) = 48.816	23.0%	1.719
1997	3.40%	.9660	(48.816) = 47.157	22.2%	1.659
1998	3.40%	.9660	(47.157) = 45.553	21.4%	1.604
1999	3.40%	.9660	(45.553) = 44.004	20.7%	1.529
2000	3.40%	.9660	(44.004) = 42.508	20.0%	1.496

Measured Res (On)	=	8.210
Inferred Res (On)	=	4.600
Undiscovered (On)	=	6.900
Measured Res (Off)	=	-
Inferred Res (Off)	=	-
Undiscovered (Off)	=	-
		19.710 TCF

MINIMUM APPROACH

HISTORIC & PROJECTED PRODUCTION OF REGIONS #8, 9, 10, 11 + MISCELLANEOUS

NONASSOCIATED & ASSOCIATED NATURAL GAS PRODUCTION - TCF/YR

Year	Annual % Withdrawal	Multiplier		(TCF) Remaining Reserve	(54.170) % ORG Remaining	Production
1965	1.87%	.9813	(24.538) =	24.080	44.5%	.458
1966	1.91%	.9809	(24.080) =	23.619	43.6%	.461
1967	2.06%	.9794	(23.619) =	23.132	42.7%	.487
1968	2.14%	.9786	(23.132) =	22.636	41.8%	.496
1969	2.10%	.9790	(22.636) =	22.161	40.9%	.475
1970	2.28%	.9772	(22.161) =	21.656	40.0%	.505
1971	2.24%	.9776	(21.656) =	21.171	39.1%	.485
1972	2.24%	.9776	(21.171) =	20.696	38.2%	.475
1973	2.32%	.9768	(20.696) =	20.216	37.3%	.480
1974	2.50%	.9750	(20.216) =	19.710	36.4%	.506
1975	2.64%	.9736	(19.710) =	19.189	35.4%	.521
1976	2.73%	.9727	(19.189) =	18.665	34.5%	.524
1977	2.81%	.9719	(18.665) =	18.141	33.5%	.524
1978	2.90%	.9710	(18.141) =	17.615	32.5%	.526
1979	2.90%	.9710	(17.615) =	17.104	31.6%	.511
1980	2.90%	.9710	(17.104) =	16.608	30.7%	.496
1981	2.90%	.9710	(16.608) =	16.126	29.8%	.482
1982	2.90%	.9710	(16.126) =	15.658	28.9%	.468
1983	2.90%	.9710	(15.658) =	15.204	28.1%	.454
1984	2.90%	.9710	(15.204) =	14.763	27.3%	.441
1985	2.90%	.9710	(14.763) =	14.335	26.5%	.428
1986	2.90%	.9710	(14.335) =	13.919	25.7%	.416
1987	2.90%	.9710	(13.919) =	13.515	24.9%	.404
1988	2.90%	.9710	(13.515) =	13.123	24.2%	.392
1989	2.90%	.9710	(13.123) =	12.743	23.5%	.380
1990	2.90%	.9710	(12.743) =	12.373	22.8%	.370
1991	2.90%	.9710	(12.373) =	12.014	22.2%	.359
1992	2.90%	.9710	(12.014) =	11.666	21.5%	.348
1993	2.90%	.9710	(11.666) =	11.327	20.9%	.339
1994	2.90%	.9710	(11.327) =	10.999	20.3%	.328
1995	2.90%	.9710	(10.999) =	10.680	19.7%	.319
1996	2.90%	.9710	(10.680) =	10.370	19.1%	.310
1997	2.90%	.9710	(10.370) =	10.069	18.6%	.301
1998	2.90%	.9710	(10.069) =	9.777	18.0%	.292
1999	2.90%	.9710	(9.777) =	9.494	17.5%	.283
2000	2.90%	.9710	(9.494) =	9.218	17.0%	.276

MINIMUM APPROACH

HISTORIC & PROJECTED PRODUCTION OF REGION #11A (ATLANTIC COAST OFFSHORE)

NONASSOCIATED & ASSOCIATED NATURAL GAS PRODUCTION - TCF/YR

Year	Annual % Withdrawal	Multiplier	(TCF) Remaining Reserve	(5.000) % ORG Remaining	Production
1965	0%	100%	5.000	100%	0
1966					
1967					
1968					
1969					
1970					
1971					
1972					
1973					
1974					
1975					
1976					
1977					
1978					
1979					
1980					
1981					
1982					
1983					
1984					
1985	.025%	.99975	(5.000) = 4.999	100%	.001
1986	.125%	.99875	(4.999) = 4.993	99.9%	.006
1987	.225%	.99775	(4.993) = 4.981	99.6%	.012
1988	.305%	.99695	(4.981) = 4.966	99.3%	.015
1989	.415%	.99585	(4.966) = 4.945	98.9%	.021
1990	.525%	.99475	(4.945) = 4.920	98.4%	.025
1991	.635%	.99365	(4.920) = 4.888	97.8%	.032
1992	.755%	.99245	(4.888) = 4.851	97.0%	.037
1993	.84%	.9916	(4.851) = 4.811	96.2%	.040
1994	.94%	.9906	(4.811) = 4.765	95.3%	.046
1995	1.035%	.98965	(4.765) = 4.716	94.3%	.049
1996	1.15%	.9885	(4.716) = 4.662	93.2%	.054
1997	1.27%	.9873	(4.662) = 4.603	92.1%	.059
1998	1.385%	.98615	(4.603) = 4.539	90.8%	.064
1999	1.50%	.9850	(4.539) = 4.471	89.4%	.068
2000	1.625%	.98375	(4.471) = 4.398	88.0%	.073

Worldwide crude oil and gas production

Oil (1,000 b/d)	June 1976	May* 1976	6-month average — Daily production 1975	1976	Change from Vol.	%	Gas (billion cu ft) June 1976	May 1976	Cum. 1976
WESTERN HEMISPHERE									
Argentina	386	386	399	386	− 13	− 3.3	22.7	21.5	144.0
Bolivia	45	45	38	45	7	18.4	11.2	11.3	70.5
Brazil	170	170	174	172	− 2	− 1.1	4.9	4.9	28.4
Canada	1,465	1,341	1,379	1,280	− 99	− 7.2	258.9	265.4	1,639.9
Chile	25	25	25	25	...	...	20.6	10.6	73.1
Colombia	146	146	162	146	− 19	− 11.5	9.7	5.0	35.9
Equador	113	203	137	182	45	32.8	1.2	1.1	7.2
Mexico	780	780	681	762	81	11.9	65.9	65.9	395.7
Peru	75	75	72	75	3	4.2	1.0	1.0	7.2
Trinidad	185	185	210	185	− 25	− 11.9	10.7	4.2	32.4
United States	8,108	8,120	8,450	8,141	− 309	− 3.7	1,602.7	1,658.9	10,191.0
Venezuela	2,371	2,410	2,529	2,201	− 328	− 13.0	32.5	32.5	195.0
Total	13,869	13,886	14,259	13,599	− 660	− 4.6	2,042.0	2,082.3	12,820.3
WESTERN EUROPE									
Austria	37	37	42	37	− 5	− 11.9	6.5	7.4	44.6
Denmark	3	3	3	3	...	...			
France	20	20	21	20	− 1	− 4.8	18.6	24.0	136.0
West Germany	110	110	113	110	− 3	− 2.7	57.5	39.4	280.7
Italy	18	18	20	18	− 2	− 10.0	46.4	54.1	292.4
Netherlands	30	30	32	30	− 2	− 6.3	360.0	363.6	2,047.3
Norway	282	169	124	243	119	96.0	...	...	...
Spain	40	40	35	40	5	14.3	...	...	...
United Kingdom	185	185	6	144	138	@	155.7	133.4	767.8
Yugoslavia	70	70	76	70	− 6	− 7.9	5.7	5.5	32.4
Total	795	682	471	714	243	51.6	650.4	627.4	3,601.2
MIDDLE EAST									
Abu Dhabi	1,574	1,542	1,201	1,552	351	29.2	...	...	...
Bahrain	59	59	64	58	− 6	− 9.4	0.1	0.1	0.8
Dubai	331	297	2,157	1,552	− 605	28.1	...	...	...
Iran	6,102	5,600	5,433	5,486	53	1.0	140.0	141.2	849.8
Iraq	1,760	1,240	2,157	1,907	− 250	− 11.6	8.6	10.0	50.3
Israel	1	1	90	1	− 89	− 98.9	0.1	0.2	1.0
Kuwait	1,659	1,449	1,890	1,624	− 266	− 14.1	15.6	15.6	92.6
Neutral Zone†	403	400	486	410	− 76	− 15.6	...	...	...
Oman	356	362	314	368	54	17.2	8.7	1.2	52.2
Qatar	494	496	456	489	33	7.2	...	...	...
Saudi Arabia	8,325	8,250	6,575	7,970	1,395	21.2	...	...	...
Sharjah	43	39	40	39	− 1	− 2.5	...	...	...
Syria	175	175	174	175	1	.6	...	...	...
Turkey	55	55	60	55	− 5	− 8.3	...	...	...
Total	21,277	20,525	19,191	20,085	894	4.7	173.1	168.3	1,046.7
ASIA-PACIFIC									
Afghanistan							8.7	3.0	52.2
Australia	423	432	420	429	9	2.1	15.1	18.5	86.7
Burma	23	23	20	23	3	15.0	0.3	0.4	2.1
Brunei-Malaysia	285	285	260	285	25	9.6	3.8	4.0	18.8
India	175	175	165	175	10	6.1	3.2	3.2	20.0
Indonesia	1,480	1,515	1,244	1,490	246	19.8	19.1	19.1	110.0
Japan	12	12	13	12	− 1	− 7.7	8.4	8.9	50.9
New Zealand	...	...	...	...	...	...	4.8	4.9	27.9
Pakistan	6	6	6	6	...	...	11.8	11.8	72.0
Taiwan	5	5	5	5	...	...	1.6	1.7	10.0
Total	2,409	2,453	2,132	2,425	293	13.7	76.8	75.5	450.6
AFRICA									
Algeria	1,000	1,000	904	1,000	96	10.6	16.7	2.5	100.2
Angola	30	15	23	8	− 15	− 65.2	5.7	6.0	11.7
Cabinda	112	88	141	45	− 96	− 68.1	...	...	...
Congo	40	40	38	40	2	5.3	0.2	0.4	...
Egypt	315	315	210	311	101	48.1	3.2	8.0	19.2
Gabon	200	200	200	204	4	2.0	0.1	1.5	1.6
Libya	1,962	1,940	1,150	1,831	681	59.2	35.4	12.0	212.4
Morocco	1	1	1	1	...	...	0.3	0.2	1.2
Nigeria	2,050	2,082	1,714	2,009	295	17.2	60.6	1.4	363.6
Tunisia	80	80	97	81	− 16	− 16.5	17.2	0.7	103.2
Zaire	18	18	...	18	18	@	...	...	...
Total	5,808	5,779	4,479	5,549	1,070	23.9	139.4	32.7	813.1
COMMUNIST									
China	1,650	1,650	1,400	1,588	188	13.4	124.0	124.4	679.3
Rumania	290	290	290	290	...	...	71.3	71.2	427.4
U.S.S.R.‡	10,317	10,244	9,655	10,204	549	5.7	916.8	917.8	5,590.5
Other	110	110	110	110	...	...	62.4	60.0	353.6
Total	12,367	12,294	11,456	12,192	736	6.4	1,174.5	1,173.4	7,050.8
World Total	56,925	55,619	51,989	54,563	2,574	5.0	4,256.2	4,159.6	25,782.7

*Figures adjusted. †Shared by Kuwait/Saudi Arabia. ‡Includes gas liquids.

U. S. ENERGY SUPPLY

1975 through 1985

Sources: EEEe Petroleum & Natural Gas Projections
Dr. Herman Franssen, *Towards Project Interdependence:*
Energy in the Coming Decade
John Duane, numerous articles
F.E.A. *1976 National Energy Outlook*
Exxon *Energy Outlook 1975-1980*
A.G.A. *1974 Gas Facts*, Page 58

SUPPLY	1975 Actual	1980 Maximum	1980 Minimum	1985 Maximum	1985 Minimum
Domestic Production:					
Petroleum (Billion bbls/yr.)	3.65	3.40	3.40	3.44	3.09
Natural Gas (Trillion cf/yr.)	19.72	15.75	15.48	15.46	13.81
Coal (Million short tons/yr.)	640	810	720	1030	850
Nuclear (Mega-watts capacity)	38,888	73,700	52,600	150,000	100,000
Hydro (Mega-watts capacity)	65,800	71,800	68,200	86,200	71,800
Domestic Synthetics:					
Syngas, Naptha, and Syncrude(TCF)	.4	.7	.5	1.5	.9
Other Domestic Sources:					
Shale Oil (Billions bbls./yr.)	0.00	0.00*	0.00*	.10	0.00
Geothermal (Mega-watts)	0.00*	0.00*	0.00*	2000	1000
Solar: Electric (Mega-watts)	0.00*	0.00*	0.00*	500	300
Heating & Air Conditioning(Bbls)	0.00*	0.00*	0.00*	.022	.012
Solid Wastes	0.00*	0.00*	0.00*	0.00*	0.00*
Net Imports (Excluding Petroleum):					
Natural Gas (Trillion cf/yr.)	1.0	.5	.3	.2	0.00
Liquefied Natural Gas (Tcf/yr.)	0.00	.6	.2	1.0	.5
Coal (Million short tons/yr.)	0.00	0.00	50	0.00	200

* Negligible Production

INTERNATIONAL PETROLEUM PRODUCTION ANALYSIS — U. S. IMPORT POTENTIAL

Million Barrels Per Day

Country	1972 Prod'n	1972 Exports To U.S.	1974 Prod'n	1974 Exports To U.S.	1976 Prod'n (Est.)	1976 Exports To U.S.	1/1/76 Measured Reserve (Billions)	Actual & Estimated Exports to U. S. 1975	1980	1985
Non-Arabic										
Canada	1.537	1.112	1.690	1.068	1.279		7.10	.844	.137	0
Venezuela	3.227	.962	2.975	.978	2.200		17.70	.699	.685	.685
Remaining S. America	1.162	.041	1.268	.312	1.216		8.17	.321	.301	.274
Caribbean Refineries	-0-	1,271	-0-	1,164	-0-		-0-	.986	1.096	1.096
Mexico	.507	.022	.652	.008	.822		9.50	.071	.164	1.644
Indonesia	1.085	.164	1.375	.301	1.501		14.00	.389	.959	.959
Remaining S.E. Asia	.808	.019	.860	.019	.929		7.23	.025	.055	.110
Nigeria	1.822	.252	2.255	.712	2.000		20.20	.762	1.233	1.973
Angola	.140	.016	.167	.049	.082		1.30	.074	.082	.082
Congo & Zaire	.008	Neg.	.060	.003	.060		2.95	.003	.005	.011
Remaining S. Africa	.126	.003	.203	.027	.249		2.50	.030	.041	.055
United Kingdom	.008	.008	.008	.008	.173		16.00	.011	.014	.016
Norway	.033	Neg.	.036	Neg.	.301		7.00	.016	.055	.055
Remaining Europe	1.150	.162	1.112	.175	.329		2.50	.071	.063	.055
Subtotal Free World	11.613	4.032	12.661	4.824	11.141		116.15	4.302	4.890	7.015
Soviet Bloc w/China	8.910	.019	10.951	.030	12.200		103.00	.030	.055	.110
Subtotal Non-Arabic	20.523	4.051	23.612	4.854	23.341		219.15	4.332	4.945	7.098
Arabic & Middle East										
Bahrain	.071	.014	.068	.014	.060		.31	.016	.055	.055
Iran	5.038	.142	6.022	.468	5.501		64.50	.279	.466	.411
Iraq	1.449	.003	1.975	-0-	1.918		34.30	.003	.027	.055
Kuwait	3.008	.044	2.277	.005	1.644		68.00	.016	.055	.110
Oman	.282	Neg.	.290	Neg.	.370		5.90	.003	.014	.027
Qatar	.485	.003	.518	.016	.488		5.85	.019	.055	.110
Saudi Arabia	5.748	.189	8.211	.460	8.170		148.60	.715	1.726	2.740
United Arab Emirates	1.208	.074	1.688	.074	3.142		40.80	.119	.274	.548
Yemen	-0-	Neg.	-0-	Neg.	-0-		-0-	Neg.	Neg.	Neg.
Algeria	1.055	.093	1.008	.189	.959		7.37	.282	.274	.274
Tunisia	.088	.008	.088	.014	.082		1.07	.003	.008	.014
Libya	2.247	.123	1.521	.005	1.863		26.10	.233	1.233	1.233
Egypt	.233	.008	.148	.008	.310		3.90	.005	.027	.027
Subtotal Arabic	20.912	.701	23.814	1.253	24.507		406.70	1.693	4.214	5.604
Total Production & Exports to the U.S.	41.435	4.753	47.427	6.112	47.849	6.575	-0-	6.025	9.159	12.726
U. S. Production*	9.468		8.775		7.904		33.00			
World Totals	50.903		56.202		55.753		658.85			

*Excluding NGL's

TOTAL ANNUAL U. S. ELECTRICAL ENERGY PRODUCTION SPECTRUM 1950-1975

Source of Energy, Heat Input, Heat Output

	Actual Tot. Elect. Prod. Bil. kwh	Coal	Nuclear	Oil	Gas	Hydro	Wood Waste & Geoth.
		P e r c e n t o f s o u r c e e n e r g y					
1950	389	47.1	---	10.3	13.5	29.2	--
1960	842	53.6	---	6.1	21.0	19.3	--
1970	1,640	46.2	1.4	11.9	24.3	16.2	--
1974	1,866	44.6	6.1	16.0	17.1	16.1	.1
1975	1,918	44.5	9.0	15.1	15.6	15.7	.2

Computed elec. prod. by source of energy in Bil.kwh.(10^9kwh)

		Coal	Nuclear	Oil	Gas	Hydro	Wood Waste & Geoth.
1950	389	183.2	---	40.1	52.5	113.5	--
1960	842	451.3	---	51.4	176.8	162.5	--
1970	1,640	757.7	23.0	195.2	398.5	265.7	--
1974*	1,866	829.8	113.6	299.3	319.9	301.0	2.7
1975*	1,918	852.8	171.9	288.8	299.7	301.5	3.4

Computed heat output (@3,413 Btu/kwh) Trillion Btu (10^{12})

		Coal	Nuclear	Oil	Gas	Hydro	Wood Waste & Geoth.
1950	1,328	625	---	136	179	387	--
1960	2,874	1,539	---	175	603	555	--
1970	5,597	2,586	78	67	1,360	907	--
1974	6,369	2,832	388	1,022	1,092	1,027	9.0
1975	6,546	2,910	587	986	1,023	1,022	12.0

Computed heat input (@10,660 Btu/kwh) Trillion Btu (10^{12})

		Coal	Nuclear	Oil	Gas	Hydro	
1950	4,148	1,952	---	425	559	1,209	
1960	8,976	4,807	---	547	1,883	1,733	
1970	17,481	8,077	245	2,081	4,248	2,833	
1974	19,892	8,846	1,211	3,187	3,410	3,209	
1975	20,446	9,091	1,832	3,079	3,195	3,214	

Sources:
* News release Oct. '76 F.P.C. and Statistical Abstract of the U.S. 1975 Table 886

U. S. NUCLEAR ELECTRIC POWER HEAT CONVERSION RELATIONSHIPS

			1970	1973	1974	1975
1.	Total elec. power prod.*	Bil.kwh.(10^9)or 10^{12} wt.hrs.	1,640	1,959	1,866	1,918
2.	Nuclear power production	Bil.kwh.(10^9)or 10^{12} wt.hrs.	23.0	88.2	114	172
3.	Thermal heat in. nuclear 10,660 Btu/kwh	Tri.Btu (10^{12})	245	940	1,211	1,832
4.	Nuclear capacity **	Thous.kw (10^3)	5,622	19,745	31,607	38,888
5.	Btu/kw capacity - input	(3) ÷ (4)	43,578	47,607	38,314	47,109
6.	Elec. heat output nuclear elec. 3,413 Btu/kwh	Tri. Btu (10^{12})	78.5	301.0	388	587
7.	Btu/kw capacity - output	(5) ÷ (4)	13,963	15,244	12,276	15,094
8.	Nuclear capacity - (4) x 8760 hrs/yr	Bil.kwh.(10^9)or 10^{12} wt.hrs.	49	173	277	341

		1970	1973	1974	1975
% nuclear power thermal eff.	(6) ÷ (3)	32.0%	32.0%	32.0%	32.0%
% nuclear power prod. of cap.	(2) ÷ (8)	46.7%	50.9%	41.1%	50.4%
% nuclear power of total elec. power	(2) ÷ (1)	1.4%	4.5%	6.1%	8.9%
% elec. heat input of total energy					26.0%

* Reference: Statistical Abstract of United States table 886
** Reference: Statistical Abstract of United States table 890

BIBLIOGRAPHY

Alternative entry has been employed in the bibliography. Primary consideration has been given to authors of books and known scientists in their individual efforts. Scientific, economic, and governmental organizations have been employed as the primary entry if these organizations have published a series of books or articles with continuity in the energy field, employing a number of authors. The bibliography is not complete as we have omitted hundreds of newspaper articles and almost all editorials and commentaries by columnists. We also have omitted reference to publications that are totally concerned with the subject and represent a source of information in themselves such as the *Oil and Gas Journal*. We have been selective in recording only responsible and relatively complete articles, but we have not eliminated economic treatises and position papers that ignore factual information and reach conclusions with which we cannot agree.

THE LITERATURE REVIEW

THE GENERAL BOOKS

The publishing experience of *The Energy Balloon* is the most helpful in gaining perspective on the availability of energy information. The book is authoritative: Stewart Udall, the principal author, was Secretary of the Interior in the Kennedy and Johnson Administrations which covered the critical years of decision setting up the vulnerability of the United States to the Arab boycott. In many respects, Secretary Udall published his confession of errors and his plea for a national energy policy that would correct those errors and reverse the country's collision course with economic disaster. The book is readable: Secretary Udall's co-authors, Charles Conconi and David Osterhout, are competent writers and they maintained the balance of required historic perspective with brevity for popular appeal. The book was timely and its publisher was competent. McGraw-Hill brought the book to the public in 1974 after the Arab boycott had created the greatest public awareness of the developing energy problem. The publisher's editor was not unhappy with his reviews, and he felt that his initial advertising budget was adequate. The book was neither a financial nor a circulation success: sales did not support the continued advertising budget; secondary or indepth reviews did not develop; two years after publication, the publisher's general books editor is emphatically not interested in any further ventures with energy books. There have not been many.

Two years before *The Energy Balloon* was published, Dr. Richard Runyon, Dean of the Science Department at Long Island University, and Dr. Lawrence Rocks, a research chemist at the same university, brought out *The Energy Crisis* with a less well known publisher. The physical scientists restricted their perspective to the 50 year development of energy dependence. They cover the sun, oil shale, and a breakthrough in atomic fusion. The book anticipated the Arab power ascendancy and predicted dire economic consequences of energy shortage in the immediate future. Again, the book was not a circulation success and the publisher has been reluctant even to discuss supplying the remaining market, four years after publication.

In marked contrast with the books focusing on the energy problem, Anthony Sampson's *The Seven Sisters* is a circulation success as well as an important source of basic information on the oil industry beginning with the 1859 Pennsylvania find and Rockefeller's early control of the industry. Solidly researched, Sampson's book covers the economic history of the petroleum business and the drama of the individuals who have controlled that business up to the April 1975 board meeting of the Gulf Oil Company. This book leaves little doubt as to the myth of the marketplace influence on petroleum prices at the wellhead or the gasoline pump. Only during the few years before Rockefeller restored order to the market, and later before the Texas Railroad Commission found a legal basis for its price control is there any history of a free market until the hundred year production glut was absorbed by the developed world consumption and dependence on this single energy resource became obvious to the natives. Then the free market handed the control of prices to the Organization of Petroleum Exporting Countries.

John Kenneth Galbraith's *Money* made the best seller list at the end of 1975 and it should not be ignored for its contribution to an understanding of the energy problem. It is a history of pecuniary economics — the only economics that economists recognize — paralleling the petroleum history of the same time span. Money and petroleum have had very nearly equal influence on the United States and world economy during the last hundred years. *Money* and *The Seven Sisters* should be read together.

The general literature books that focus on the population problem, the broad aspects of growth limits, and ecology have not met with the public rejection that has been the experience of the energy books. It is now fifteen years since Rachel Carson's *Sea Around Us* and later *Silent Spring* became best sellers, and we are now in the second generation of ecological organizations nationwide. There is solid, grass roots support in the ecology movement today, and, although there are few converts in the community of economists and active business interests, and although the ecologists are not available as apostles of physical economy, they have a substantial political influence and they represent a substantial market for their literature. The fact that this market does not spill over into a demand for books on energy economy only demonstrates the insulation of the intellectual market and the problem of gaining acceptance for physical economics.

The population problem directly parallels the energy problem in its long term aspects, and opposition to population control is more vocal than the opposition to energy economy, but the population literature has its best sellers. These include Paul Ehrlich's *The Population Bomb* and *The End of Affluence*, 1968 and 1974 releases. In 1967, William and Paul Paddock brought out their book titled *Famine 1975! America's Decision: Who Will Survive?*, a most specific prediction of the consequences of inadequate population control running against the limits of the world's agricultural capacity. This book generated strong opposition and still does, but its predictions have been fulfilled to a surprising degree. *Population and the American Future*, the report of the commission authorized by the President in 1969 — published in 1972 — is both a government publication and a successful addition to the general literature in paperback form. The most authoritative statement of the population problem is Garret Hardin's *Population, Evolution, and Birth Control* first published in 1964. This book could be classified as an addition to the academic library.

Alvin Toffler's *Future Shock* and *The Eco-Spasm Report* as well as Charles Reich's *The Greening of America* add perspective on the sociological aspect of the limits problem. All three books are imaginative and were widely circulated.

The direct attack on pecuniary economics and unlimited expansion is represented in *The Limits to Growth*, a report for the Club of Rome's project on the predicament of mankind. This 1972 publication precipitated the unqualified opposition of the pecuniary economists. *Mankind at the Turning Point*, the second report of the Club of Rome, which reduced the attack on growth, was proportionally more acceptable, and introduced the concept of non-material growth. Both of these books contributed to the understanding of the basic conflict between the facts of petroleum availability and the western world's commitment to growth in the resolution of social problems.

Omitted from this list of general books are the discussions of the specifics of atomic energy, available now and in the future, and the geological base for projecting the quantity of the remaining petroleum, natural gas, and coal resource. A responsible treatment of the atomic energy potential in book form for popular consumption has not been identified. We are dependent on periodicals and technical bulletins, and in these media we have found a wealth of material.

THE GENERAL PERIODICALS

The limited number of general books on the significance of energy limitation has been balanced by an outpouring of articles in the daily, weekly, and monthly press, each publisher selecting authors with the expected perspective.

The *New York Times* series began in March, 1974 tracing the origins of the Arab boycott each week in the *Sunday Magazine* section. *Harper's* and the *Atlantic Monthly* each produced excellent, readable, objective analyses of the physical problem and its social and economic implications during 1974 and 1975. *The Wall Street Journal* opened its editorial pages to a variety of points of view including the proponent of a planned economy, Wassily Leontief, but the *Journal* carefully balanced each such opening with its own editorial defending unlimited expansion. Reacting to the news release from the U. S. Geological Survey announcing the first auditable inventory of the U. S. oil and gas resources which reduced the remaining oil reserve to 27% of the estimate which they had published only three years before, *The Wall Street Journal* handled this news on Page 5 under the heading, "Fuel Recovery Seen Much More Feasible If Prices Climb." This was June 20, 1975 and the serious monthly periodicals had already dealt with the petroleum and energy problem. The news was given headlines only in a few liberal dailies. Time is a critical element in the periodical press both for potentially quick response to the evidence and for the quick decay of the product. The currently most significant treatment of the energy problem appeared in the

January 3 and 10, 1976 issues of the *New Republic*. Robert Samuelson's article titled *Too Little Too Late* lays out the problem and required solution to the U. S. petroleum supply and contrasts the U. S. legislative response.

The most interesting manipulation of the news which I have observed was the handling of the American Geological Institute's White House Conference on Earth Sciences July 21, 1975. The Conference invited the principal scientists representing the sixteen organizations supporting the Institute to discuss their potential contribution to the national energy problem. The Conference was precipitated by the release of the new U. S. Geological Survey findings that had so drastically deflated the undiscovered gas and oil estimates. This was not good news for the petroleum geologists who dominate the earth scientists organizations. The press was barred from the official session but invited to a reception where reporters were given news releases that were verbatim reproductions of every speech. No discussions had been entertained during the business session. These papers praised the survey but presented unsupported criticism of the conclusion. The press cooperated fully in attending the party and publishing not one word so far as I have been able to determine. The geological event having the most significant effect on the U. S. economy remains a statistical resource reserved for specialists in petroleum geology uninterpreted for economists and the informed public.

THE SCIENTIFIC PERIODICALS

The monthly and quarterly periodicals serving the natural sciences are a much more responsible reference base and these periodicals began their analysis of the energy problem earlier. In September 1971, *Scientific American* published Dr. M. King Hubbert's analysis of the energy resources of the earth including reference to his historic 1956 paper forecasting the peaking of U. S. petroleum production, which had then been realized to the satisfaction of most observers. The *American Scientist* began its series on the energy problem in 1973 as did *Science*, starting in June.

As the energy problem developed, a limited edition, weekly report service became available, published by Llewellyn King, reporting and editorializing on the current news from Washington. This service can bring the business community into instant contact with the political responses.

The world petroleum resource is best identified by H. R. Warman, Chief Geologist of the British Petroleum Company in an article, *The Future of Oil* that appeared in the Geographical Journal, Volume 138, 1972.

Publications by the economists' organizations have been principally concerned with ignoring both the reality of limits and also the implications of the steady reduction in U. S. petroleum production. They have concentrated on the political error of price control and the avoidance of the free market mechanisms. The main line economists support this view with few qualifications.

THE ACADEMIC PRESS AND PRIMARY RESOURCE BOOKS

Until 1976, the energy problem rested on the foundation of multiple disciplines, uncoordinated and independent. The source of energy is the responsibility of the physical sciences. Its use, its control, and its influence is economic, political, and broadly social. No interdisciplinary bridge is more difficult to negotiate than the span which connects the physical sciences with the arts and social disciplines.

The energy problem has brought on to center stage the interdisciplinary problem of the western world's colleges and universities. The necessity for coordination of disciplines has been demonstrated but the response has been limited and halting.

For the economists, Kenneth Boulding introduced the concept of spaceship earth in 1966 with his *Environmental Quality in a Growing Economy*. In 1972 Herman Daly delivered a paper at Yale University analyzing the necessary parameters of a steady state economic system and opening an attack on the conventional economics which he identified as "Growthmania". Nicholas Georgescu-Roegen introduced the concepts of entropy in physical economics publishing *The Entropy Law and The Economic Process* in 1972. Each of these economists has continued to publish articles and present his views, but there has been next to no response from their colleagues in the economic discipline. The main line economists have been adamant in their defense of growth as a social and economic necessity. In Paul Samuelson's 9th Edition (1973) of his classic text, *Economics*, no mention is made of the possibility of material limits affecting economic principles or practices. The persons concerned with limits are noted and the cost-push inflation is lamented, but no connection is drawn. The economist remains in his cave studying the price and index shadows of the material world, trusting the invisible hand of the price mechanism and debating the merits of alternative expansion stimulants.

All of the general readership books concerned with the material limits of economic expansion have been written by engineers, professors of management, and physical scientists. They have been supported by academic papers and the scientific publications mentioned earlier, but until 1976, none has attempted an academic text which identifies the interdisciplinary nature of the energy problem and fully documents this conclusion in the form that can be recognized as a potential new discipline. Earl Cook's *Man, Energy, Society* released by his publisher, W. H. Freeman & Company in May of 1976, may be that text. It is the most broadly based and fully documented treatment of the energy problem in the necessary perspective of man's million years on the planet. Dr. Cook recognizes the two halves of economics, physical economics and pecuniary economics, and he provides a language and a reference base for the necessary discussion.

Several texts support Dr. Cook in his perspective without reaching the full energy focus. Dr. Cook was preceded in 1974 by Wilson Clark and the research of David Howell. Their book, *Energy for Survival, the Alternative to Extinction,* was published by Anchor/Doubleday. It is encyclopedic in its coverage of the facts and opinions on energy in the United States through 1974. Clark is perceptive — avoiding false information and criticism — and accurately interprets the necessity for understanding and decision. He spells out the terrible probabilities for western civilization.

Earlier texts which anticipated the developing problem and now provide perspective for Dr. Cook's broad coverage include, C. D. Darlington's *The Evolution of Man and Society*, a geneticist's universal history of the human development, published in 1969; William McNeill's *The Rise of the West*, another universal history identifying the influence of western culture published in 1963; Harrison Brown's *The Challenge of Man's Future,* a 1954 publication directly paralleling Dr. Cook's perspective; and for a better understanding of the economists, Robert Heilbroner's 1970 *The Worldly Philosophers*, focusing on Adam Smith and his successors through John Maynard Keynes.

THE GOVERNMENT PRINTING OFFICE CONTRIBUTIONS

Productions from this source are particularly important, and they have been released under circumstances that appear to have been planned to discourage circulation. Our first two recommended readings carry the inscription on the front page, "Printed for the use of the Committee....." and one was released on December 23rd effectively discouraging the employment of the press release. Government offices most concerned with the information have been unaware of its existence.

U. S. Energy Resources, a Review as of 1972, by M. King Hubbert, was released by the Senate Committee on Interior & Insular Affairs in July 1974. The importance of this book is the complete record of Dr. Hubbert's forecast of petroleum reserves, demonstrating the methodology and the developing proof of the accuracy of his conclusions. In this same book, the totally unsupported and unsupportable estimates of the U. S. Geological Survey are reproduced in their entirety including the 1974 press release which was the interim estimate of resources, preceding their release of Circular 725 in 1975. The contrast between documented research and bureaucratic abuse of discretion is clear.

The second and most important Government Printing Office contribution is the work of Dr. Herman T. Franssen of the Library of Congress for the Joint Committee on Atomic Energy. It is titled *Towards Project Interdependence: Energy in the Coming Decade* dated December 1975. The report details the sources of information relating to the availability of U. S. and world gas and oil resources and concludes that the objectives of Project Independence cannot be realized in 1985 and probably cannot be realized in any future year.

The Federal Energy Administration has published two giant reports, *Project Independence Report of November 1974* and *National Energy Outlook 1976.* Both must be read with reservations. The organization was created to handle the Arab petroleum embargo and continues to carry the burden, for both Congress and the Administration, for the defense of unlimited exploitation of natural resources and uninhibited economic expansion. The rationing program and the complicated system of price and quantity controls are administered without a coordinated policy. The 1974 report is an elaborate compilation of petroleum statistics employing an econometric model that forecast virtually unlimited production of U. S. petroleum at higher and higher prices. The 1976 report is a compromise between the evidence of U. S. petroleum resource limits available at that time and the economic theories of increasing supply with increasing price. Current F.E.A. news releases promise holding the price line obedient to the Congressional mandate and political expedience in the election year.

The Energy Research and Development Administration is more responsive to the physical facts of energy materials availability, but this organization is also subservient to the political instruction. Its report, *A National Plan for Energy Research, Development and Demonstration: Creating Energy Choices for 1976,* is published in two volumes. There is much concrete information on the quantities of energy available from alternative sources assuming the resolution of technical and sociological problems with atomic energy. ERDA has identified five national policy goals relating to energy which fairly well interpret the political environment of conflicting objectives not possible of achievment. ERDA avoids compounding errors in the overstatement of the availability of physical resources but avoids conflict with other administrative

agencies, accepting the conclusions of these agencies without reservation.
The failure of the ERDA plan is a direct consequence of a failure of the
Legislature and the Administration to develop an energy policy.

The United States Congress Office of Technological Assessment published
its second evaluation of ERDA in May titled, *Comparative Analysis of the 1976
ERDA Plan and Program*. This 204 page publication is more concise than the
ERDA reports as a summary resource and it is more candid and broader in its
perspectives, but this report reflects the constraints of Congressional instruction which are very little different from the ERDA constraints of Administrative instruction. Both are influenced by the same economic and political interests. Neither ERDA nor OTA has been given a comprehensive energy
responsibility. The critical transportation problem is practically ignored
by both. ERDA has no budget for considering the alternatives to the petroleum dependence of transportation and neither is realistically aware of the
level of the U. S. petroleum resources and their year-to-year availability.
This void encompasses half the country's energy problem and the most necessary immediate concern.

TWO ECONOMISTS' VIEW OF THE FUTURE

Two texts were neglected in my preparations, not because of their
limitation but because they were not specific to the building blocks of
my reading. Their conclusions, which were discovered after completing
my own writing, closely parallel my own. E. F. Schumacher is an economist,
a German transplant to England who became the Director of that country's
coal industry. His *Small Is Beautiful* is a frontal attack on the conventional
economic theory of unrestricted growth, mechanization, and unaccountable
environmental exploitation. He advocates the reduction of scale, humanization
of economic activity, and a return to reason. His in depth experience with
the industrial world and his broad perspective on the developing world is
complemented with deep philosophic insights.

Dr. Schumacher identifies the impossibility of resolving the third
world economic problems on the basis of transplanted advance technology
and he presents positive alternatives. His in depth analysis of alternative capitalist and socialist structures and their equal dependence on indus-
trialization and growth fills in the foundation missing in my own analysis.

Dr. Schumacher fails to come to grips with the population problem or
suggest a political solution to our dilemma, but he has laid the foundation
for the solutions by destroying the illusions that have so long stood in the
way of constructive reasoning.

Robert Heilbroner's *An Inquiry Into The Human Prospect* provides the perspective on the same problem by an American economist. Dr. Heilbroner does not ignore the population and political problems. His is a short summary, an overview and a prescription for change.

These two books provide the sequel to my discussion of energy and the critical decision for the United States economy. The future is immediate and for a long time. The decision is difficult. Dr. Schumacher's specifics of the economic problem and Dr. Heilbroner's perspective on the population and political problem will be needed. There is no conflict in our common identifications of problems and solutions. There is also no assurance that it will be possible to maintain the minimum requirements of a free society. There is no question about the necessity for change and the sacrifice of prerogatives. Representative government will not survive on the basis of primary concern for special interests.

AUTHOR INDEXED LISTING OF CONTRIBUTING BOOKS

American Academy of Political and Social Science: *The Energy Crisis: Reality or Myth*, The Annals Volume 410, November, 1973; *Adjusting to Scarcity*, The Annals Volume 420, July 1974

American Astronautical Society and American Institute of Aeronautical and Astronautics Conference Papers, April 21-24, 1975: *System Aspects of Ocean Thermal Energy Conversion* by Robert H. Douglass, 75-715; *Ocean Thermal Energy Conversion System Evaluation* by Lloyd Trimble and Bernard Messinger, 75-616; *Tropical Ocean Thermal Power Plant & Potential Products* by G. L. Dugger, 75-617; *One Hundred MWe Solar Power Plant Design Configuration & Operation* by F. A. Blake, 75-624; *Photovoltaic Systems With Concentration* by C. E. Backus, 75-627; *Solar Electric In Thermal Conversion Systems in Close Proximity to the Consumer* by K. W. Boer, 75-628; *The Oceanic Biomass Energy Plantation* by Howard A. Wilcox, 75-635; *The Satellite Solar Power Station: An Option for Energy Production on Earth* by Peter E. Glaser, 75-637; *Derivation of a Total Satellite Energy System* by G. R. Woodcock and D. L. Gregory, 75-640; *Overcoming Two Significant Hurdles to Space Power Generation: Transportation and Assembly* by R. Kline, 75-641; *The Adaptation of Free Space Power Transmission Technology to the SSPS Concept* by William C. Brown, 75-642; *Gulf Stream Based Ocean Thermal Power Plants* by J. G. McGowan, 75-643

American Gas Association, *1974 Gas Facts*

American Geological Institute, *The White House Conference Concerning U. S. G. S. Circular 725*, regarding U. S. petroleum and gas inventory as of July 1975, published speeches and press releases.

American Enterprise Institute: *The Oil Crisis and World Monetary Arrangements* by Edward J. Mitchell and Weitze Eizenga, 1974; *The Energy Dilemma - Which Way Out?* by Edward J. Mitchell, 1974; *The Future of Electric Utilities* by Murray L. Weidenbaum, 1975; *Price Controls & The Natural Gas Shortage* by Paul W. MacAvoy and Robert S. Pindyck, 1975; *Is Nuclear Power Safe?* by Melvin R. Laird (Moderator), 1975

American Petroleum Institute: *1971 Petroleum Facts & Figures; Reserves of Crude Oil, Natural Gas Liquids, and Natural Gas in the United States and Canada and United States Productive Capacity as of December 31, 1974*, Volume 29, May 1975; *Basic Petroleum Data Book*, updated through April 1976 for U.S. Production; *Technical Report No. 2, Organization and Definitions for the Estimation of Reserves and Productive Capacity of Crude Oil*, First Edition June 1970; *Seminar on Reserves & Productive Capacity*, April 1975

Anthony, John Duke (edited by), *The Middle East: Oil, Politics, & Development*, a conference sponsored by the Middle East Studies Committee of the International Studies Program School of Graduate Studies, University of Toronto and Canadian Institute of International Affairs, 1975

Beckerman, Wilfred, *Two Cheers for the Affluent Society, A Spirited Defense of Economic Growth*, 1975

Bethe, H. A., "The Necessity of Fission Power", *Scientific American*, January 1976

Binzen, Peter and Joseph R. Daughen, *The Wreck of the Penn Central*, 1971

Boulding, Kenneth E., "The Economics of the Coming Space Ship Earth", In Henry Jarrett edition, *Environmental Quality in a Growing Economy*; "Truth or Power?" editorial, *Science*, October 31, 1975

Borchgrave, Arnaud de, *Intervention Wouldn't Work*, 1975

Bronowski, J., *The Ascent of Man*, 1973

Brown, Harrison, *The Challenge of Man's Future*, 1954

Christian Science Monitor: *Energy: The Crisis that Could Help Us* by Robert Cahn, December 17, 1973; *Energy: Wake Up America*, June 25, 1976

Clark, Wilson, *Energy for Survival, The Alternative to Extinction*, 1974

Commoner, Barry, "A Reporter at Large (Energy - L, II, III)", *The New Yorker Magazine*, February 2 through 16, 1976

Commission on Population Growth & the American Future, *Population and the American Future*, 1972

Committee on Ways and Means, U. S. House of Representatives, Committee Print: *Background Readings On Energy Policy*, WMCP:94-14, March 1, 1975; *Summary of Energy Facts and Issues*, WMCP:94-18, March 4, 1975

Congressional Research Service, Library of Congress, *U.S. Energy Policy ... Major Issues & Options* by Alfred Riefman, Henry Canaday, Herman Franssen, David Gushee, and Clyde Mark, March 3, 1976

Cook, C. Sharp, "Energy: Planning for the Future", *American Scientist*, January-February 1973

Cook, Earl, *Man, Energy, Society*, W. H. Freeman & Company, 1976

Daly, Herman E., *A Model for Steady-State Economy*, paper presented at Yale University School of Forestry & Environmental Studies, October 1972, Reprint in Forensic Quarterly; *Steady-State Economics versus Growthmania: A Critique of the Orthodox Conceptions of Growth, Wants, Scarcity, and Efficiency*, paper presented at Symposium on "Economic Growth and the Quality of Life" sponsored by the College of Liberal Arts, Oregon State University, May 1973; "In Defense of a Steady-State Economy", *American Journal of Agricultural Economics*, Vol. 54, No. 5, December 1972; "The World Dynamics of Economic Growth, The Economics of the Steady State", *The American Economic Review*, May 1974; "Energy Demand Forecasting: Prediction or Planning?", *A.P.I. Journal*, January 1976

Darlington, C. D., *The Evolution of Man and Society*, 1969

Darmstadter, Teitelbaum and Polach, *Energy In The World Economy*, Johns Hopkins Press, 1971

Department of Commerce, *Statistical Abstract of the United States*, 1975

Doerr, Arthur H., "The Bounds of Earth", *The Rotarian*, April 1976

Duane, John W., *The Impending Energy Crisis - A Vital Challenge*, paper prepared for Ontario Petroleum Institute annual conference, October 1974; *A Discussion of Growth Versus No Growth*, November 1974; *World Oil Supply, Demand and Future United States Policy*, report prepared for Consumers Power Company; *An Independent Appraisal of the Project Independence*, November 1974; *Petroleum - The Closing Frontier* (a response to Barry Commoner), February 1976; *Michigan's Future Natural Gas Supply*, prepared for Consumers Power Company, February 1976

Electrical World, *It's Time for a Reappraisal*, Annual Electrical Industry Forecast editorial, September, 1975

Ellis, A. J., "Geothermal Systems and Power Development", *American Scientist*, September-October 1975

Ehrlich, Paul, *The Population Bomb*, 1968; *The End of Affluence*, 1974

Energy Reports, Weekly publication edited by Llewellyn King

Energy Research & Development Administration, Robert C. Seamans, Jr., Administrator, *A National Plan for Energy Research, Development, and Demonstration: Creating Energy Choices for the Future*, Vols. 1 & 2, 1976

Exxon, *Energy Outlook 1975-1990*, 1975

Federal Energy Administration: *Project Independence Report*, November 1974, Administrator John C. Sawhill; *Final Report of Oil & Gas Resources, Reserves and Productive Capacities*, submitted in compliance with Public Law 93-275, Section 15 (b), October 1975 (ten year forecast of 59 oil and gas fields representing 52% of proved reserves of crude oil and 28% of proved reserves of natural gas); *National Energy Outlook 1976*, Administrator, Frank G. Zarb

Federal Reserve Bulletin, *U.S. Energy Supplies & Uses*, a staff economic study, December 1973 and later reports

Fancher, George H., *The Oil Resources of Texas, A Reconnaissance Survey of Primary and Secondary Reserves of Oil*, The Texas Petroleum Research Committee, The University of Texas, 1954

Forester, J. W., "The Road to World Harmony", *The Futurist*, October 1975

Ford Foundation, The, *A Time to Choose America's Energy Future*

Fortune Magazine articles: *Capturing Clean Gas & Oil from Coal* by Lawrence Lessing, November 1973; *Clearing the Way for the New Age of Coal* by Edmund Faltermayer, May 1974; *Oil, Trade, & the Dollar* by Lawrence A. Mayer, June 1974; *Modest Men Who Manage Billions*, April 1974

Franssen, Herman T., *Towards Project Interdependence: Energy in the Coming Decade*, 1975, prepared for the Joint Committee on Atomic Energy U.S. Congress, Congressional Research Service, Library of Congress, U. S. Government Printing Office 61-173; *Effects of Offshore Oil & Natural Gas Development on the Coastal Zone*, a study for the use of the Ad Hoc Select Committee on Outer Continental Shelf, House of Representatives, March 1976; "Federal Energy Planning: Scenarios for Disaster", *World Oil*, April 1976

Freeman, David S. Director of Ford Foundation energy studies.

Friedman, Milton, *A Monetary History of the United States*, 1867-1960, 1963

Galbraith, John Kenneth, *Money, Whence It Come, Where It Went*, 1975

Georgescu-Roegen, Nicholas, *The Entropy Law & The Economic Process*, Harvard University Press, 1972; "Energy and Economic Myths", *The Southern Economic Journal*, Vol. 41, No. 3, January 1975; *Process In Farming Versus Process In Manufacturing: A Problem of Balanced Development*, International Economic Association Conference, Rome, 1965; *Macmillan*, 1969; "Entropy: The Measure of Economic Man", *Science*, October 31, 1975; "The Entropy Law and the Economic Problem", *The Ecologist* (London), Vol. II, No. 7, July 1972

Gilliland, Martha W., "Energy Analysis and Public Policy", *Science*, September 26, 1975

Harvard Business Review: *What Happens When Our Oil Runs Out?* by Alan S. Manne, July - August 1975, Dix Letter September - October, 1975; *Political Approach to the World Oil Problem* by Christopher Tugendhat "The oil consuming countries must take the offensive and make OPEC interest more compatible with theirs."

Hardin, Garrett, *Population, Evolution, and Birth Control,* 1964

Heilbroner, Robert L., *The Worldly Philosophers,* 1970; *An Inquiry Into the Human Prospect,* 1974

Hill, Dr. Richard F., Chief Engineer, Federal Power Commission, *Energy Technology III,* 1976

Hubbert, M. King, "Energy Resources of the Earth", *Scientific American,* September 1971; *U. S. Energy Resources, A Review As Of 1972* in a national fuels and energy policy study, Committee of Interior and Insular Affairs, U. S. Senate, Serial No. 93-40 (92-75), July 1974: *Comments on Barry Commoner Article "Energy I" (The New Yorker,* February 2, 1976) - Hubbert manuscript not published at this printing

Huxley, Aldous, *Brave New World,* 1932

Illinois State Geological Survey, *The U. S. Energy Dilemma, The Gap Between Today's Requirements and Tomorrow's Potential,* EGN-64, July 1973

Javits, Jacob K., Senator, "The Need For National Planning", *Wall Street Journal,* July 8, 1975

Joint Economic Committee, Congress of the United States: *Reappraisal of U. S. Energy Policy,* March 8, 1974; *Gasoline & Fuel Oil Shortage,* hearings May and June 1973; *Potential Heating Oil Shortage,* hearings September 1973

Karnitz, Michael A., "Energy Parks and Energy Park Modeling", *Power Engineering,* March 1976

Keyfitz, Nathan, "World Resources and the World Middle Class", *Scientific American,* July 1976

Kirkbride, Chalmers K., Science Advisor to the Administrator, Energy Research and Development Administration, *New Technology, Planning for Utilization,* a paper delivered March 29, 1976 to the Third Energy Technology Conference in Washington, D. C.

Koenig, Herman, Thomas Edens and others, *Resource Management in a Changing Environment,* 1976, Michigan State University, DMRE

Kreisinger Development Laboratory, *Combustion/Fluids & Process Technology*, Combustion Engineering, Inc.

Landsberg, Fischman & Fisher, *Resources in America's Future*, 1963

Lanouette, William J. "Nuclear Fuel: Will It Run Out?", *National Observer*, April 24, 1976

Lieberman, M. A., "U. S. Uranium Resources - An Analysis of Historical Data", *Science*, Volume 192, Number 4238, April 1976

Leilich, Robert H. *A Study of the Economics of Short Trains*, June 1974, Peat,

Llewellyn, Richard, *How Green Was My Valley*, 1940

Malthus, Thomas Robert, *An Essay on the Principle of Population*, 1798

Marine Engineers' Beneficial Association, *The Energy Cartel, Big Oil Vs. The Public Interest* by Norman Medvin, Iris J. Lav and Stanley H. Ruttenberg

Marx, Karl, *Capital*, 1867

McKenzi and Utgard, *Man and His Physical Environment*, 1972

McNeill, William, *The Rise of the West, A History of the Human Community*, 1963

Meadows, Donella H. and Dennis L., "A Summary of Limits to Growth - Its Critics and Its Challenge" in *Futures*, February 1973, Yale University Lecture, September 1972; also note principal authors of *Limits to Growth*, Club of Rome 1972

Menard, H. W. and George Sharman, "Scientific Uses of Random Drilling Models", *Science*, October 24, 1975

Mesarovic, Mihajlo and Eduard Pestel, *Mankind at the Turning Point*, 1974

Michigan Commission on Electric Power Alternatives, Governor's Advisory, James H. Brickley, Chairman, Preliminary report, April 1976

Michigan Department of Natural Resources: *Future Oil & Gas in the Michigan Basin* by G. D. Ellis; *Michigan's Oil and Gas Fields*, annual statistical summary by Ells and others, 1973

Moore, C. L., *Discovery and Recovery of Petroleum in the United States*, Gompertz curves fitted to historic patterns of petroleum discovery and recovery, 1890 - 1973, U.S.G.S. (not published)

Myhra, David, "The Elasticity Argument in Electricity Demand:, *Public Utilities Fortnightly*, June 6, 1974

National Academy of Sciences, *Mineral Resources and the Environment*, 1975

National Geographic: *New Energy from an Old Source: The Wind* by Roger Hamilton, December 1975; *Solar Energy, the Ultimate Power House* by John L. Wilhelm, March 1976

National Petroleum Council, *U. S. Petroleum & Gas Transportation Capacities*, 1967

National Railway Publication Company, *Official Railway Equipment Register*, 1975

National Science Foundation, *Report on Effect of Fuel Price Increases on Energy Intensiveness of Freight Transportation*

New York Times Magazine Section: *The Richest Oil Company in the World* by Leonard Mosley, March 10, 1974; *Unradical Sheiks Who Shake The World* by Edward R. F. Sheehan, March 24, 1974

Oak Ridge National Laboratory, *Report on Energy Intensiveness of Passenger and Freight Transport Modes*, 1950 - 1970

Ophuls, William, "The Scarcity Society", *Harper's*, April 1974

Office of Technology Assessment, *Comparative Analysis of the 1976 ERDA Plan and Program*, Director Emilio Q. Daddario

Paddock, William and Paul, *Famine 1975! America's Decision: Who Will Survive?*, 1967

Peach, Dr. W. N., University of Oklahoma, *The Energy Outlook For The 1980's*, a study prepared for the use of the Subcommittee on Economic Progress, December 1973

Pestel, Eduard and Mihajlo Mesarovic, *Mankind at the Turning Point*, 1974

Resources for the Future (Ford Foundation Corporation): *Exploring Energy Choices*, 1974. (Note major work *Resources in America's Future* listed under principal author Lansberg); *Low-Cost Abundant Energy: Paradise Lost?*, December 1973; *Resources* (periodical covering many subjects including "An Abundance of Shortages", January 1974)

Rhodes, Richard, "Delusions of Power, The Benefits, Costs, and Risks of Nuclear Energy", *The Atlantic*, June 1976

Roberts, Ralph, "Energy Sources and Conversion Techniques, What is our capability of meeting the energy needs of the future within the limitations of known energy resources and energy conversion technology?" *American Scientist*, January-February 1973

Rocks, Lawrence and Richard P. Runyon, *The Energy Crisis*, 1972

Rose, David J., "Energy Policy in The U. S., The President's appeal for U. S. energy self-sufficiency by 1980 cannot be regarded as realistic," *Scientific American*, January 1974

Sampson, Anthony, *The Seven Sisters, The Great Oil Companies & The World They Shaped*, 1975

Samuelson, Paul A., *Economics*, 1973 Edition

Samuelson, Robert "Too Little Too Late, Two years after the Arab embargo, America is still without an oil policy that deserves the name," *The New Republic*, January 3-10, 1976

Saturday Review, July 12, 1975 issue, "The American Economy, Can Capitalism Survive Another Thirty Years?", articles by William Simon and Harvard professors principally challenging dooms-sayers

Schumacher, E. F., *Small Is Beautiful*, 1973

Smith, Adam, *An Inquiry into the Nature and Cause of the Wealth of Nations*, 1776

Stanford Research Institute, *Nuclear Power Prospects*, by Kopelman & Alich, 1975

Science editorials: *Alaskan Gas: The Feds Umpire Another Confused Pipeline Debate*, October 24, 1975; *Icebergs & Oil Tankers: U.S.G.S. Glaciologists are Concerned*, November 14, 1975

Shell Oil Company: *The National Energy Problem, The Short-Term Supply Prospect*, June 1973; *The Changing Role of the International Oil Industry* by H. Bridges, President, 1975

Shils, Edward, "The Intellectuals and Their Discontents," *The American Scholar*, Spring 1976

Starr, Chauncey, "Energy and Society", *Aware*, April 1976 (lecture to Stanford University, School of Earth Sciences)

Stobaugh, Robert B., "The Hard Choices on Energy", *Wall Street Journal*, December 9, 1974

Subcommittee on Transportation and Aeronautics, House Committee on Interstate and Foreign Commerce: *Surface Transportation Act (HR5385)*, *Transportation Improvement Act (HR12891)*, *Pickle Freight Car Bill (HR11317)*, *Freight Transportation Improvement Act (HR13487)*, and *Fastcor (S1149)*

Teller, Edward, "The Energy Disease," *Harper's*, May 1975

Texaco, *Balancing Regulation and Energy*, address by Maurice F. Granville, Chairman of the Board, September 1973

Tillman, David A., "Status of Coal Gasification," *Environmental Science & Technology*, January 1976

Toffler, Alvin, *The Eco-Spasm Report*, 1975

Toynbee, Arnold, *Mankind and Mother Earth*, 1976 and *The Study of History*, 1947

Udall, Stewart, Charles Conconi and David Osterhout, *The Energy Balloon*, 1974;

Udall, Stewart, *The Quiet Crisis*, 1963

U. S. Corps of Engineers, *Interim Report on Atlantic Coast Deep Water Port Facilities*, June 1973

U. S. Department of Interior, Bureau of Mines: *U. S. Energy Through The Year 2000* by Walter G. Dupree, Jr. and James A. West, December 1972; *U. S. Energy Through The Year 2000 (Revised)* by Walter G. Dupree, Jr. and John S. Corsentino, December 1975; *Mineral Yearbook*, 1972; *Commodity Data Summaries*, 1975; *Mineral Industry Surveys*, monthly publications of crude petroleum, petroleum products, and natural gas liquids; *International Petroleum Annual 1974*, printed March 1976; *U. S. Petroleum and Natural Gas Resources*, February 14, 1974

U. S. General Accounting Office, *Implications of Deregulating the Price of Natural Gas*, by the Controller General of the United States

Underground Storage of Gas in the United States and Canada, December 31, 1975

U. S. Geological Survey: Circular 641 - *Selected Sources of Information on United States and World Energy Resources* by Paul Averitt and M. Devereux Carter, William T. Pecora, Director, 1970; Circular 650 - *Energy Resources of the United States* by P. K. Theobald, S. P. Schweinfurth, and D. C. Duncan, V. E. McKelvey, Director, 1972; Circular 682 - *Summary of the United States Mineral Resources*, 1973; Circular 725 - *Geological Estimates of Undiscovered Recoverable Oil and Gas Resources in the United States* by Betty M. Miller, Harry L. Thomsen, Gordon L. Dolton, Anny B. Coury, Thomas A. Hendricks, Frances E. Lennartz, Richard B. Powers, Edward G. Sable, and Katharine L. Varnes, V. E. McKelvey, Director, 1975; Professional Paper 820 - *Oil Shale, Bitumen-Bearing Rocks, Coal, Geothermal Resources, Nuclear Fuel, Oil & gas*, 1975

Warman, H. R., Chief Geologist, British Petroleum Company, Ltd., "The Future Of Oil", *Geographical Journal*, Volume 138, 1972

Wall Street Journal, Spring 1976 articles: *Population of World Growing Faster Than Experts Anticipated* by Jonathan Spivak, April 12, 1976; *Energy Scare's Impact on the Stock Market Fades Into History* by Charles Elia, May 4, 1976

Weinberg, Alvin M., "Some Views of the Energy Crisis", *American Scientist*, January-February 1973

Yergin, Daniel, "European Energy: A Policy Evolves?", *European Community*, January-February 1976

Zareski, Gordon K., Chief of Planning and Development Division, Bureau of Natural Gas, Federal Power Commission, *A Realistic View of U. S. Natural Gas Supply*, January 1975; Statement before Subcommittee on Energy and Power of the Committee on Interstate and Foreign Commerce, U. S. House of Representatives on January 27, 1976

TABLES OF EXHIBITS, FIGURES,
AND TABULATIONS

Exhibit		Page
1	Remaining Recoverable Petroleum Resources, U.S.G.S. Cir. 725	14
2	Forecast of U. S. Liquid Hydrocarbon Production & Demand	16
3	U. S. Liquid Hydrocarbon Production and Additions to Reserves	18
4	Forecast of U. S. Natural Gas Production & Demand	24
5	U. S. Gas Demand by Priority & Total Projected Supply Source	27
6	Perspective on Solar Power Potential	34
7	U. S. Energy Supply and Demand	40
8	International Petroleum Production Analysis-U.S. Import Potential	45

Figure | |
---|---|---
1 | Estimates of Original Recoverable Oil in Place, Graph | 64
2 | Estimates of Original Recoverable Oil in Place, Analysis | 66
3 | Remaining Recoverable Petroleum Resources | 69
4 | M. King Hubbert Forecast Methodology | 70
5 | M. King Hubbert 1972 Forecast | 73
6 | Summation of Potential U. S. Petroleum Production Through 1985 | 75
7 | U. S. Proved Reserves of Crude Oil | 77
8 | Historic U. S. Petroleum Discoveries | 79
9 | Annual Withdrawal & Demand Rates Percent of U. S. Proved Reserves 1947-1975 | 81
10 | Conterminous U. S. Historic Rate of Withdrawal for Crude Oil | 83
11 | Forecast of U. S. Liquid Hydrocarbon Production | 85
12 | Summation of U. S. Liquid Hydrocarbons & Crude Oil Production | 87
13 | Wellhead Price of Domestic Petroleum, U. S. Consumption of all Petroleum Products 1915-1975 | 89

Tables of Exhibits, Figures
and Tabulations

Figure   Page

14   Wellhead Price of Domestic Petroleum Annual Proved Reserve
        Additions, U. S. Petroleum Production for the Lower 48 States   91
15   Forecast Comparison with 1974 F.E.A. Projection   95
16   Forecast Comparison with 1976 F.E.A. Projection   97
17   Forecast Comparison with U. S. Department of Interior & Dr.
        M. King Hubbert's Forecast   99
18   Significant World Petroleum Statistics   101
19   1974 Seven Year Petroleum Imports Projection 1974 thru 1980   103
20   Remaining Recoverable Natural Gas Resources   104
21   Summation of U. S. Natural Gas Production & Demand   107
22   Comparison of Significant Discoveries and Ultimate Gas
        Reserves by Year of Discovery   109
23   The Two Faces of the Future of U. S. Gas Production   111
24   U. S. Gas Forecast Comparison with F.P.C. Forecasts   113
25   U. S. Gas Forecast Comparison with F.E.A. Forecasts   115
26   U. S. Gas Consumption by Sectors of the Economy   121
27   Summation of U. S. Natural Gas Production and Demand   123

Tabulations (All listed in Appendix)

A   Summation of Historic U. S. Petroleum Production and Ten
        Year Known Oil Forecast
B   Domestic Demand for Refined Products
C   The Declining Supply of Domestic Crude Oil
D   Historic Domestic Production of Liquid Hydrocarbons
E   Conterminous U. S. Crude Oil Production with Maximum Resource
F   Conterminous U. S. Crude Oil Production with Minimum Resource
G   Summary of Domestic Liquid Hydrocarbon Production with Maximum Resource
H   Conterminous U. S. Crude Oil Projected Production with Maximum Resource
I   Alaska Crude Oil Projected Production with Maximum Resource
J   Summary of Domestic Liquid Hydrocarbon Production with Minimum Resource
K   Conterminous U. S. Crude Oil Projected Production with Minimum Resource
L   Alaska Crude Oil Projected Production with Minimum Resource
M   F.E.A. "1976 National Energy Outlook", Revised Domestic Production
        Projections
N-1   Summary of Historic & Projected Natural Gas Regional Production - TCF/Yr.
N-2   Projected Production of Prudhoe Bay as Per F.E.A., 93-275, Sec. 15(b), 10/75
N-3   Historic & Projected Production of Alaska (Exc. Prudhoe Bay) Nonassociated
        & Associated Natural Gas Production - TCF/Yr.
N-4   Summary of the Historic & Projected Production of Region #1 NA & Assoc.
        Natural Gas Production - TCF/Yr.

Tables of Exhibits, Figures
and Tabulations

Tabulations

N-5   Maximum Approach Historic & Projected Production of Region #2 (On & Off) NA & Assoc. Natural Gas Production - TCF/Yr.
N-6   Maximum Approach Historic & Projected Production of Region #3 NA & Assoc. Natural Gas Production - TCF/Yr.
N-7   Same (Region #4)
N-8   Same (Region #5)
N-9   Same (Region #6)
N-10   Same (Region #6A Gulf of Mexico)
N-11   Same (Region #7)
N-12   Same (Regions #8, 9, 10, 11 + Miscellaneous)
N-13   Same (Region #11A Atlantic Coast Offshore)
P-1   Summary of Historic & Projected Natural Gas Regional Production - TCF/Yr.
P-2   Projected Production of Prudhoe Bay as Per F.E.A., 93-275, Sec. 15(b) 10/75 NA and Assoc. Natural Gas Production - TCF/Yr.
P-3   Historic & Projected Production of Alaska (Exc. Prudhoe Bay), NA & Assoc. Natural Gas Production - TCF/Yr.
P-4   Summary of the Historic & Projected Production of Region #1, NA & Assoc. Natural Gas Production - TCF/Yr.
P-5   Minimum Approach Historic & Projected Production of Region #2 (On & Off) NA & Assoc. Natural Gas Production - TCF/Yr.
P-6   Minimum Approach Historic & Projected Production of Region #3, NA & Assoc. Natural Gas Production - TCF/Yr.
P-7   Same (Region #4)
P-8   Same (Region #5)
P-9   Same (Region #6)
P-10   Same (Region #6A Gulf of Mexico)
P-11   Same (Region #7)
P-12   Same (Regions #8, 9, 10, 11 + Miscellaneous)
P-13   Same (Region #11A Atlantic Coast Offshore)
Q   Worldwide Crude Oil and Gas Production, 1975 & 1976
R   U. S. Energy Supply 1975 through 1985
S   U. S. Import Potential - Million Bbls./Day
T   Total Annual U. S. Electrical Energy Production Spectrum 1950-1975
U   U. S. Nuclear Electric Power Heat Conversion Relationships